Samuel Gompers
and the Origins of the
American Federation of Labor
1848-1896

Samuel Gompers in the late 1890's
By Courtesy of the AFL-CIO, Washington, D.C.

Stuart Bruce Kaufman

Samuel Gompers and the Origins of the American Federation of Labor 1848-1896

Contributions in Economics and Economic History
Number 8

Greenwood Press
Westport, Connecticut o London, England

Library of Congress Cataloging in Publication Data

Kaufman, Stuart Bruce.
  Samuel Gompers and the origins of the American
Federation of Labor, 1848-1896.

  (Contributions in economics and economic history,
no. 8)
  Bibliography: p.
  1. Gompers, Samuel, 1850-1924. 2. American
Federation of Labor. I. Title.
HD8073.G6K38 1973   331.88'32'0924[B] 76-176430
ISBN 0-8371-6277-7

Library of Congress Catalog Card Number: 76-176430
ISBN: 0-8371-6277-7

First published in 1973
Greenwood Press, a division of Williamhouse-Regency Inc.
51 Riverside Avenue, Westport, Connecticut 06880

Manufactured in the United States of America

To Phyllis

Contents

Acknowledgments

This work has been immeasurably improved through the advice of other members of the craft, none of whom need bear responsibility for the final product. J. Harvey Young of Emory University saw the manuscript through several drafts. His reading of it was penetrating, unsettling, and invaluable. Robert Wheeler and Charles Strickland of Emory raised questions which troubled me and led to a good deal of revision. Greenwood Press submitted the manuscript to David Brody, whose critique was a model of encouragement and constructiveness. Dan Carter, my colleague at the University of Maryland, read the work in its late stages and provided further suggestions as I reworked it for the last time. Finally, the editors at Greenwood did me another service for which I owe a considerable debt. They assigned the manuscript to Judith H. Johnson, who improved the style and the clarity of writing in hundreds of ways.

Following many other labor historians of this period, I too found the staffs of vital archives for this period proficient and hospitable. The Library of Congress was my home for a year; the State Historical Society of Wisconsin smoothly handled my hurried demands for a portion of a summer. At Catholic University's archives, a routine was arranged whereby I could use the Powderly Papers after archive hours. The staffs of the Illinois Historical Survey, the University of Michigan archives, and the New York Public Library, seemed well practiced in providing professional service to scholars on limited leave. The Tamiment Institute Library steadily provided microfilm on loan from its fine labor collection. The Samuel Gompers Memorial Library has a well-earned reputation for warm and personal service.

Most of all, I am grateful to my wife Phyllis. She staked me in this project, she listened, she helped me pick up the pieces again and again.

College Park, Maryland
December 1972

Introduction

At thirty-six years of age the first president of the new American Federation of Labor exhibited confidence and single-mindedness of purpose. A hard-jawed defender of the self-sufficiency of his federation to achieve the workers' emancipation, he was soon the nemesis of populists and socialists who sought his cooperation in some grander movement for the masses of deprived Americans. They, and historians who followed them, could find little that was radical in the "pure and simple" trade unionism on which Samuel Gompers took his stand.

What goals did Gompers have for the labor movement in its formative decade? Selig Perlman, writing in 1918, found nothing beyond the immediate aims of higher wages, shorter hours, and improved working conditions. Appeals from well-meaning advocates of seemingly more ambitious movements could not penetrate Gompers' "pure wage-consciousness." To Perlman, the advent of Gompers "signified a labour movement reduced to an opportunistic basis, accepting the existence of capitalism and having for its objective the enlargement of the bargaining power of the wage-earner in the sale of his labour." A dozen years after Perlman, Louis Reed concluded that Gompers was not actually hostile to socialism in these early years; he simply did not often think about the possibility of substituting a new social order for capitalism.[1]

Recently, Marxist historians have paid renewed attention to the apparently radical aspects of Gompers' thought in the late nineteenth century. Bernard Mandel sees in some statements of the period, manifestations of Gompers' earlier close associations with members of the First International and subsequent socialistic organizations. Mandel particularly stresses Gompers' class consciousness, his militancy, and his expressed belief in the inevitability of radical change some time in the future. But he is disturbed by the ambiguity with which Gompers spoke of the ultimate goals of the labor movement, and doubts that he was really a serious theoretical thinker. Gompers "did not always believe what he said," Mandel decides. He utilized a radical vocabulary only to "fend off criticism" of the narrow objectives to which he wished to confine the AFL's efforts. Behind this front he could not transcend the limitations of his own pragmatic, opportunistic mind. He was "constitutionally allergic to speculative thought." In the same school, Philip Foner has concluded that the vagueness of Gompers' statements on the nature of the future society veiled a basically opportunistic and bureaucratic mind concerned primarily with career advancement: "He knew enough to advocate radical principles when these would advance his own position in the labor movement, and he was fully prepared to abandon them the moment he felt that they were proving to be an obstacle to his career."[2]

More subtle is the tendency of socio-psychological analysis of the origins of the AFL to lead away from a serious consideration of the role of ideas in its formation. Granted, as Robert Weibe argues in his synthesis of the period, the Gilded Age appears to have witnessed the beginning of the end of an age of island communities, particularism, parochialism, and dispersed power, and their replacement in sector after sector with organizational order suited the needs of an urban-industrial life. In that sense the federation was a natural result of a groping for hierarchical order and control over forces "feared and not fully understood." The impingement of technological innovation and a national economy upon trades and trade status created an insecurity for many who looked to their unions to consolidate their power over their crafts, which they did, and preserve the workers' "slender hold within the middle class." Business unionism's strongest buttress may well have been the craftsmen's "passionate urge toward respectability." But did this mean that "the apparent 'class' consciousness of such men as Samuel Gompers actually represented no more than a generalized version of this extreme craft and organization consciousness"?[3] Does not such a characterization eliminate consideration of ideas as motives and tell us less than we need to know about the sources of creative, inspired leadership?

What I am suggesting is that Gompers' more radical professions and more glimmering ideals seem less like rhetorical flourishes to me than they do to many of my colleagues. That I can take him more nearly at his word than they, I can attribute only to the way in which I have come to know him. I have studied his teachers and companions. As nearly as I could I have tasted their ideas as he did. I have found the roots of their ideas in the works of Karl Marx and in their correspondence with Marx. The way Gompers thought in the 1880s and 1890s came as no surprise to me. The same thinking was at work in the 1860s and 1870s and it is reflected in Gompers' own words as soon as he became an articulate labor leader in the 1870s.

This study was completed as a dissertation in 1970 and was virtually in production at Greenwood Press before I had the benefit of reading William M. Dick, *Labor and Socialism in America: The Gompers Era* (Port Washington, N.Y.: Kennikat Press, 1972). I am impressed that we should have independently reached many of the same conclusions about Samuel Gompers and the early AFL. Our studies, which essentially do not cover the same ground, should complement each other in substantially revising the historical assessment of the man. Our main difference may be that Dick finds Gompers to be a syndicalist. I don't believe pure and simple unionism can be understood without its political dimension, its promise that the political movement of the workers would emerge from a groundwork of success in the economic struggle.

A difficulty the reader may find with this work is that Gompers himself is only occasionally to be found in half or more of its chapters. He darts in and out of the picture, staying barely long enough to establish his presence. This is unavoidable. I see Gompers as at the tail end of a tradition. Before his ideas can be dealt with intensively, the coterie of leaders with whom he was intimate in his formative years must be introduced. This in turn cannot be done meaningfully without beginning where they did—with Karl Marx in mid-century England.

Samuel Gompers
and the Origins of the
American Federation of Labor
1848-1896

1
Karl Marx
and the Trade Unions
1884-1872

Samuel Gompers' susceptibility to Marxist influence can perhaps be traced to his childhood in England. Ten years old in 1860, he left school and worked in a cigar shop until his father moved the family to the United States in 1863.[1]

There was a body of Marxist thought particularly suited to the practical outlook of the nineteenth-century English workshop. Karl Marx wrote in the middle and late 1860s with English workers very much in mind. One cannot help but feel that Samuel Gompers' brief three years in an English cigar shop as a boy established a temperamental bond between the young cigarmaker and the writings of the revolutionary leader.

British workers at this time exhibited a mixture of idealism and practicality that Karl Marx found auspicious. They easily identified with a variety of mass causes abroad, sympathizing in succession with Mazzini's movement in Italy, the plight of the slaves in the American Civil War, and the

insurrection of the Poles. They were thinking of the fight
for social justice in universal terms.[2]

International developments with a more practical bearing
on the workers' well-being also occupied the thoughts of the
Englishmen. If cigarmakers, for instance, found drama in
the American war against human bondage, they also eyed
the United States as a potential home for surplus members
of their crowded trade, the more so as alteration of the
tobacco duties in 1863 depressed the entire industry. Their
trade society, while frantically trying to convince continental
labor that emigration to England was unwise, established its
own emigration fund to relieve the trade by subsidizing the
passage of English cigarmakers to the United States. One
of those to accept emigration assistance was Samuel Gompers' father, Solomon Gompers.[3]

Karl Marx developed much of his analysis of the trade
unions and their role in the coming revolution after
intensely studying the British workers. As the Gomperses
left England, Marx already had found much of a very radical nature in practical aspects of the British labor movement. He was, in effect, developing an approach to trade
unionism that was to seem very relevant to Samuel Gompers
not long after the Gomperses settled in the United States.

Marx wrote in the face of dismay among many revolutionaries with the practical and conservative trend of labor
organization in Britain. Since the early 1850s, a disciplined
"new model" unionism had grown in favor among British
unions. New model unions charged high dues and offered
attractive benefits to workers who could afford to join. They
were moderate in their demands upon employers and government. Their aim was a gradual increase in the economic
security and cultural opportunities of the skilled craftsmen.[4]

Revolutionary leaders found new model unionism regressive, particularly in its tight control over access to trade

employment through restrictive apprentice regulations, but they could not convince union leaders to organize the entire British proletariat.[5] Yet to Marx, the British workers' idealism about international events in the early sixties suggested radical potential developing alongside this conservative trend. He was to demonstrate how the spirit of these workers, and their practical organizations, might auger revolution in capitalism's future.

In the basic document which Marx had previously furnished his followers, the *Communist Manifesto* (1848), he had already tried to impress upon the workers that capitalism actually provided their class with the power it needed to achieve its emancipation. How dependent the capitalists were on the workers, he exulted, for though the capitalists controlled the productive process in modern society, they could not operate it without the collective efforts of all members of society. All of what Marx saw as features of capitalistic modernization, from the initial capital accumulation, to the continuing revolution and centralization of the instruments of production, to the replacement of the decentralized forms of feudal agricultural and industrial production with a centralized capitalistic structure, had depended upon the cooperation of the working class. And in the competitive world economy that capitalism had created, the continued elimination of those producers economically incompatible with the modernizing of the productive forces was also a cooperative effort. Backward elements of the bourgeoisie, from the small tradesman or shopkeeper to the handicraftsman and peasant farmer, did not have sufficient capital to carry on at the scale at which modern industry functioned or had specialized skills which new methods of production made obsolete. These "reactionary" or "petit bourgeois" elements were being eradicated, despite their aggressive attempts to "roll back the wheel of history," because they could not command the labor of the workers and utilize it to augment their capital.[6]

Marx was predictive as well as descriptive in 1848, for he discerned in the' massing together of the workers and in the obliteration of the old distinctions in labor through centralization and modernization, the seeds of the destruction of the capitalistic system. Formerly the workers had supplied their labor docilely because they were in competition with other workers. The occasional resistance of a workman to his employer had resulted only in his replacement by a competing worker. But with mechanization stressing the similarity of all laboring men, and with centralization increasing their communication with one another, the workers were gaining a sense of their common class interest. Inevitably the "collisions" between workers and capitalists would lose their individual character and take on the character of class conflict.[7]

To mobilize the workers for struggle as a class was, for Marx, the most important function of labor organizers. Their significance lay not so much in the immediate gains they achieved, but in the ever-expanding union of the workers which they facilitated. The organizers drew the workers of isolated localities into contact with one another and centralized local struggles into a national class confrontation. In so doing, they not only advanced the workers' economic class interests, but enhanced their political class power as well. This, Marx believed, was so because political and economic power were interrelated. The economic advance of any class was always accompanied by corresponding political advance of that class. It was by this means, for instance, that the bourgeoisie had achieved "exclusive political sway" in the modern representative state. So too, once the workers were organized as a class, would each economic advance bring with it equivalent political power, for "every class struggle is a political struggle." As the workers wiped out job competition "by their revolutionary combination, due to association," they would constitute themselves a political party. Thus the bourgeoisie was itself supplying the proletariat with "its own elements of political and general education."[8]

The *Manifesto*, however, contained only a limited groundwork for Marx's later appraisal of the revolutionary role of trade unions. Its major concern was with the prospects of a German rather than an English revolution. There was an air of immediacy in the document, for, despite the peculiar backwardness of the German homeland, Marx believed the highly advanced theoretical understanding of the German intellect would shortly precipitate a bourgeois revolution against feudalism. This revolution, he predicted, would not be successful, for backward Germany had not yet developed a middle class capable of making revolution. But once the bourgeois leadership had fallen away, the revolutionary proletariat under the leadership of an intellectual vanguard would continue the revolution in the name of the inhuman conditions the workers had suffered. The workers would then not be satisfied without the dissolution of the entire existing social order, and this German proletarian revolution would bristle through the interdependent world economy created by capitalism, initiating permanent revolution throughout Europe.[9]

If there was a second national influence in the *Manifesto*, it was French rather than English. Paris had served as the informal revolutionary capital of Europe since the 1830s, holding this dominating position primarily because of the intellectual stimulus which revolutionaries found in contemplating the French Revolution. Marx's analysis of the coming of the German revolution reflected his preoccupation with the catalytic effect of the French bourgeoisie's initial

challenge to the ancien régime in 1789. Theirs had proven
to be only the first in a series of insurrections in which moderate factions were displaced by progressively more radical
factions, causing the revolution to burst its original bounds.
The *Manifesto* also evinced a conditioning by the French
Revolution to think in terms of cataclysmic change in the
social order, speaking as it does of the sweeping away by
force of the bourgeois forms of production.[10]

A decade after the *Manifesto*, Marx had already gone a
long way from his French mood and German preoccupation, achieving a frame of mind in which he could devote
more attention to the revolutionary role which the trade
union movement, particularly that of England, might play.
By late 1850, having witnessed the demolition of the European revolutions of 1848, Marx had begun to stress that
more damage than good was done by prematurely inciting
proletarian revolutions. What was needed, he submitted,
was a period of organizational and educational groundwork
within the proletariat to forearm and prime it for its final
class confrontation. Marx had originally written the *Manifesto* as a guide for the Communist League, a revolutionary
exile group conspiring in the late forties to seize control of
the simmering radical movement in Germany for purposes
of revolution. Now he opposed revolutionary conspiracy
without preparation, and held this conviction strongly
enough by September 1850 to risk schism in the revolutionary forces in its defense. At the meeting of the League's
Central Authority in London, he dismissed as overly
enthusiastic those who sought an immediate mandate for
armed rebellion. Advocating the postponement of revolution in the name of proletarian readiness, Marx said that
he "opposed ephemeral notions of the proletariat" and
believed the party of the proletariat to be "precisely rather
far from achieving power." He called for devotion to the

development of this party and warned that even if the achievement of power prior to preparation were possible, it would be undesirable. It would yield petit bourgeois measures rather than revolution.[11]

Aware of the hazards of precipitate revolution, Marx propounded a clear responsibility for revolutionary intellectuals like himself. In the *Manifesto* he had already assigned to such intellectuals the decisive role in the historical development of the proletariat. He had predicted that, as the class struggle intensified and reached its decisive stage, a portion of the bourgeoisie would go over to the proletariat, particularly "a portion of the bourgeois ideologists" who by their unusual educational opportunities "have raised themselves to the level of comprehending theoretically the historical movement as a whole." These intellectuals would be the only part of the working class party "clearly understanding the line of march, the conditions, and the ultimate general results of the proletarian movement."[12]

In the fifties Marx began to emphasize not so much the role of the intellectuals in an imminent revolution as their duty to impress upon the workers the historical dangers of premature proletarian insurrections and to use their analytical skills to demonstrate the organizational prerequisites of revolution.

Because Marx stressed this preparatory role, he was less attracted to the conspiratorial Communist League with which he had been associated in the late forties. Since the European revolution no longer seemed pending, there was less need for what Bertram D. Wolfe calls the "party-of-the-moment" such as the Communist League. This did not mean that Marx no longer thought of forming the working class into a party. He simply insisted upon distinguishing between an "ephemeral" clique and the development of the party of the proletariat. The former

had been a party of convenience, a mere episode in the formation of the proletarian party. The latter Wolfe has
described as "a phenomenon of nature growing spontaneously out of the soil of modern society . . . the party in
the great historical sense." This might not resemble a political party in the traditional sense at all.[13]

Marx's interest in the trade union movement grew in
proportion to his interest in preparation and he became
more concerned with England, where the organization of
the working class by trade unions had made its greatest
progress. England was pivotal to the permanent European
revolution for it was the only advanced industrial nation,
the "demiurge of the bourgeois cosmos" or heartland from
which exploitive capitalism had spread across the world,
creating an international market and interdependent world
economy. He now believed that the revolutions of 1848 on
the Continent had been only peripheral political uprisings.
They could not have approached more general success
because they did not involve the bourgeois heartland. The
permanent revolution needed a proletarian impulse from
England.[14]

The difficulty Marx faced was that it was precisely in England that revolution seemed least likely. The productive
forces of English capitalism, he mused, had inflated to their
most expansive phase at mid-century, creating industrial
prosperity and stabilizing conditions at a level, which, for
the time, provided for some degree of proletarian comfort.
Under such conditions the workers seemed satisfied to
move in the direction followed by one faction of the former
Chartist movement, toward the poorly defined workers' suffrage goals of the Bright radicals, with no thought of an
independent class program. Meanwhile the English bourgeoisie had consummated a peculiar alliance with the aristocracy, precluding the possibility of an English bourgeois

revolution in the near future. What seemed to be happening in England was well described by Friedrich Engels in 1858, writing to Marx on the defection of the left-wing Chartist, Ernest Jones, to the cause of worker suffrage and collaboration with the middle class:

> It seems to me that Jones' new move . . . is really bound up with the fact that the English proletariat is actually becoming more and more bourgeois, so that this most bourgeois of all nations apparently aims . . . at a bourgeois aristocracy and a bourgeois proletariat alongside the bourgeoisie. . . .[15]

Marx surmised that if a revolutionary proletariat was to develop in England, the independent self-image of the English working class must somehow be restored. And he predicted that if the independent day-to-day struggle for economic and political reform, in which the trade unions took a leading role, was encouraged, it would rekindle the fighting spirit and class consciousness which he believed had characterized the true Chartist movement. The growing consciousness of its class interests and isolation which this would impart to the English working class would then induce it to join the international revolutionary movement.[16]

In 1864 Marx found what he fancied was the instrument for stimulating the independent activities of the English trade union movement, educating its leaders, imbuing it with a sense of independence, and binding it to the revolutionary movement on the Continent. This was the International Workingmen's Association (IWA) or First International, whose inauguration in 1864 culminated developments on both sides of the channel. Within England there existed in the early sixties a climate of opinion among

positivist and radical intellectuals influential among the
workers favoring international working-class solidarity. New
model union leaders, meanwhile, were beginning to fully
grasp that they were now operating in an international
labor market that could only be controlled through practical
cooperation among the labor movements of the various
countries involved. Also, for the English workers in the
early sixties a sense of domestic isolation was inescapable.
They found little middle-class support for the position of
labor during the London builders' strike at the beginning
of the decade. They were conspicuously apart in their sympathy for the emancipationists in the American Civil War
and for the Poles in their insurrection shortly thereafter.
But they had stood alone before and an inner resource of
independence, derived from the Owenite and Chartist
movements of earlier decades, was not far below the surface.[17]

On the Continent workers still responded to the drum
of international solidarity which pulsed from the French
Revolution and was amplified by subsequent European
upheavals and a growing, though diverse, European
revolutionary movement. English workers, as has been seen,
were not untouched by this emotional brotherhood. More
tangible connections between the French and English workers developed in the early sixties after French unions
sprouted under a very limited toleration conceded by
Napoleon III. Permitted to exist in the form of unthreaten-
ing "friendly societies," they were encouraged by the French
government to send delegates to the London International
Exhibition in 1862, where they might pick up ideas of mod-
eration and discard their radicalism under the influence of
the supposedly more sedate new model tradition. The
Frenchmen were graciously received by the London Trade
Council and returned again in 1864 with nascent concep-

tions of an international organization. When they joined in founding the IWA that year, it was conceived as a practical effort by French and English trade unionists to explore the international community of trade union interests.[18]

Marx knew that since 1862 the French workers had also joined the English on a more idealistic plane. Parallel labor protests against Russian oppression in Poland had led to a joint protest by French and English workers in July 1863. It was, in fact, only after the Polish crisis began that British labor leaders began actively to pursue closer cooperation with the French. In an address "To the Workingmen of France from the Workingmen of England," in December 1862, the English spoke of the need for a "fraternity of peoples" in which the united effort on behalf of Polish freedom would be only the first project.[19] It was, therefore, with a mixture of practical and idealistic concerns, much as has already been noted among the English cigarmakers, that the English trade unions looked upon the international scene as the convening of the IWA in September 1864 approached.

A vital task for Marx as one theoretician of the First International was to cultivate this initial English support. He understood that an ideology that slighted the practical in its pursuit of the ideal could not strike a sympathetic chord in many British workshops. On the other hand, if he could develop theoretical guidelines that avoided the doctrinaire in deference to the day-to-day constructiveness that trade unionists associated with progress, he would probably emerge as the organization's leading theoretician. In attempting to reach this status Marx seems to have had the inside track due to the strong position which his friends George Eccarius and Herman Jung, members of London's revolutionary German exile community, had achieved among the English trade union leadership.[20]

With initial English support, Marx was called upon to deliver the International's inaugural address. Not unexpectedly, he devoted special attention to praising the recent manifestations of idealism among the English workers. What had prevented European intervention in the American Civil War, he claimed, was "not the wisdom of the ruling classes but the heroic resistance to their criminal folly" by the English working class. To the assassination of "heroic Poland" by Russia, the workers of England and Europe had reacted, when all else failed, with "simultaneous denunciations" whose effect was to invoke the "simple laws of morals and justice." Such experiences were gradually leading the workers to the conclusion that they must stand together in their struggles for emancipation regardless of country, or else "be chastised by the common discomfiture of their incoherent efforts."[21]

Marx gave equal credit to the more practical activities of the English working class in bringing about this growing class unity. In the *Manifesto* he had treated the English workers' achievement of securing passage of the ten hours' bill of 1847 as a manifestation of the class organization of workers and the intensification of the collisions of proletariat and bourgeoisie. Nothing was said then of the possible constructive value of the measure itself, for the impoverishment of the proletariat was supposedly equally a part of this phase of the class struggle and such measures could therefore have little ameliorative effect. The Inaugural Address now found that the measure had resulted in "immense physical, moral and intellectual benefits" for factory workers, a conclusion made more consistent by playing down the idea of increasing impoverishment and speaking more of increasing social contrast in society: ". . . every fresh development of the productive powers of labour must

tend to deepen social contrasts and point social antagonism."[22]

Having testified to the practical importance of the bill,
Marx pointed to its even more important contribution to
the development of the workers as an independent class.
Ameliorative in nature, the measure at the same time was
a milestone in the history of the social consciousness of the
working class party. Passed in the face of bourgeois predic-
tions that it would result in "the death knell of British
industry," it had proven a success even by the admission
of the bourgeois theoreticians themselves. The political
economy of the middle class, "blind rule of the supply and
demand laws," had been defeated by the political economy
of the proletariat, "social production controlled by social
foresight." Similarly, the successful cooperative factory
movement of the English workers was more than a palliative. In opposition to the political economy of the middle
class, the workers in these cooperatives had demonstrated
that "hired labour is but a transitory and inferior form,
destined to disappear before associated labour."[23]

In sum, Marx was proposing that the workers had
reached a major watershed without departing from their
practical interests. And he offered certain observations to
serve as the IWA's provisional "rules," guidelines for proceeding with the very practical work of revolution: (1) The
source of workers' "social misery, mental degradation and
political dependence" lay in the system justified by the political economy of the bourgeoisie, one based upon "the
economical subjection of the man of labour to the monop-
olizer of the means of labour, that is the sources of life."
(2) The workers must therefore proceed as an independent
class if they wished to substitute a political economy based
on "equal rights and duties, and the abolition of all class

rule"; in other words, "the emancipation of the working class must be conquered by the working classes themselves." (3) As the workers proceeded as an independent class, they would use the political power they conquered not "for class privileges and monopolies" but for their emancipation: "The economical emancipation of the working classes is therefore the great end to which every political movement ought to be subordinate as a means." (4) The first step in constituting the working class as a party in the broad sense and achieving power involved unification, "to combine the disconnected workingmen's societies of their respective countries into national bodies, represented by central national bodies, represented by central national organs."[24]

In the eight years after the Gomperses left England, the period 1864-1872, Karl Marx achieved his status as the main theoretician of the First International. The internal history of the International during this period pitted Marx against a host of competing groups, each arrayed behind an ideology against which he was forced to sharpen his own. He argued against the Proudhonists' contention that private property could be retained, reformed of its exploitive features. He rejected the spontaneous and destructive incendiarism of the Bakuninists as being no substitute for the orderly development of revolutionary class consciousness under the nurture of an intellectual vanguard. He equally disputed the notion of the Blanquists that the revolutionary vanguard should constitute itself a revolutionary elite, forcing the workers into revolution by conspiracy, rather than pacing itself by the preparedness of the workers for that revolution.[25]

In the process, Marx also marked out in more elaborate detail the revolutionary role of the trade union movement. In 1864 he had still regarded crafts unions of the type that prevailed in England as very temporary societies, useful in

achieving occasional breakthrough victories for the proletarian political economy, but bound to become meaning-
less as the crafts themselves became mechanized and crafts
skills useless. By 1866 he had come to envision an evolution
of these unions into something greater than craft guilds.
Serving as nuclei around which the entire working class of
each nation could be organized and disciplined, they would
become instruments for that revolutionary combination of
workers of which he had written in the *Manifesto*. Their
mold would provide the form in which the working class
could most quickly emerge as an independent political
force, exacting concessions and ultimately overthrowing the
bourgeois state. In the *Instructions* he wrote for the guidance
of the General Council's delegation to the Geneva Congress
of 1866, Marx appealed to the unions of all countries to
expand their organizational efforts to all fields of labor, and
especially to unskilled workers.[26]

While he was placing the trade unions at the core of the
historical workingmen's party, Marx was also working on
his theoretical analysis of bourgeois society, which demarcated the field of economic operations for the trade unions
within the system of private property, and located as well
the point at which the trade unions must depart from that
system. The unions' role was to lead the assault on capitalistic profit, for all profit, Marx strove to demonstrate, was
confiscated labor. In *Value, Price and Profit*, an address given
to the IWA General Council in 1865, and in the first vol-
ume of *Capital* in 1867, Marx argued that prices, from
which profits and wages were drawn, were totally determined by the quantity of labor crystallized in the commodity. Values and prices being social functions of commodities
"having nothing at all to do with the natural qualities," their
exchange rate could be fixed only by reducing them to the
one common social substance contained in them, which was

labor But if laborers created all the value of a commodity, what determined the percentage of the value for which labor was paid, and the percentage of unpaid (i.e., confiscated) surplus labor or profit? Marx saw no absolute minimum for wages other than that amount necessary to keep the worker alive and supply him with energy. It was in the employer's self-interest to pay this much. If, however, a worker who could sustain himself on the value of six hours of work could be forced to work twelve, half of the total value he created would be the object of confiscation by his employer. If he wished to dispute the possession of the confiscated portion of the value of his labor, then his actual wages and his employer's profit would be determined by

> the continuous struggle between capital and labour, the capitalist constantly tending to reduce wages to their physical minimum, and to extend the working day to its physical maximum, while the workingman constantly presses in the opposite direction.[27]

Marx believed that in this economic battle for wages the workers were fighting a losing cause. The centralization of capital (that imminent law of capitalism which dictated that "one capitalist always kills the many") had generated what he described as a progressive change in the composition of capital. Capitalist competed with capitalist, mechanizing to cheapen commodity production, increasing production to achieve economies of scale and compensate for declining price value per commodity, and all toward the invariable expropriation by the larger of the smaller competitor, whether farm or factory. In the process, the proportion of fixed capital in modern production was continually increasing, that of labor (variable capital) decreasing, creating a technologically unemployed contingent of workers which Marx referred to as the "industrial reserve army." At the same time, machinery was radically altering the means of production so that a new stratum of lesser skilled men, and of women and children, was now available for exploitation as part of the unemployed pool. The existence of a competitive unemployed army was a tremendous imperative for a division of unpaid labor more and more favorable to the employers.[28]

Though a losing battle, the struggle for economic betterment was essential. It reinforced the workers' sense of their own manhood: "By cowardly giving way in their every day conflict with capital, they would certainly disqualify themselves for the initiating of any larger movement." More importantly, such temporary successes as the workers did sustain served to aggravate the contradictions inherent in the capitalistic system. Since, for instance, profits resulted only from the expropriation of human labor, the successful achievement by the workers of a legally regulated working day forced the employers to immediately consider ways of systematically getting more work from their workers in the shorter time period. Through mechanization the employers were able to substitute more intensified labor for labor of more extensive duration. Nor could the workers resist this intensification; they were compelled to furnish more labor because of the availability of unemployed workers who would gladly do so in their place.[29]

But the starkness of the contradiction, in which potentially liberating improvements were repeatedly converted into instruments for making labor more precarious and more exhausting, served to educate the workers. In their trade unions, Marx relates, the workers had begun to organize "a regular cooperation between employed and unemployed in order to destroy or to weaken the ruinous effects of this natural law. . . ." At the same time, the artificial acceleration of mechanization, which the reduction of hours stimulated, would inevitably generate a movement for a further reduction of hours. In the last analysis, Marx projected, a practical shortening of the working day, one which left enough energy for "free development, intellectual and social" in the workers' spare time, could only be achieved as the employer class "is more and more deprived of the power to shift the natural burden of labour from its own shoulders to those of another layer of society." The movement for the shorter working day could find its last limit only in the reduction of the working day to that time necessary for the subsistence of the worker (with the understanding that the workers "would lay claim to an altogether different standard of life"), and the maintenance of a fund for reserve and accumulation. But this could only be accomplished by the more even division of labor among all ablebodied members of society, through the "generalisation of labour" and the suppression of the capitalistic form of production. This was the lesson of the economic struggle.[30]

Because the trade unions led the battle for wages, they were, for Marx, the "centres of resistance against the encroachments of capital," with an important revolutionary role in bourgeois society. A Marxist could find worthy occupation working alongside other trade unionists. What distinguished a Marxist from the others was his dedication not only to the protection and advancement of the working class, but also to its complete emancipation as an ultimate end. He must keep in mind that conservative movements "fail generally from limiting themselves to a guerilla war against the effects of the existing system," whereas the revolutionary movement simultaneously worked for the abolition of the wage system by using the organization perfected in everyday struggles as a lever for the workers' emancipation. Force would have to serve as this lever in most Continental countries, Marx said in his final speech to the International. But in a special signal to the movements of England, the United States and, hesitantly, Holland, he added "I must not be supposed to imply that the means to this end will be everywhere the same. We know that special regard must be paid to the institutions, customs and traditions of various lands." The workers of the three countries "may hope to secure their ends by peaceful means."[31]

By the 1870s a substantial body of Marxist thought could have a striking appeal to a trade unionist. Without slighting the practical work of the union, Marx elevated the avocation of the unionist. Trade unionism as a revolutionary calling was a rugged profession. It had duties of exhausting commitment and scope. In return it offered righteousness and a comprehension of the human existence and its direction —in essence, the rewards of a religion. This tradition of ideas was subject to transfer much as were the Gomperses in their migration abroad.

2
The First International in America

The First International itself did not survive the sectarian struggles that characterized its eight years in Europe. Marx eventually arranged for the transfer of its headquarters to the United States, in order to prevent its capture by his opponents and let it die a quiet death. But in America the IWA for a time enjoyed an unexpected second life, due, in no small measure, to the vigor of the leadership there. Among the trade unionists of this leadership, the concept of a radical role for the trade union movement survived, and became a recurring theme in a tradition leading toward the founding of the American Federation of Labor.

Samuel Gompers entered the trade union movement under the influence of the trade unionists who had led the International in America. Before he became involved with them, he limited his participation in the trade union movement to a casual attendance at meetings of Local Cigarmakers' Union No. 15 of New York City. If he became a union member in 1864, as he says, he was one of the last members to be admitted so young. At the second convention of the Cigarmakers' National Union, held in 1865, a law was adopted in the interest of national uniformity, reading: "No person shall be eligible to membership in this union, unless he be a white male of age 18 years, and has served an apprenticeship of not less than three years." Gompers would have been only fourteen at the time he joined the union.[1]

As a boy in a man's organization, Gompers found a more satisfying outlet for his fraternal instincts in the popular judge and jury clubs of the day. He was a member of the Court Empire City of the Ancient Order of Foresters and, before reaching its retirement age of twenty-one, had risen to become the Court's Chief Ranger. Not to be denied fraternal pleasures after "retirement," Gompers, in the early seventies, helped organize two lodges of the Independent Order of Odd Fellows and as late as 1873 proudly took on the responsibilities of the first Noble Grand of the Stephen A. Douglas Lodge, which at the least suggests that he was something less than preoccupied with trade unionism at the time.[2]

Other interests and circumstances also probably reduced Gompers' availability for union activities. There were the Cooper Union lectures: "Nothing humanly possible ever kept me from attending those Saturday night lectures." In 1866 and early 1867 he was courting, which involved long journeys to Brooklyn two or three evenings a week. Shortly after his marriage on January 18, 1867, unemployment and the responsibilities of a family forced him to make his residence first in Hackensack and later in Lambertsville, New Jersey, for about two years.[3]

Nor was the state of Local 15 such as to attract the enthusiasm of its new recruits. When Gompers returned to

New York, his union was emaciated by the effects of new ways of organizing the production of cigars, both through family production in employer-owned tenement houses, and through the use of a new tool, known as the mold, which made the use of unskilled labor possible. The National Cigarmakers determined to combat the introduction of molds, but insofar as Gompers participated in the resistance it was more by reason of his personal associations than his union membership: "The crowd of boys with whom I was associated voted for a strike and I followed along." The strike failed, the National Union having no funds with which to support it, and Local 15 limped into the seventies with less than fifty members.[4]

Then, in less than six years, Gompers' relationship to the labor movement changed completely, so that on a Saturday evening in October 1876 he could be found participating in the most advanced councils of the radical labor leadership in America. On that evening the *Labor Standard* picked him out as among the eight men who engaged in debate at a meeting of the American Section of the Workingmen's Party of the United States in New York City's Jefferson Hall. The issue was the preservation of the purity and independence of the working class movement and Gompers joined the section in resolving unanimously:

> Whereas, All issues raised by the political parties of the propertied class are in the interest of the class and of no advantage to the working class.
>
> Be it resolved, That it is the duty of the working class to ignore not only all the existing political parties but their issues and to support only those questions raised by and coming from recognized Trade and Labor bodies, made in the interest of the working class.[5]

The meeting was of the same sort Gompers had been attending for several years, at which small groups of "brainy" men spoke in Marxian terms about trade unions. The sessions were first connected with, and later the legacy of, the First International in America.[6]

The resolution unanimously endorsed defended a principle that had been severely tested during the decade. Though loyalty to Marx's dictum that "the emancipation of the working classes must be conquered by the working classes themselves" came naturally to long-time followers of Marx and the International, there were newer recruits who wished to mold the American IWA according to their own bourgeois reform ideas. While most of the original architects of the International in America were of foreign origin, American sections had emerged from middle-class reform organizations, particularly one known as New Democracy. Their program for the workers' emancipation ran a gamut of proposals from free love to women's suffrage to broad schemes of banking and monetary reform and socialism. Gompers shared the disgust of the older leaders toward these experimentalists, later describing their leaders as "a brilliant group of faddists, reformers, and sensation-loving spirits." Yet these bourgeois reformers did serve a purpose in the IWA. They forced the leaders of the North American Federation to defend the faith. The challenge helped to sustain and enliven the career of Marxian trade unionism in America.[7]

It had been by no means clear at the beginning of the 1870s that the foreign, but supposedly theoretically advanced, members of the vanguard of the International could retain control of the organization they were building in the United States. The American reformers had a good claim to the leadership, for they could argue, as they did in their appeals to the General Council in London, that they composed the only native American sections in the American branch of the International. For example, Friedrich A. Sorge, who would become the leading light of the International in America, was a German refugee. He had participated in the Baden revolution of 1849, and had been in Switzerland and London before coming to New York in 1852. The most powerful section in America, No. 1 of New York City, had its roots in the Communist Club of New York, founded in 1857 by Sorge and two other German immigrants, Conrad Carl and Siegfried Meyer. In 1868 the club had joined with the General German Workingmen's Union, founded in New York by German Lassalleans in 1865, to form the Social Party of New York under Sorge's leadership. After making an insignificant showing in the election of 1868 it reorganized and, with Sorge as its leading spirit, became Section No. 1 of the International in America in December 1869. German in membership, it was soon joined by one French and one Bohemian section and together the three formed a Provisional North American Central Committee of the IWA. With the expectation of becoming the permanent council of North America, the Provisional Central Council assigned itself a duration of one year, beginning in mid-December of 1870. By the following April it claimed to represent eight sections, five German and one each French, Bohemian, and Irish.[8]

The resourcefulness of the American sections in turning toward London to appeal for power forced the Sorge leadership into a productive consultation with Marx. The correspondence in a few years accumulated a small but significant Marxist syllabus for the trade unionist in America. No sooner had the Provisional Central Committee been organized than the native American sections, led by Section 12, gained a receptive hearing at the highest councils of the International. Marx himself hinted to Sorge in March 1871

that a Central Committee composed solely of foreign sections would be of questionable influence in the United
States. He seemed unimpressed by Sorge's argument that
the so-called foreigners were not temporary residents, as
many were in London, but full citizens of the United States,
who were well represented in every trade and labor society
and composed the entire membership of some of the most
powerful unions.[9]

As Marx continued to press for a broadening of the
American movement, Sorge shifted to a more detailed
analysis of the American scene, to the special institutions,
customs, and traditions Marx had earlier found of primary
importance in the strategy of each national movement. The
American movement must be judged according to circumstances "widely differing from those of European countries," Sorge pleaded in 1871. The great majority of workingmen in the most industrial sections of this country were
immigrants who had come to America in order to rise to
a position of wealth denied them at home. Employers in
America devoted themselves to preserving the illusion that
determined individual effort on the part of workers could
lead to the realization of such dreams. Little did it matter
if all the time employers were actually making the attainment of such goals by the workers all the more difficult.
The visionary ideal of individual progress discredited those
who suggested the necessity of unified worker resistance.
Workers clung instead to the religious and political prejudices that divided them from their fellow workers.[10]

Such arguments appealed to Marx. As recently as April
9, 1870, he had written to Siegfried Meyer and August Vogt
of the International in America, bemoaning a similar
antagonism among the workers of England as "the secret
of the impotence of the English working class, despite their
organization." Marx had counseled these leaders to work

for "a coalition of the German workers with the Irish (as
well as with those English and American workers who are
ready to do so)." And Sorge could easily have taken his cue
in the first place from Marx's reference in *Value, Price and
Profit* to the favored position of laborers in colonial
countries. Marx had noted that capitalists in America

> cannot prevent the labour market from being con-
> tinuously emptied by the continuous conversion
> of   wages   laborers   into   independent,   self-
> sustaining peasants. The function of a wages
> labourer is for a very large part of the American
> people but a probational state, which they are sure
> to leave within a longer or shorter term.[11]

This measure of the American workers became characteristic of the trade unionists of the Internationalist tradition.
Their strategy began with a Marxian characterization of the
conservative mentality of the American workers whom they
had to mold toward emancipation.

Sorge did not argue that the internal divisions in the
American working class could not be overcome, but he
believed they would not be overcome as long as the bourgeoisie maintained its stranglehold on the labor movement.
He felt that American labor leaders, whether for honest or
selfish reasons, had fascinated their followers with issues of
relevance only to the bourgeoisie. They had beguiled
American labor into a series of National Labor Congresses,
meeting annually since 1866, each one more remote than
the previous from legitimate labor issues. Instead of concerning themselves with the defense of trade unions, the
right to strike, the abolition of convict labor and the tenement house system, and the enactment of the eight-hour
day, the American workers had been captivated by a pro-

gram for the reform of the monetary system.[12] It was difficult for Sorge to see how the workers could develop any consciousness of their class interests while devoting themselves to "a question brought up by the parties of the ruling classes." If the International in America was to wean the American working class from the bourgeoisie, he insisted, it must first rid itself of the group of well-meaning scientists, philanthropists, and the like who were coaxing the workers into reform parties. This group was convincing the workers that amelioration of their conditions through the peaceful and easy means of "universal suffrage, glittering educational measures, benevolent and homestead societies, universal language or other schemes or systems" would somehow lead them to the achievement of the "welfare of mankind."[13]

During the fall of 1871 Sorge continued to prod Marx, deploring the American trade unions' alienation from politics and blaming the false leadership of outsiders and bourgeois issues. He reported that the National Labor Union, increasingly dominated by middle-class reformers, was virtually boycotted by the important trade unions. Except for the miners none attended the annual labor congress in 1871.[14]

At the end of November Marx sent a very important letter to Friedrich Bolte, a cigar packer on the Central Committee, in which, finally, he accepted Sorge's analysis. Drawing on his European experience, Marx saw the general problem as that of dealing with "the socialist or semi-socialist sects," a category which included the Proudhonists, Bakunists, and Lassalleans in Europe as much as Section 12 in the United States. The very purpose of founding the First International, he reminded, had been to replace these sects with a real organization of the working class for struggle.

> The development of socialist sectarianism and
> that of the real working-class movement always
> stand in inverse ratio to each other. Sects are jus-
> tified (historically) so long as the working class is
> not yet ripe for independent historical movement.
> As soon as it has attained this maturity all sects
> are essentially reactionary.

An American movement independent of the sects could be
built on the basis of three propositions. First, before the
workers could conquer political power, there must appear
"a previous organization of the working class developed up
to a certain point and arising precisely from its economic
struggles." Second, the workers' economic struggles and
their drawing together into an organization were processes
which nourished each other in a reciprocal and accelerating
fashion: "While these movements presuppose a certain
degree of previous organization, they are in turn equally
a means of developing this organization." Finally, with the
construction of a class organization on the basis of economic
class struggle, the independent political movement of the
working class will also have been achieved, for "every movement in which the working class comes out as a *class* against
the ruling classes and tries to coerce them by pressure from
without is a political movement."[15]

With these guidelines, Marx opened the way in late 1871
for deferring the formation of an American workers' party
in the traditional sense of a political party. He required only
that the International in America train the working class
for the achievement of political power "by continual agitation against, and a hostile attitude toward, the politics of
the ruling classes." The agitation of issues on a class basis,
he encouraged, would serve a dual purpose: preventing the
American working class, while weak, from becoming a play-

thing in the hands of the ruling class, and generating a class feeling that would aid in the building of labor organizations. On this basis he was able to inform Sorge in November 1871 that in the General Council a decision had been made "against these pretensions [of Section 12] and for the present Committee."[16]

In anticipation of victory Sorge had already decided to wait no longer. The International's entire American effort was rapidly being led astray, he broadcast in October. To prevent this it was necessary to insure that all sections of the International be composed only of

> *workingmen* understanding their position toward capital and modern Society, ready to make a radical change of Society's structure and rebuild it on the basis of labor, men entirely free from present political (bourgeois) affinities and rejecting all compromise.

With this in mind he convened the Provisional Central Committee on November 19, and it dissolved itself immediately, one month short of its planned duration. Moving briskly, the German, French, and Irish sections then reconvened separately at the Tenth Ward Hotel and formed a Federal Council which would "preserve to our movement the character of a Labor movement."[17]

Marx, informed beforehand by Friedrich Bolte of the imminence of this move, assured Sorge of his support. Reviewing the International's long fight against Bakunin and other "sectarians," he noted: "Obviously the General Council does not support in America what it combats in Europe." He suggested that Sorge have the new Federal Council express its full agreement with the decisions of the London Conference for dealing with the Bakunists, which would at the same time strengthen Sorge's hand in crushing his American sectarians. Following Marx's scenario, Sorge reported on December 17 that the Federal Council had declared its full approval of the London conference resolutions. Pointing to "the great resemblance of this our American trouble with the trouble caused in Switzerland by the 'Alliance de la Democratie socialiste' [Bakunin's group]," he promised that, in the battle with Section 12, the Federal Council would stand "on the principles and statutes of the IWA and nothing else." As the London Conference had reaffirmed the IWA's insistence that working class political action remain independent of bourgeois parties, Sorge made this the keystone of his case against Section 12: "The overwhelming majority of the opposing delegates are shopkeepers and so-called independent men (belonging to the middle class)." He also claimed that the expulsion of the bourgeoisie was the first step in "the task of harmonizing and fraternizing the two most numerous and important component elements of the working classes of this country—the Irish and the German Workingmen."[18]

In the following year Sorge solidified his position by calling a national congress of the North American Federation in which only sections of at least two-thirds wage-laborer membership could participate. He made it clear that this meant the permanent exclusion of Section 12 and those others formed on the basis of Section 12's appeal to the citizens of the country. There was some room for a reconciliation with selected native sections, but only assuming two-thirds of their members were wage workers and that they would agree to raise no issue that was not part of the labor question.[19]

Section 12 reacted to its exclusion by forming its own Federal Council on Prince Street, thereafter referred to as either the Prince Street or Spring Street Council after its alternate meeting places. Backing Sorge, the General Council called for the reunion of the two councils on the basis of Sorge's criteria, suspending Section 12 pending the next General Congress of the International. The suspension of Section 12 completed what Sorge termed the "purefaction of our organization" and the use of this term might supply a key to the early derivation of what Gompers referred to as the "pure and simple" program upon which he built the American Federation of Labor. What made a labor organization pure, according to the usage of the word among the Internationalists in these years, was its orientation around working-class issues as defined by the working class itself. Thus Sorge said of the goals of the International: "we want to keep it pure and unpolluted for the future affiliation of the organized Trades-Unions, who will never connect with organizations tainted by adventurous ideas and actions." Friedrich Bolte referred to a "pure labor organization" as one "simply aiming at 'the protection and advancement and complete emancipation of the working classes.'" By contrast he scorned the Prince Street group for proposing "social remedies" foreign to this purpose and for interpreting the IWA rules and statutes "after its own fancy." This he said proved that they had exalted themselves above the workingmen, "who wanted to defend their own class interest." Again in May 1873 Sorge, speaking by then for the IWA General Council located in New York City, told the Congress of the British Federation that the Hague resolution for support of political action independent of the bourgeoisie would leave "perturbing spirits . . . out in the cold." In this spirit he encouraged, "Hold aloof from all entangling alliances, keep our standard pure and our ranks clean!"[20]

In sum, what Marx in the early 1870s had helped transmit to the United States was an organization charged with

the development of a pure working-class movement committed to the conquest of political power "as its final object."
The conquest of political power and the destruction of the
bourgeoisie would be achieved, it was expected, as a natural
consequence of the struggle against the economic subjection
of the workers. As Bolte pointed out in interpreting the
program of the IWA,

> it maintains the great truth that the *root* of all evils
> is the economical subjection of the man of labor,
> that therefore all our efforts must be directed
> towards the extermination of the *root*, carrying
> with itself the destruction of its natural conse-
> quences.

It did not represent an abandonment of the quest for political power so much as a recognition of its economic basis.
And this, after all, was precisely the lesson Samuel Gompers
claimed to have taken from Marx.[21]

Gompers began attending Internationalist meetings only
in the aftermath of the North American Federation's
"purefaction," in a period when the Tenth Ward Council
was launching an intensive effort to organize and centralize
the trade unions as the basis of a pure working class movement. Charles Praitsching of the Tenth Ward reported in
June 1872 that "to this effect committees have been sent,
from here to Boston, Philadelphia, and other centers of
industry and a lively correspondence is going on to the
same end." As part of this drive the Tenth Ward participated in the struggle among city workers for the eight-hour
day. An eight-hour movement had developed in New York
City as the national economy in 1868 began to recuperate
from its post-war slump. Beginning with the Bricklayers'
International Union strike in 1868, it culminated in 1872

with a massive three-month strike of some 100,000 city workers, mostly in the building trades, which ended successfully in June. A movement for eight hours had been centered nationally in Massachusetts since the mid-sixties under the leadership of Ira Steward and George E. McNeill. But where the Massachusetts leaders concentrated on the enactment of eight-hour legislation, the New York movement involved a shop-by-shop confrontation between workers and employers. The Tenth Ward leaders participated not because they believed the achievement of an eight-hour day would reform the capitalistic system, as Steward contended, but because the campaign would unify the workers and draw them into trade unions independent of the bourgeoisie. For this reason Praitsching was not unduly alarmed by the fact that "very few trades will obtain, and still less . . . preserve the eight hours, for the time being," believing that a more centralized workers' organization might "spring from this movement."[22]

It is doubtful that Gompers was yet working with the Tenth Ward group when these initial organizational efforts were made in the first half of 1872. In his autobiography Gompers recalls the "great workingmen's parade" in June but seems unaware that the Tenth Ward leadership considered the parade a tragic failure. On the eve of the parade, Theodore Banks of the Prince Street Council released a letter to the press threatening violence if the eight-hour day was not granted. The Tenth Ward had hoped to unify the trade unions through a joint participation in the movement, but the most important trade unions now quickly repudiated the Banks letter and refused to appear for the procession. On top of this, Praitsching reported, the letter now brought the repressive forces of the government down upon the workingmen of the city:

> . . . the police authorities of the City whistled up
> their courage and made several brutal attacks on
> unarmed peaceable workingmen trying to per-
> suade their fellow laborers to join the ranks of the
> strikers. A number of Workingmen were brutally
> beaten and wounded. . . .[23]

This episode only served to renew the determination of
the Tenth Ward to carry on its organizational work. It
resolved that "there is enough of parades and that time and
money should be devoted to better and nearer ends," and
was gratified to see workingmen in a protest meeting at
Cooper Union in June show "their rather late appreciation
of our constant advice." This advice was that before going
into battle the workers must first "perfect and improve their
organization in organizing the shops and factories and cen-
tralizing them." Meanwhile Friedrich Sorge returned from
the Hague Congress of 1872 bringing the General Council
headquarters with him. He quickly used his position at the
head of the Council to concentrate the influence of the
entire International in the same direction. During the next
year he sent out a barrage of correspondence to trade
unions and federal councils throughout the world, sup-
plemented by addresses to the IWA membership in general,
attacking secessionists and arguing for a reunification of the
International's forces on the basis of the organizational task
before them.[24]

Perhaps the most encouraging organizational development for the IWA leadership in America was the revolution
in the organization of the cigar trade. For this a twenty-
eight-year-old newly arrived Hungarian immigrant cigarmaker and Internationalist, Adolph Strasser, was largely
responsible. Strasser arrived in New York City in 1872 after
having lived in London for a time. By the end of the year,

with the aid of certain other Internationalists, he was engaged in organizational work in the cigar trade independent of the Cigarmakers International Union (CMIU). Bolte remarked at this time that

> trades unionists commence to feel that the basis on which the trade unions hitherto have been founded are [*sic*] not sufficient for the elevation of the working class as they call it and that another plan of organization ought to be adopted.

Strasser worked outside the Cigarmakers International Union, organizing among the mass of cigarmakers who could not meet the CMIU's high admission requirements. His results quickly impressed the leaders of New York Local 15. Long in need of an infusion of new members, the local began to follow Strasser's lead. Through a series of shop and mass meetings it organized the United Cigarmakers, open to all those city cigarmakers formerly excluded from the CMIU. It duplicated the work of Strasser's group and was soon merged with his. The combined personnel were divided into one Bohemian and one German section, and with Local 15 itself serving as the American section of the trade the three sections began to coordinate their efforts through a central council. In March 1873 Strasser was sent by the city cigarmakers to the state CMIU convention. There he gained approval for the new city cigarmakers council, while establishing himself as an important state labor leader.[25]

Strasser's work produced the organizational sensation of the year. The *Workingmen's Advocate* of Chicago published a letter from a Baltimore correspondent which reflected a new excitement in the CMIU. The writer lectured his brothers:

We have tried nine years of legislating for the
minority and found that we could not induce the
mass of the trade to come in with us. Now let us
try the system of legislating for the majority, and
see if we cannot induce those who are outside of
the folds of the International Union to join hands
with us. I am happy to see a movement of that
kind on foot in New York City.

Friedrich Bolte of the International Workingmen's Association singled out the development as one of the most important of the year, and in his annual report called on others
to follow this lead,

to organize the workingmen as a class, and to
create that class feeling, which never will allow the
labourer to leave the organization but which leads
to the great aim of the International Workingmen's Association, The Emancipation of Labour![26]

Most probably Samuel Gompers began to make his commitment to the labor movement in 1873. In that year he
started working at the shop of David Hirsh and became a
protégé of a Swedish shopmate named Karl Ferdinand
Laurrell. Gompers came to Laurrell with a very limited formal education, four years in the Jewish Free School, three
more in Hebrew night school, all in Britain before he was
fourteen. But he sensed that he had been cheated, and in
his young, impressionable years in America, he now discov-
ered an alternate route to education. The radical movement, as Theodore Draper has observed, "has been a university as well as a faith."[27]
Laurrell was both a member of the purified Federal

Council of the North American Federation of the International and an associate of Strasser's in the work of reorganizing the cigarmaker's trade. Under Laurrell's tutelage, Gompers read socialist literature, Marx, Engels, Lassalle, and others. He also attended meetings of the Tenth Ward and in his autobiography could later remember as "friends," three men in addition to Laurrell who served on the first Federal Council: Friedrich Bolte, Conrad Carl, and Karl Bertrand. He seems as well to have had considerable contact with Sorge himself, remembering that "I met him frequently at meetings that I began attending after I went to Hirsh's."[28]

Both Laurrell and Gompers were deeply involved in the cigarmakers' trade reorganization in New York when the Detroit convention of the CMIU met in the fall of 1873 and rejected the demand for easing the membership requirements upon which the success of the Strasser program depended. In reaction, Strasser, Laurrell, Gompers, and several other New York cigarmakers decided to concentrate all their efforts on building a strong independent city organization through the city cigarmakers' council, without regard to "sex, nationality or method of work." Though organizing outside the CMIU, they retained their local charter in the hope that they might yet use this connection to reform the entire union.[29]

While both men worked together in the cigarmakers' trade, Laurrell seemed reluctant in 1873 to have Gompers become involved in the affairs of the International Workingmen's Association. Though a member himself of the innermost councils of the North American Federation, Laurrell was pessimistic about its future in America. According to Gompers, "his keen mind seemed to have grasped the fact that a new movement must be born out of the experience of the old and that there must be leaders unhampered by past affiliations." Laurrell was in a position to appreciate the weaknesses of the North American Federation. In addition to the New York City cigarmakers' reorganization, Friedrich Bolte had found only two other encouraging signs in his annual report of 1873. The Internationalist Carl Speyer had organized the American furniture workers that year, though he was unable to convince the new union to join the international union of cabinetmakers that had appeared in Belgium. And an Industrial Congress composed of the trade union remnant of the National Labor Union had met in Cleveland. Although the congress displayed a general interest in starting a labor federation, no greater organizational effort materialized. During the same year the Federal Council's campaign to make inroads into the State Workingmen's Assembly of New York failed miserably. Despite appeals to that body beginning in the spring of 1872, Bolte was forced to conclude a year later that the Assembly was "now in the hands of a few political quacks and nearly dead."[30]

Laurell must also have understood that serious signs of disintegration had appeared within the International in America. If the North American Federation had weathered the challenge of the American middle class, it was in great part because of the ideological clarity with which Sorge was able to defend his position. His opponents were, after all, the bourgeoisie, and the tenets of Marxism were most definite in their insistence on the independent route that the working class must take to its emancipation. But since its "purefaction" the Federation had given a priority to "perfecting" the organization of the American working class, through a program which placed proportionately heavy emphasis on economic class struggle. As Sorge explained through the General Council delegate to the IWA Congress of 1873, all agricultural and industrial workers

must be organized into trade unions "not only on the narrow basis of obtaining higher wages but on the broad basis
of the complete emancipation of labor, the demand of a
normal working day being the first step to it." The trade
unions, drawn into central bodies, might then join with the
national branches of the IWA in conducting the political
movement of the workers. But this stage would develop
"whenever such movement shall be deemed opportune,"
and the form of political action was not to be fixed by convention, for "every movement of the combined workingmen
as a class for the advancement of their interest of course
is a political movement." Finally, he proposed, international
connections between central trade union bodies should be
established through the good offices of the General Council.[31]

Though Laurrell believed that the perfection of the labor
movement along the lines indicated by Sorge had to precede the achievement of political power by the working
class, he also had to be aware by this time that a growing
number of American Internationalists were impatient with
the trade union emphasis of the past year. The International had enjoyed an impressive growth between 1871 and
1873, picking up a large number of new sections in the
cities of the East and Midwest, primarily in the communities
of recent German immigrants, though to a lesser extent
among Bohemian, French, Irish, Scandinavian, and American groups as well. Among these newcomers there was a
distinct preference for another approach by the IWA based
upon deeply held loyalties to different concepts of socialist
tactics. A power struggle that might wreck the North
American Federation seemed imminent and, with Gompers
absorbed in the work of perfecting the organization of the
cigarmakers, Laurrell could easily believe his protégé was
already moving further toward the movement of the future

than he could by joining the International for its last gasp. Laurrell gave Gompers two pieces of advice: to attend Internationalist meetings attentively, but to avoid membership in preference for his union work. Not long thereafter the IWA, once feared as an International socialist monolith, did indeed crumble over unresolvable ideological differences.[32]

3
The Depression Seventies and the United Workers of America

In the early 1870s disciples of the German socialist, Ferdinand Lassalle, helped accentuate the differences that were developing among American Marxists over the tactics of the North American Federation of the First International. Lassalleanism had become popular in Germany a decade earlier, shortly after representatives of German labor attended the London International Exhibition of 1862 and returned inspired by the trade unions and cooperative ventures of the English working class. The backwardness of their own movement by comparison made the German workers restless. A new rebelliousness spread through the educational societies in which the German middle class had at first hoped to win German labor to bourgeois liberalism. This was the impulse that Lassalle gathered in and projected to national importance in the two years of intensive propaganda preceding his death in 1864. The General German Workmen's Association, founded in 1862, adopted Lassalleanism as its revolutionary program.[1]

Lassalle was haunted by the Malthusian law of wages. If wages were invariably bound to the subsistence level, he wondered, how could anyone hope to strengthen the economic organization of the workers as a basis for working class political power? He looked instead to the German Volkgeist, which he sensed was restless with the inhibitions of laissez-faire, and hoped to see the workers mount direct political initiatives and fashion an alliance with the monarchy against the bourgeoisie. Perhaps the monarchy might be shaken loose from its feudal background in such an alliance. In any case the workers would soon be the stronger of the two partners and they would demand the instrument of their emancipation, universal manhood suffrage.[2]

Under Lassallean influence, the General German Workmen's Association pursued the franchise, intent on seeing the state finance worker cooperatives as the basis of the new economic system. Marx complained that cooperatives that were the gift of the state could never emancipate the workers. Had not the whole thrust of the First International been that "the emancipation of the working classes must be conquered by the working classes themselves"? Such concessions could only prove illusory, he insisted. If, as the *Rules* of the IWA noted, the political action of the proletariat was to be directed toward its emancipation, it was independent political action, based upon a developing revolutionary class consciousness and culminating in a political class revolution against the state, that Marx envisioned. In Marx's view, Lassalle avoided the fundamental organizational and educational responsibilities of the intellectual vanguard by compromising the independence of the labor movement in an unholy alliance with the monarchial establishment.[3]

The Lassalleans, however, did not compose the German delegation to the International, at first because they were not invited and later because the leaders who organized the German Social Democratic Party were favored over them. Led by Wilhelm Liebknecht and August Bebel, the Social Democratic Party opposed alliance with the autocrats for the achievement of universal suffrage, calling it a step toward Caesarism whereby absolute power would be created through apparent concessions to the masses. The party instead exploited the growing popularity of the English trade union example in Germany, forming and loosely federating trade unions under the eased regulations passed in Germany in 1869. Marx and Engels supported the Social Democrats in Germany and in turn were given solid backing from the party's delegates to the International. The Lassallean challenge in Europe was thus confined to Germany until the General Council transferred to America. There a much less significant International leadership confronted a powerful German Lassallean exile group and its friends.[4]

The guidelines that Marx willed to his defenders in their war with the Lassalleans in America contained ambiguities which even a quarter century of argument failed to untangle. In the *Rules*, which Marx wrote in 1864, he spoke of the necessity for independent political action by the workers as a means to their economic emancipation. But the Lassalleans, too, favored political action on the part of labor, and Marx's disciples sought to dissociate theirs from the Lassallean brand. The clause in the *Rules* which most appropriately distinguished Marxian political action read: "That the economical emancipation of the working classes is therefore the great end to which every political movement ought to be subordinated as a means." From the inception of the International, English and French trade unionists had taken this to commend only political action auxiliary to the work of perfecting the independent industrial organizations of the working class. They judged that the discipline and order of such organizations made these, rather than political parties, the core of the Marxist workingmen's party and the instrument of the workers' emancipation. Some reasoned that until the workers had developed a revolutionary consciousness, any political action that might open the labor movement to infiltration by bourgeois politicians ought to be avoided. Since Lassalle played down the value of conventional nonpolitical trade union activity in a laissez-faire society, there was additional reason to suspect that Marx intended to emphasize trade union over political party activity in order to nurture the independence of the working class. And Marx may in fact have encouraged this belief, putting the trade unions in the spotlight as the price he had to pay for their support of his ascendancy in the International. The group that followed this line of thought, though obviously not apolitical, came to be identified as the "economic" wing of the International.[5]

But the same clause in the *Rules* of the IWA was subject to a second possible interpretation. It could be argued that Marx had intended to emphasize that, notwithstanding the value of trade union activity, political action was the essential means to economic emancipation. All working-class politics that preserved the integrity of the final class goals was to be encouraged, even if it was of limited practical benefit at the time. While Lassallean collaboration with the autocracy was ruled out, this interpretation left room for an almost unlimited amount of labor party activity. What is more, though Lassalleans might shun this type of political class independence in Germany, it was the only type of political activity open to them in the United States. Here they would find a bourgeois rather than a feudal society and the question of collaboration with the monarchy was a moot point. Both the Lassalleans and the political Marxists could agree that politics in a bourgeois society should be independent of the bourgeoisie. Both could agree as well that the trade union Marxists' emphasis on the primary importance of organization and agitation through economic rather than political action was inherently conservative. They were identified together as the political activists of the movement. Trade union "economic" Marxists, with credentials as good as their politically minded colleagues, could only view such impatient tacticians as the hawkers of empty enthusiasm about which Marx had warned the intellectual vanguard. In such an atmosphere Marx was quoted against Marx, with the question of which group was the legitimate heir to Marxism in America being settled by each in its own favor. This study does not attempt to dispute the legitimacy of either group but rather to follow the development of the trade union group in the context of its own assumption that it was a legitimate heir to the International in America.

Gompers' reminiscences of the period are best understood as a product of this conflict within Marxism. In his autobiography he insisted on making a distinction between Marx's views and those of the Socialists, remarking that Marx was "the severest critic of Socialism . . . his denunciations of the Socialists in attacking trade unions has [sic] no superior even in our own time."[6] Gompers recognized that Marx was "not consistent in all his writings" but still felt that the most vital lesson Marx contributed was "the necessity for organization of wage-earners in trade unions and the development of economic power prior to efforts to establish labor government through political methods." He claimed that letters Marx addressed to Carl Speyer, Friedrich Bolte, and Friedrich Sorge of the International's inner circle in America bore out his belief that Marx "approved the course of our trade unionists—the group with which I was working." But if trade unionists like Gompers believed themselves to be heirs to a Marxian tradition, it was Marxism as they understood it to have been in the third quarter of the nineteenth century, and not Marxism as they had watched it become thereafter. As Gompers noted, "Terms as Marx used them often had a very different meaning from what became fixed in later years. To understand Marx one must read him with an understanding of the struggle from the 'fifties to the seventies.' "[7]

The socialist unity of the First International, already threatened by ideological dissension, broke apart in America in the mid-seventies on the rock of depression. In New York most of the Internationalists, along with many reformers and trade unionists not connected with the International, at first cooperated in a joint effort to promote public depression relief. At a Cooper Union meeting on December 11, 1873, convened on the joint call of trade groups and Section 1 of the IWA, several thousand workers called for a minimum wage, an eight-hour day, an income tax, and a debt moratorium for the unemployed. They created a Committee of Safety to rouse the workers in support of this program and to build a labor party.[8]

Within a month the press was alerting the public to the coming of another Commune and New York police were being mobilized in readiness. Statements of worker spokesmen contributed to the provocation. Bricklayer Patrick Dunn promised to unleash the unemployed to "help themselves" if jobs were not provided by the city, and a young Lassallean socialist Committee of Safety member, P. J. McGuire, spoke publicly of plans to provision the starving with food to be commandeered and billed to the city. Then on January 13 the Committee of Safety precipitated a mass protest meeting in a city tensed in anticipation of revolution. The Committee learned only too late of the revocation of its meeting permit, of the technical illegality of its demonstration about to begin at Tompkins Square. The converging of families of laborers upon the square for a peaceable protest, their wonderment at the unfathomable attack upon them by mounted and foot police—these were the images born into the depression by the New York labor leadership, in bitterness and, for some, in guilt as well.[9]

For Gompers the coming of the depression meant a first taste of personal leadership in the trade union movement under the encouraging approval of his tutor, Laurrell. When the depression first hit New York in late 1873 the city cigarmakers' council moved quickly to do it battle on a variety of fronts. In the first year of the depression the council began to operate a cooperative store, which continued in existence for many years thereafter. It also battled the tenement house system through agitational meetings in the local sections of the council and through a mass meeting at which Gompers gave his first public speech on labor.[10]

For Gompers' cigarmaker co-workers, Laurrell and Strasser, the depression meant involvement in activities outside the union as well, growing out of their previous Internationalist affiliations. By the time of Tompkins Square the North American Federation was no longer in a position to coordinate the depression efforts of its members. A playground for two factions, it could serve neither well. Even as a debilitating maneuvering for its control ground on in early 1874, members of both its political and economic wings were turning to other instruments to meet the immediacy of the depression. In effect, the Federation had been drydocked by the spring of 1874. Its hulk would remain for all to see, but for the remaining two years of its existence a goodly portion of its most vigorous personnel

moved out in a variety of directions to meet the problems
of economic distress. Perhaps this was the most face-saving
way for the Federation to respond to a depression crisis for
which its members had a surfeit of solutions each in need
of testing. Laurrell and Strasser, proceeding along different
lines, fairly represented the two major competing tendencies Internationalists were developing to cope with the
challenge.[11]

In the aftermath of the so-called Tompkins Square riot,
the political activists of the International commenced building their own independent organization, which emerged in
May 1874 as the Social Democratic Workingmen's Party. Its
members intended to meet the challenge of the depression
by taking political action on behalf of the workers. Strasser
was chosen as its executive secretary and P. J. McGuire
became one of its leading propagandists, but the party,
which combined nine existing societies, was not a purely
socialist enterprise. In the face of the economic emergency
the Social Democrats agreed that political action could be
taken either independently or in cooperation with radical
bourgeois parties, and the party drew to itself elements formerly associated with the Prince Street Council. This same
coalition participated in the New York City mayoralty campaign of 1874 as the Industrial Workingmen's Party. P. J.
McGuire, acting secretary of the party, and the labor journalist, John Swinton, made a poor showing as its candidates
in the race. Of long-range significance were the new contacts the Social Democrats cultivated with native American
groups, none more important than the Boston Eight Hour
League.[12]

More central to the development of the trade unions were
the activities of Ferdinand Laurrell. He was associated with
a group concerned with furthering the economic organization of the workers as a means to emancipation, which
included such Internationalists as Friedrich Bolte, Karl Ber-

trand, J. H. Monckton, Robert Blissert, J. P. McDonnell, and David Kronburg. In addition to general Marxian analysis and the central place accorded the trade unions by Marx under the International in Europe, this group's emphasis on labor organization owed its inspiration to a more recent confirmation from Marx of the validity of this approach. Marx had emphasized organizational work in conveying to Bolte in November 1871 his vision for the future of the working class in America. He looked forward, he had said, to the day when the American working class would be "far enough advanced in its organization to undertake a decisive campaign against collective power, i.e., the political power of the ruling class."[13]

On top of this, in the following months Bolte had helped lead a purification eliminating the bourgeois reformers from the International in defense of the tenet that "the emancipation of the working classes must be conquered by the working classes themselves." Those purged were reproved for their quixotic attempt to remake history to their own fancy. This only served to reemphasize that the role of the vanguard intellectuals could not be simply to displace the demands of the workers with supposedly more far-reaching demands of their own. They must begin, rather, with a recognition that the workers' present demands were an integral part of the ongoing process of evolving class consciousness: ". . . may these demands of the working class in any country be ever so small or low," Bolte exulted, "their ultimate aim is the economical emancipation of the man of labor." The workingmen, he insisted, "must pass through various phases of development in order to gain a full knowledge of their own class-situation and to obtain that class-feeling which will secure their emancipation."[14]

Since Internationalists of the Bolte group believed the first step toward emancipation was the economic organiza-

tion of the workers, they were not attracted to the Social
Democratic Workingmen's Party. Instead they launched a
central union of workers in 1874, known as the Association
of the United Workers of America. The General Rules of
this Association did not state that the emancipation of the
working class was to be "conquered" by the working classes,
the wording originally used in the General Rules of the
IWA. Taking no chance that the term be used to justify
precipitate action, the founders stated that the workers
would "accomplish" their emancipation and were invited to
do so through an organization that would work for a "practical solution" to this "mighty problem of modern society."
In periodic meetings of the United Workers, the great principles of emancipation would be grasped through "mutual
intercourse and exchange of thoughts and ideas." Then
they would be propagated through the fraternal union of
"communication and co-operation" that the United Workers
had created.[15]

The United Workers made every effort to identify Internationalist aspirations with the immediate practical goals
pursued by the existing class organizations of the workers,
the trade unions. Thus, while the work of the Association
was to "lead to and culminate in" the complete emancipation of the working class, the United Workers would grow
to the task by affording the workers, in the meantime, a
means of working together for more immediate economic
protection and advancement. The ability of members of the
Bolte group to find revolutionary import in even the most
mundane of union demands had been illustrated by a statement by Bolte as early as January 1873, that "by claiming
a fair remuneration for a fair days' work" the trade unions
were "making a fair step toward the final emancipation of
labour by abolishing wages at last and substituting associa-
tive labor for private enterprise."[16]

Although political activity was not prohibited, members of the United Workers were required to pledge to "disavow all alliance with existing American political parties" or those of the future whose programs did not "aim at the emancipation of labor." The only political movements which required the members' loyalty, the rules stated, were those which "aimed directly" at the workers' emancipation. But clearly the leaders of the United Workers believed they were aiming as directly as possible toward that emancipation by involving the workingmen themselves in the struggle. If there was no prohibition against outside political party activity, there was also no reason for it. So, where the rules of the United Workers spoke of the necessity of constituting the workingmen into a political party to face the collective power of the capitalists, and where the *United Workman*, organ of the United Workers, spoke of itself as the organ and property of the united proletarian party of America, it was not of the party-of-the-moment that they spoke. Gompers understood this in reflecting that "It is evident that the word 'party' is used in a special sense. In those early days neither our ideas nor our terminology were formulated and crystallized."[17]

Since the United Workers downgraded political activity, its most immediate preoccupation was bound to be the common union concerns of economic protection and advancement, the struggle for which had long been seen by Marxists to provide a basis for the development of proletarian class consciousness. The United Workers adopted verbatim the 1864 rule of the IWA stating "that the economical emancipation of the working classes is, therefore, the great end to which every political movement ought to be subordinate as a means." Gompers paraphrased the statement in his autobiography as "Economic betterment is the first step to the desired end, to its achievement all political effort must be subordinated."[18]

A series of resolutions drafted in the name of the General Council of the International appeared in April 1874, apparently giving sanction to the depression activities of the United Workers while raising serious questions as to the propriety of the Social Democrats' approach. They contained an injunction that most forms of working class political activity should be avoided for the time being, and that "all co-operation and connection with political parties formed by the possessing classes" was prohibited. By parties of the possessing classes the Council meant not only the Republican and Democratic parties, but "independents, or Liberals, or Patrons of Industry, or Patrons of Husbandry (Grangers), or Reformers, or whatever names they may adopt." Members of the International who accepted a place in such a party were threatened with suspension from the International for the period in which they were so engaged. The resolutions approved of political action directed toward "obtaining legislative acts in the interest of the working class proper," suggesting along these lines

> the normal working day, the responsibility of all employers in case of accidents, the securing of wages, the abolition of working of children in manufactories, sanitary measures, the establishment of bureaus of statistics of labor, the abolition of all indirect taxes.

As far as entering into "a truly political campaign or election movement" was concerned, they advised waiting until the workingmen could "exercise a perceptible influence" at the polls. And when that time did come, it was envisioned that the movement would arise in the first place out of local movements, which, once successful, could then be "transferred to the larger communities . . . according to circumstances. . . ."[19]

By the mid-seventies, then, an approach to trade unionism closely attuned to Marxian and IWA guidelines appeared on the verge of beginning an institutionalized life segregated from the politically activist socialists in America. Sorge himself announced in a pamphlet in 1876 that the socialist movement in North America had begun, that its origin lay in "the gallant endeavors" of the workers in their trade unions. "They will transcend the narrow limits they made for themselves," he contended, "they will expand and embrace the whole class of workers in this country as soon as they have overcome some prejudices, the natural outgrowth of their national conditions and then, perhaps, they will lead the van." And looking to the future expropriation of the means of production he wondered whether the employers would submit peacefully to such a measure: "Perhaps they then will consent themselves to such a measure . . . perhaps they will use their ample means to resist the common demand. . . ."[20]

4

The Workingmen's Party of the United States and the Dialogue over Marxist Tactics

Had the split institutionalized by the Social Democrats and the United Workers at mid-decade been uninterrupted, the legitimacy of a trade unionist offspring of the International in America might never have been so severely disputed. Both in continuity of leadership and proximity of time the United Workers bore a family relationship to the International, and its program had been designed within IWA councils toward the fulfillment of a Marxist revolutionary dream. But in the year following its creation, the Association of United Workers perceived the possibility of utilizing the IWA's international connections in combating international competition of cheap labor. A relatively small organization, it affiliated with the International and surrendered its independence.[1]

By the middle of 1875 a majority of the Social Democrats, led by Adolph Strasser and G. C. Steibeling, had concluded that political success depended upon drawing the native trade unions into the party. Steibeling even suggested that control of the party would be surrendered to the unions once their representation became substantial. The party convention in July 1875 resolved that members devote themselves to the work of organizing workers into trade unions. Meanwhile the most solidly Lassallean party of socialists, the Labor Party of Illinois, turned reluctantly from political to economic organization after being crushed in the municipal elections in the spring of 1874. After a year of splinter-group activity the factions were pulling together again. Samuel Gompers became involved in this growing movement for unity.[2]

In the year it had taken to reverse the separatist trend, Gompers had become one of the major labor leaders in New York City. By the summer of 1875 the city organization of cigarmakers, which he had helped build, was strong enough locally and in the esteem of the Cigarmakers International Union membership to apply for a charter without fear of rejection. In November a charter was granted, creating Local 144 of the CMIU, with Gompers as president and Strasser as financial secretary. During the next six months the local's prestige continued to rise. *The Cigarmakers' Official Journal* reported admiringly that at a mass meeting held by the local in March 1876, sixty-eight new members were added "and a great many who did not have the required initiation fee with them, promised to join at the regular meeting of the union. . . ." The journal noted that this success was achieved during a period of general depression in the trade, identified the organizers for Local 144 as "A. Strasser and L. Gomperts [*sic*]" and closed with the observation that "Union No. 144 has among its members many earnest workers, men who are well fitted for this arduous yet noble work of reorganization . . . who think but to act. . . ." Gompers later agreed that "our group was as brainy a crew as ever gave their hearts and minds to protect wage-earners against exploitation and injustice" and singled out among others, Louis Berliner, Henry Baer, Fred Bloete, Karl Laurrell, and Adolph Strasser. The list is significant in that these same men were importantly involved in the first steps toward uniting the estranged Internationalist forces.[3]

The movement for socialist unity appeared in concrete form in connection with the activities of a loosely organized New York group known as the Economic and Sociological Club. The club was formed in the aftermath of the experiences of 1874, especially Tompkins Square, and was based on a common interest in the labor problem, if not a unanimity of opinion about it. In addition to Gompers and those on the list of his cigarmaker associates, the club also included Friedrich Bolte, David Kronburg, J. P. McDonnell, Conrad Carl, George Steibeling, Hugh McGregor, J. H. Monckton, Carl Speyer, and James Lynch. Gompers chose to list only these few of the members in his autobiography but made it clear that the group had a large membership and maintained informal relations with a wide group of labor leaders.[4]

During 1876 the Economic and Sociological Club customarily met at 10 Stanton Street; at that location in April delegates of local unions, including Local 144, CMIU, formed the Trade and Labor Council of New York and Vicinity. Adolph Strasser, Social Democrat, acted as secretary of the founding meeting, and Robert Blissert of the United Workers was elected temporary president. "United we stand—Divided we Fall," was proclaimed on the first page of the *Socialist*. It was unity wholly for the purpose of trade union organization and economic measures. "Being fully cognizant of the fact, that the united capital in the hands of an employing class tends to reduce the recompense of labor to a mere pittance, or even less; we, the workingmen must organize and unite, to oppose the former to advantage." The Council would call public meetings and meetings of special branches of work to arouse the workers to organize. It would seek to establish the eight-hour day and the responsibility of employers for injuries "inflicted" on their workers, and to abolish both child labor under fourteen years of age and tenement house industry. No delegate was to be admitted to meetings unless he actually worked at the trade he represented.

Many of the New York leaders were also responsible for a national reconciliation. Hugh McGregor, jewelry worker and member of the Economic and Sociological Club, had been chosen General Secretary of the New York Social Democrats' Committee on Organization, and in the committee's name he appealed in September 1875 for the help of all socialists in overcoming the "minor points on which we differ." Initially, the Social Democrats suggested as the basis for discussion the formation of a confederation of socialist groups working through a general congress, with each group having the right to accept or reject the decisions of that congress. They urged that any program decided upon be of a practical nature, priority to be given to proximate national goals, with the IWA's promotion of international proletarian action postponed.[6]

Before October 1875 was over, the major socialist groups were discussing unification through "a more or less pronounced system of centralization, rather than any system of federative organization" as the Social Democrats had originally proposed. Though the appearance of such an organization was delayed until the following summer due to general interest in a call by a Pennsylvania reform group for a national labor congress for April 1876, the foundation for a socialist unity existed. It may in fact have explained the willingness of the socialists to walk out of the national labor congress when their demands were not met.[7]

The national labor congress had been called to meet in Pittsburgh beginning on April 17, 1876, the appeal being issued by a Pennsylvania political group known as the Junior Sons of '76, which advocated monetary reform and the recall of public officials. It was a period of greenback fervor. As the depression dragged on, sustaining unemployment and undermining wages, laborers joined farmers in blaming the currency for a sluggish economy. Most delegates to the labor congress came to do battle with a currency shortage they believed kept interest rates high and industry inactive. Not so the Social Democrats. They arrived instructed to oppose action on monetary issues as "questions that properly belong to bankers, merchants and employers. . . ." They were prepared to unite with this movement only if "remedial measures" were incorporated into its platform. A resolution signed by seven, including Strasser, presented the Social Democrats' main plank for the congress in a Lassallean resolution reading, "we favor the loaning of money to the laboring class, by the Government, with which to enable said class to engage in co-operation in the productive branches of trade." Otto Weydemeyer, a close associate of F. A. Sorge and son of the pioneer American Marxist Joseph Weydemeyer, represented the International. He closely cooperated with the Social Democrats, advocating the "adoption of the cooperative plan," though stressing as well the need for the organization and unification of trade unions. The resolution on cooperatives was diverted into committee where it was buried, and when the congress followed this by endorsing a series of resolutions on monetary and financial reform, the socialists bolted.[8]

Inability to make inroads at the national labor congress was the final impetus toward Internationalist unity. With preliminary work already accomplished in earlier interfactional meetings, the new organization materialized quickly.

The socialist delegates reconvened separately in May and called for a congress in July to launch the Social Labor Party of the United States of America. At the May meeting they suggested a fourteen-point party program. They proposed to adopt the Social Democrats' political demands for direct election of all public officials, reform of the electoral system, a one-house legislative system, a free judiciary system, and the initiative, referendum and recall. The program also was to embrace social and industrial proposals from the Social Democrats and IWA, including the abolition of indirect taxes, monopolies, laws treating union activities as conspiracies, the contract system of labor; and the introduction of a progressive income tax, compulsory school attendance, the eight-hour day, regulated conditions for female labor, equalized wages between the sexes, a sanitary inspection system, government departments of labor statistics, and public works for the unemployed. The future industrial order envisioned was a fulfillment of the Lassallean dream of industry carried on "by free co-operative trade unions under the guarantee of the people with state credit." The program was to concede to the International that election campaigns should be avoided until the party could "exert a perceptible influence," and that political effort would first be exerted at the local level. Equally important, the new party was to organize and unify trade unions "for the improvement of our economical condition and for the spreading of our ideas and principles." Finally, the Social Democratic Party was to surrender control of its newspapers to the common ownership of the new organization.[9]

Gompers recalled in his autobiography that the question of the control of the New York *Socialist*, a Social Democratic English language paper, was of primary importance to the New York Marxists with whom he was associated: "By capturing this organ we trade unionists hoped to accomplish two points—to secure a going concern and to retard Socialistic [i.e., political] activity." In the interim preceding the congress, Carl Speyer maintained pressure on the Social Democrats through his official capacity as Secretary of the North American Federation of the International. If the *Socialist* was to have the IWA's "cordial aid and support," he wrote in May, its name should be changed and its Board of Administration should include one member each from the International and the United Workers. He then carefully dropped the intelligence that the International had been contemplating publishing a competitive English labor organ of its own, that it was refraining from doing so only "In consideration of the late proceedings at Pittsburgh," but should that joint control not work out, the International's "connection to this effect remains unbroken."[10]

The editor of the *Socialist* was Hugh McGregor, to whom Gompers referred when he said "we had friends on the paper." McGregor's activities in 1876 indicate that he was a loyal Social Democrat and a leading socialist spokesman. He was the driving force behind the Social Democratic Workingmen's Party in Philadelphia and served as its secretary after February 1876. In that position he regularly addressed party meetings on such topics as "the tendency of the system of wage slavery," "the supreme importance of establishing a paper devoted to the interests of the working classes and the propaganda of the principles underlying the labor movement," "the History and objects of Socialism," "Social Revolution," and "the present miserable condition of the working classes in America." He advocated "prompt and radical" political action and this perhaps explains why he could not remain the paper's editor after the unity congress in July. But he also looked to trade unions as "the germ of the social organization of the future" and believed that strong organizations of the workers were necessary before the workingmen would "conquer the state." He found it amusing that political economists believed trade unions were established "for the sole purpose of fomenting strikes."[11]

A party was indeed founded at the Philadelphia congress, July 1876, but not before the trade unionists exacted further concessions as the price of unity. The name Workingmen's Party of the United States (WPUS) was chosen, honoring the International Workingmen's Association as much as the Social Democratic Workingmen's Party, and the New York unionists gained their newspaper. The *Socialist* was renamed the *Labor Standard*, and Marx's former private secretary, J. P. McDonnell, was chosen as editor, easily defeating McGregor's Philadelphia associate, Victor Drury, for the job.[12] In return the party rewarded Lassallean groups in Chicago and New Haven by designating Chicago as headquarters for the party's executive committee, a governing body whose powers were to be checked only by an annually elected board of supervision located in New Haven. Accommodation was reached on the question of political action. Sorge and Weydemeyer for the International, along with Conrad Conzett of the Illinois Labor Party, made a determined stand against immediate political action.[13] Overruled in a vote of four to three on a resolution that gave the executive committee the right to permit local political activity, the three were then joined by Strasser in a majority statement on the dangers of premature political action. It recommended that workingmen "turn their backs on the ballot box" for the present and concentrate on organizing, for "organization is frequently destroyed and always injured by a hasty political movement."[14]

The platform and principles of the party adopted the general principles of the First International: the basis of the economic subjection of the workers lay in the appropriation

of the means of production by the capitalists; the struggle
for emancipation had to be carried out by a united and
independent international working class; and the final goal
was the abolition of the wage system and the creation of
a classless society. The Workingmen's Party would approach
the great labor question by eschewing political campaigns
until strong enough to exercise a perceptible influence,
starting on a local scale. It reasoned that "whereas, political
liberty without economical freedom is but an empty phrase,
therefore, we will in the first place direct our efforts to the
economical question." Toward that end the party would
work for the organization and unification of trade unions
"to ameliorate the condition of the working people and seek
to spread therein the above principles." It would also seek
the enactment of eleven specific measures:

1. Eight hours for the present as a normal
working day, and legal punishment of all vio-
lators.
2. Sanitary inspection of all conditions of labor,
means of subsistence and dwellings included.
3. Establishment of bureaus of labor statistics in
all States as well as by the National Government;
the officers of these bureaus to be taken from the
ranks of the labor organizations and elected by
them.
4. Prohibition of the use of prison labor by
private employers.
5. Prohibitary laws against the employment of
children under 14 years of age in industrial estab-
lishments.
6. Gratuitous instruction in all educational
institutions.

7. Strict laws making employers liable for all accidents to the injury of their employees.

8. Gratuitous administration of justice in all courts of law.

9. Abolition of all conspiracy laws.

10. Railroads, telegraphs, and all means of transportation to be taken hold of and operated by the Government.

11. All industrial enterprises to be placed under the control of the Government as fast as practicable and operated by free cooperative trades unions for the good of the whole people.[15]

The appearance of the Workingmen's Party was vital for the further maturation of Marxian trade unionism in the United States. The party created the framework for an exciting dialogue over socialist tactics and then provided the trade union faction with an organ for its own defense. This forced the trade unionists to remain explicit about the Marxian orientation of their brand of trade unionism, to self-consciously relate program to principle, to perpetuate a habitual intimacy between the consideration of the practical affairs of the trade unions and the understanding of their relation to working-class history and the future emancipation of the workers.

As this suggests, if a settlement was reached in Philadelphia, an understanding was not. The new program was open to different interpretations not only by the various parties to the settlement but also within the parties themselves. Strasser of the Social Democrats, for instance, now stood strongly with the trade unionists. A few weeks before the congress he made his position clear in insisting that, "The main task of the American Socialists in the near future consists in the strong and energetic promotion of the organization and centralization of the trade unions." Two months after the congress he continued to speak favorably of trade union activity, referring to the movement as "the natural and only Labor Party" and predicting that when the struggle for amelioration was centralized and invigorated, "it will lead to a revolutionary change of society." On the other hand, P. J. McGuire of the Social Democrats was willing to work within the framework of the WPUS but hoped to see it well enough organized in a very short time to permit its rapid emergence as a major political force. Two months before the congress he told a mass meeting in Meriden, Connecticut, that

> We intend to commence at the bottom and build up. We must carry the towns first, the States next, and the presidential elections last; and I believe that in 1880 we will have a party that every honest, intelligent citizen will be proud of.[16]

In the months following the convention, the ideological crossfire in the *Labor Standard*'s letters columns already promised a fractionalization of the nascent socialist unity. Attention centered on New Haven, where P. J. McGuire and W. G. H. Smart, both former Social Democrats, defended their preparations for the local electoral campaign in November. Challenged by Michael Raphael, a former Social Democrat but close associate of Strasser and Gompers in the CMIU, McGuire threatened to reevaluate the work of the Philadelphia congress. "For the sake of advancing the cause dear to our hearts, we sacrificed our well grounded objections," he warned, not permanently but only "hoping in the next congress to rectify the mistakes made in Philadelphia."[17]

Before the end of the year the controversy over politics broke wide open. In New York the American Section of the party, formed in September by the merger of the United Workers and elements of the Social Democratic Party, was the center of the trade unionist defense. It envisioned itself as of special importance to the party due to the "adhesion" of the predominantly Irish United Workers. According to one spokesman, this had the effect of "bringing together the two great foreign labor elements of this country: The German and the Irish—the other elements will readily follow." The possibility of achieving this unity had excited Marx six years earlier. The spokesman also noted that the United Workers was composed of men who were "influential among their fellow-workmen and in their Trade Unions, and who are earnestly devoted to the cause of our economical emancipation." Gompers was an active member of the section.[18]

By October the New York American Section had debated the question of "Trades Unions and their relation to the Workingmen's Party" to a far different conclusion from that of P. J. McGuire. As already noted, early in the month, the section had expressed its unwillingness to support any but those questions "raised by and coming from recognized Trade and Labor bodies, made in the interest of the working class."[19] A week later it was the "general opinion" of the members of this section that "the Workingmen's Party should be an auxiliary to the Trades Unions." The decision was reached on the basis of a discussion whose participants, it was reported, included Strasser, Berliner, and McDonnell, among others. The meeting unanimously passed a resolution on the importance of trade unions as "a great lever by which the working class will be economically emancipated" and demanded full support by the members of the party in promoting "the organization of trade unions on a national as well as an international basis."[20]

The leading propagandist for the New York American Section was the Marxist J. P. McDonnell, a member of the Bolte group that had founded the United Workers two years earlier. Taking over the editorship of the *Labor Standard* in August, he expounded a Marxian trade unionism in which both the existing trade unions and the practical demands of the workers played an important role. To McDonnell the socialist movement comprehended "the Revolution of our entire social and political system," and he defined revolution as not necessarily "a forcible and bloody overthrow" of capitalism, but certainly "a total, not a partial, not a slow or gradual change." He believed a "bloody and anarchical overthrow" to be a very real possibility, however, unless the change were governed by an organization of all the sufferers armed with scientific remedies.[21]

By sufferers, McDonnell meant those whose labor was being confiscated by the capitalists. Capital for him, as for Marx, was accumulated unpaid labor, and as capital accumulation always proceeded faster than the growth of population, an increasing majority of the people were being impoverished by the process. What is more, he saw that capital accumulation and possession were protected by the existing social system and political fabric, which, while allowing anyone to be a capitalist, left those who could not be capitalists "to the tender mercies of capital." Thus the existing socio-political world was for him, as for Marx, a reflection of the capitalistic system. It could not itself effect fundamental solutions to the mounting crisis. He believed, accordingly, that "it is much more advisable for all workers to reserve their scanty means for a powerful propaganda towards that ultimate revolution than to dabble with little reforms that will waste means without a corresponding effect."[22]

McDonnell's advice to the party sections was that they could "not overdo the work of union of all the workers in one organization, no matter what its present programs may be." He believed that program resolutions were relatively unimportant in the process of emancipating the workers, arguing that no set of resolutions, even when ratified by popular votes, could bring emancipation: ". . . it can be brought about and speedily too by a strict organization of all the sufferers all over the prominent countries . . . accelerated by a rapid propaganda of correct economical principles and theories." He therefore issued what was to be the standard line for the New York American Section: "Let us then be united in *doing*, let us discard all disputes about paragraphs and resolutions."[23]

In the *Labor Standard* during this period, McDonnell conducted an editorial campaign against immediate political action. His ideas were well received by the cigarmakers' leaders, who thereafter reprinted some of his most important editorials on the subject in their journal. In November, for instance, the *Cigarmakers' Official Journal* carried a reprint of one of McDonnell's most important editorials, "The Necessities of the Hour," in which he concluded that "any action but for the immediate improvement of our condition is reactionary and false and must be opposed because it will retard the progress of union and does not meet the necessities of the hour." He argued that "the working class, before it can destroy the present system, must be relieved from long hours and low wages," and that through the battle for immediate amelioration by practical trade union methods, the organization and intelligence of the working class would grow until the cause of labor became irresistible. On the other hand, he feared most of all a repetition of the "errors of the past" which turned men from "sane and practical methods" to "political schemes of all kinds." Similar in spirit was McDonnell's contention in the *Labor Standard*, under the title "Wages," that the demand for higher wages did not signify support for the wages system: "On the contrary every one who through necessity or principle, wars against low wages, helps in no small measure to promote the destruction of the wages system."[24]

Significantly, McDonnell traced his position on political action not only to the resolutions of the Philadelphia unity congress of July 1876 but also to the IWA's resolutions on political action two years earlier. Both recommended practical legislative goals, with electoral campaigning limited to the workers' ability to perceptively influence the polls. He observed that the most effective way "to drive the trade unions into the political field" was "just to continuously extend them and their mutual relations." He argued, like Marx, that the workers' "*general* economical interests can finally only be protected by political action, which will be forcibly felt in comprehensive organizations." As to when and how the workers would exercise political action, this "must be answered with due regard to the conditions of this country." With the political processes of the United States still completely controlled by the possessing classes, it would be a "wanton waste of power" to approach the ballot box prior to the disciplined organization of the workers on a trade union basis.[25]

Within the Workingmen's Party, the political activists were actually in a strong position in that the executive committee at the end of September 1876 granted a cautious approval to the New Haven section's political activity. Corresponding secretary Philip Van Patten announced that the committee's consent was granted "not without reluctance" because "we have no wish to establish a precedent . . . for

similar political action without . . . the necessary organization or strength to make their influence felt." But trusting
that such activity in this case would exercise a perceptible
influence and provide valuable experience he urged the section to "strike vigorously and unflinchingly." By granting
its consent the committee created consternation among the
trade unionists, particularly Sorge and Weydemeyer, who,
Van Patten later reported, sent the committee a communication that was "extremely personal and offensive."[26]

In order to reverse the trend toward local electoral campaigns by party sections, the trade unionists felt compelled
to propose a positive political program of their own as an
alternative. Such a program was being discussed as early as
November by the New York American Section, which
announced that its meeting would consider the question,
"Would it not be wise to confine ourselves for the present
to an agitation for 8 hours—the first plank of our platform?" J. P. McDonnell believed the issue vital, both as an
agitational issue to attract the workers to the trade union
movement and as a propaganda focus for the workers'
education. Appealing to the party-at-large in December, to
"begin our agitation, wherever it is in its first stages, with
the first three planks of our platform, the normal workday,
sanitary inspection and labor statistics," he argued that these
were potent because they "appeal forcibly to every laborer's
understanding." He believed that the eight-hour day was
pivotal because it carried with it its own propaganda.
Through its promulgation the workers would not only gain
"in manly spirit" but simultaneously become aware that they
were supplying surplus labor for their employers and that
"the very system of wage labor is wrong because it compels
the workers to do more or less work which is not compen-
sated. . . ."[27]

McDonnell emphasized that the so-called economical

program of the New York American Section was a political program as well. The focus on organization and eight-hour agitation was "the quickest, because it is the *only* means of an early political success," he told the party. "Our progress may for some time be slow on account of the thinness of our means, but it must be sure, and in a geometrical ratio, if we use our means economically, and do no more waste them for premature political efforts." In March 1877 he added that such a legislative program was the only practical labor political action because it did not ask the workingmen to ignore their economic interests "until the Legislatures are filled with workingmen."[28]

P. J. McGuire was not long in answering these arguments, asking in January,

> If we compromise so far as to come down to measures that are well understood and confine our action for the present, merely to popular labor issues, then will not we have afterwards the same up-hill work to spread our ideas that we have had all along?

The false emphasis on "milk-and-water" measures, he felt, came from a misunderstanding of the role of trade unions in the emancipation of the working class. In their existing form, trade unions were useless to socialists, for they were "not prepared for our ideas." Helping such unions by agitating their practical struggles, far from whetting their class consciousness, would only speed the day when they would desert the party altogether. Therefore, McGuire argued, the party must first be made numerically strong through the agitation of its principles, and "political action is our greatest means of agitation." Reversing McDonnell's order of priorities, he asked that members "keep on agitating for our Party and its principles and confine ourselves to that entirely for the present" trusting to the future to make headway in the unions, when they could be organized on a socialistic basis.[29]

Thus McGuire had reduced the controversy once again to the question of trade union versus party action. It became increasingly clear that if the trade union faction was required to choose between them, the ballot would have to suffer. This did not mean that the trade unionists of the party would abandon their goal of radically altering society, for even McGuire referred to his differences with the trade unionists as being over "the best means to advance our principles." During the time when conciliation rather than polarization had characterized the debate, as in the spring of 1876, McGuire had spoken of the importance of trade union organization, contending that, "We must organize in Trade Unions, centralize them and then strike a united blow for our liberty. Then our power will be felt." The Social Democratic Party in New York City during the same period had seized upon the demand for the reduction of the hours of labor as "the first vigorous step on the road that leads to the emancipation of the working classes." It was, then, a question of timing and priorities and, within the context of the primacy of party action, the role of the trade unions was subordinate but not always unimportant to political activists.[30]

Conversely, the trade unionists' subordination of the ballot did not reflect an abandonment of the political aspects of the movement—which they believed organically related to the economic—so much as a faith in the historical evolution of the party of the proletariat in the course of the everyday class struggle under industrial capitalism. It was for McDonnell and his associates a simple article of faith grounded in Marxist ideology, that "when millions of organized men fighting the battle of life in their respective localities, are organized all the world over [then] will the cause of labor rise triumphant." The details of the transition were only sketched in. As the organization of the workers was extended, the workers would begin to recognize from their own ranks those of knowledge and skill who could be entrusted with leading their movement toward emancipation.[31]

Among the leading participants in the defense of trade unionist tactics, David Kronburg most impressed Samuel Gompers. To Gompers' mind, Kronburg "dominated every small-room conference . . . was easily the mastermind." As a public speaker, Kronburg's reputation was that of a practical trade unionist. He customarily spoke on economic questions, particularly the eight-hour day, and in support of trade unions and party newspapers. One report of a mass meeting observed that Kronburg addressed the audience and "as usual spoke on practical subjects in a pointed manner." But before his own section in early 1877 Kronburg presented the broader context of his approach, and in April the *Labor Standard* chose to serialize this lecture, "Labor from the Real and Ideal Standpoint."[32]

One of the inner circle of the North American Federation of the IWA, a member of the Bolte group, and a chief architect of the Workingmen's Party, Kronburg was an important socialist theoretician. His message to the American section followed closely the Bolte-McDonnell approach. Kronburg's insights on socialist strategy were reminiscent of Marx's important letter to Bolte in 1871. First, organization derived from the workers' economic struggles was necessary to a certain point before the achievement of political power by the working class. "Political success cannot be secured by the guerilla tactics of a few quasi-philosophical skirmishers," Kronburg argued, recalling the coldness and

apathy with which the masses had greeted doctrinaire political theoreticians since the 1840s. Nor, he held, would the
misery of the workers soon precipitate them into a social
revolution, for they had already suffered bitter misery and
deprivation during successive crises in America without
turning to revolution.

Second, Kronburg held that the economic struggles of the
workers actually were at one with the political movement
of the working class whenever carried on in the context of
the general centralization of the trade union movement.
"These centralized organizations will express in a collective
form the aspirations, the sentiments, and the will of the
working-classes," he said. In this way the workers would
achieve political success by their united efforts "themselves,
to achieve a definite economic aim obviously calculated to
procure a direct practical advantage."

Third, Kronburg believed that the collectivized economic
struggles and the development of an organized working
class movement were interdependent. Organization of the
unorganized masses could not be accomplished except on
the basis of "questions they can comprehend, and for
objects that can be attained," for in Kronburg's view, the
workers currently had "neither energy, time nor inclination
to study anything over and above the satisfaction of their
immediate physical needs." Though the workers were not
yet prepared "to pass by a violent transition, from one system to another," they would become progressively better
organized in the process of pursuing their economic
struggles. Soon, "these millions of workmen, compacted
into solid organizations will be in a position to enforce their
rights," he predicted. Then the emancipation of the working class would be achieved "by a long series of rights wrung
by conquest."

Finally, believing that he had delineated the "real working

class movement," Kronburg adopted Marx's distinction
between this movement and the "socialist and semi-socialist
sects." He recalled how many of the latter he had encoun-
tered under a variety of names, such as "Social Reformers,
Communists, Collectivists, Positivists, Socialists, Spiritual-
ists," how each had initially given laudable attention to
ameliorating the condition of the working class, and how
each in turn had become doctrinaire in its program, drifted
away from its founders' goals, and become reactionary. He
feared that "the social movement of the United States" was
once again drifting into a "reactionary phase" led by
theoreticians who "endeavored to engraft a religious character upon the social movement; excommunicating all those,
who in the independent exercise of their own judgment
repudiated their sectarian dogmas. . . ." Meanwhile they
ignored the ongoing process of historical class development
represented in its present stage by the "natural and progressive tendency among the workers of the modern world
towards organized effort to ameliorate their present conditions." Adopting a concept which had appeared in the *Communist Manifesto* two decades earlier, he called for acknowl-
edgment that "the present encloses the germ of the future"
and therefore for more attention to "the waking realities
of this work-a-day world." And he termed it "the height of
arrogance" for a small number of men to turn from these
realities "to lay a plan for the redemption and regeneration
of the world, by passing resolutions at their meetings or in
their congresses." These resolutions were the product of
those who, "styling themselves radical, are in fact reactionary, otherwise they would not undertake to build a house
commencing with the roof."

Stimulated by these ideas, Gompers and a fellow young
cigarmaker, Louis Berliner, followed closely, and even
became briefly involved in, the skirmishes between the two

factions of the party. Their involvement took place at the New York City level, where, in December 1876, Berliner attacked ideas of a fellow party member, John Shafer. Shafer, formerly a Social Democrat and now a member of the German section of the Workingmen's Party in the city, had contended that "a political class organization and the Ballot box could solve the question." Berliner held, on the contrary, that it was wishful thinking to believe that any but a small minority of the working class could comprehend the concept of the abolition of the wage system as put to them by socialist politicians. It must be put to them in practical terms as the trade unions were doing in their call for the eight-hour day and more pay. In fact he maintained that

> there is and only can be one class organization and that is the economical or industrial organization of the whole wages class into one solid phalanx. Class rule and class privileges will then be abolished and the whole present system, *without the use of one ballot*.[33]

Though Gompers would not have gone so far as to dismiss the ballot, he was drawn into the argument on Berliner's side. Shafer answered Berliner's arguments by proposing a "social-political class organization" as a superior alternative to economical or industrial organization. He did not attempt to refute the validity of Berliner's arguments; he was simply presenting an alternative. Gompers felt Shafer was avoiding the proper order of debate and appealed to him to address himself properly to the question. Berliner had claimed not only that organization and centralization of the trade and labor unions "accomplished more and better bread," he emphasized, but that it created as well "a power felt by the ruling classes." This, Gompers explained, was why Berliner had deemed it "more practical and earnest and sensible" to favor "organizing the masses into purely industrial or economical class organizations with less hours and more *wages* for their motto." Should Shafer not choose to meet this argument head on, then, Gompers felt, he forfeited the right to propose an alternative. The vigor and detail of Gompers' critique suggest how deeply he had become absorbed in the growing conflict over social-ist tactics.[34]

5
Developing the
Union Approach

The Workingmen's Party had been the lineal descendant of the First International in America, recognized as such by trade unionists and political activists of that tradition alike. It was therefore bound to give an appearance of legitimacy to the faction able to control it. Initially neither faction dominated the party. That the political activists were able to take control may have been due as much to their opponents' default as to their own political skill. Inherent in the trade union faction's approach was the tendency of its members to exert their main energies and make their most important personal contacts in the pursuit of activities for which party organization was not essential. In the trade union world they tended to be identified more as ardent trade unionists than as socialists, and perhaps it was only natural that the party apparatus, peculiarly suited to assault by ballot, would gradually slip into the hands of the political party action group in the last years of the 1870s.

This pattern was already evident during the party's first year. Criticized by party members more politically inclined than they, the trade unionists redoubled their efforts to build the larger movement upon a trade union base. Michael Raphael, for instance, presented the Cigarmakers' convention of 1877 with proposals for the unification and centralization of the trade union movement, a theme which had been central to the program of the First International from its founding in 1864. He proposed that the executive of the CMIU be instructed to communicate with all other unions in the country concerning the formation of a central body. Its purposes would be to stimulate organization and provide both a means of protection and a means of educating the workers "into a thorough knowledge of the Economic question." Its principles would be the same as those incorporated in the platform of the Workingmen's Party. Until this central body could be established, Raphael proposed that the CMIU amend its constitution to provide for the formation of lyceums attached to every local union, "by which means after the regular business of the unions, or on other occasions, lectures and discussions may take place."[1]

Meanwhile, J. P. McDonnell addressed himself to the problem of organizing the "thousands of laborers who have no Trade properly speaking" and those who "have a changing occupation and therefore cannot join any of the existing Trades Unions." Could not these men be reached by the trade union movement through the establishment of "mutual protective" unions, "especially in smaller towns where separate unions cannot be maintained . . . or several such in large cities?"[2] The idea was a precursor to the International Labor Union which would appear in early 1878 and, more remotely, to the American Federation of Labor's federal trade unions.

Important in any calculations for initiating the larger movement was the need for an agitational issue to attract the interest of the workers. Members of the trade unionist faction were agreed upon the importance of the eight-hour issue for this purpose. There had already been considerable contact with the Boston Eight Hour League leaders, Ira Steward and George McNeill, and both men were very close to the group that comprised the Economic and Sociological Club of New York. Hugh McGregor, while still editor of the *Socialist*, had promoted an alliance between the Social Democrats and the Boston League, arguing "there is no reason why we should not work side by side until the first step in the march of the wage-workers toward emancipation is achieved; until the eight hour system has become an accomplished fact." Gompers recalled not only a close acquaintance with Steward and McNeill, but his own understanding that the eight-hour day was adopted as "a revolutionary force."[3]

By the end of 1876 the ideas and activities of the leading eight-hour advocates were receiving close attention from the *Labor Standard* and the New York American Section of the Workingmen's Party. The American section as early as October 1876 deemed a visit from McNeill worthy of a special reception and, after the section began discussion that month on the advisability of concentrating on the eighthour plank of the party platform, it was encouraged by what was termed an "able letter" received from Steward. Early in 1877 McNeill was reported to have attended the meeting of the section at which Kronburg spoke on "Labor from the Real and Ideal Standpoint." McNeill defended certain of Kronburg's points in the discussion that followed and "was warmly received."[4]

What most recommended the eight-hour spokesmen to the trade union faction, however, was their deftness at counteracting the work of McGuire, Smart, and other New England political activists. In December 1876, for instance, Steward issued a warning "to our sincere labor friends in the city of New Haven," in which he argued that honesty and earnestness could not prevent a "political labor machine" from gradually succumbing to the practice of "trading." This he said had been the "painful experience" of Boston, that the capitalistic party can always find well-meaning labor politicians who will wipe their ticket clean of any truly important or radical demands, in return for support on such peripheral issues as "branch libraries" or free city gas. This demonstrated that, unlike the abolitionists who saw "an impassable gulf" between themselves and the slave owners, "the political labor reformer today sees no such dividing line between himself and the capitalistic party." Steward proposed therefore that the first step in solving the labor problem was "to introduce a sufficiently large number of 'economical' labor reformers to each other."[5]

Early in 1877 face-to-face challenges by the eight-hour spokesmen to the political activists were frequently reported by George Gunton, who, under the name "Middleton," was the *Labor Standard*'s New England correspondent. Gunton had emigrated from England in 1874 to become a founder and secretary of a New England amalgamated union of cotton operatives. His reports usually involved his activities in connection with George McNeill, co-founder with Steward of the Boston Eight Hour League and deputy chief of the Massachusetts Labor Bureau. In 1877 Gunton and McNeill often found themselves addressing meetings jointly with McGuire, Smart or others of the political action group, as part of a general campaign to resist the repeal of Massachusetts' ten-hour law. Differences were tempered but never submerged in these joint affairs.[6]

Antagonism often surfaced casually and, sometimes, only indirectly. McNeill, introducing McGuire to one assemblage, endorsed the platform of the Workingmen's Party but confessed that he "did not agree wholly with Mr. McGuire's views" (though he hoped they were "intelligent enough to agree to disagree"). In general, McNeill's addresses methodically ticked off the arguments in favor of shorter hours' legislation. When he mentioned the party program it was primarily the first plank, on the eight-hour day, that he advocated. When McGuire spoke the audience could expect to hear a denunciation of the wage system as a whole with an appeal for the final plank of the program, universal cooperation.[7]

In question and answer periods after the speeches the most direct confrontations could develop. In one instance Smart told a meeting that he found only the last two planks of the program acceptable, believing that the present condition of labor called for immediate government seizure and ownership of private property. Gunton then contended that the program of the party called for the government to place industrial enterprise under the control of free cooperative trade unions only "*as fast as practicable.*" From this he argued that only the first planks were intended to be the present demands of the party.[8]

As a live, viable alternative to party electioneering the issue-oriented legislative politics of the eight-hour advocates hit a responsive chord among party trade unionists. George Gunton smarted under attacks on the Eight Hour League for its supposed resistance to politics. Was it not obvious that the league had "done more political work *for* labor than any other labor organization (English Trades Unions excepted)"? He brandished its impressive efforts in the passage of the eight-hour law for children, the ten-hour law, factory inspection legislation, and the legislation establishing

the Massachusetts Labor Bureau. He also praised the work
of the executive political committee set up by the league
as a legislative watchdog and lobby. J. P. McDonnell agreed.
When the move to repeal the ten-hour law was defeated
the *Labor Standard* gave the chief credit to "the herculean
efforts of Geo. E. McNeill, 'Middleton' and other good
men," comparing this "wise political action" to that proposed by "members in the W.P.U.S. who have politics on
the brain." Unless more workingmen awoke to their legislative responsibilities, McDonnell warned, their economic
organizations would be crippled by "a network of legal
despotism."[9] The cooperation begun within the Workingmen's Party between the Boston labor reformers and the
trade union Internationalists, a coalition of men who agreed
on practical first steps but not on basic principles, was to
contribute to the establishment of the American Federation
of Labor a decade later.

By 1877, organizations in which the trade union faction
had been able to establish a base of support characteristi-
cally backed the eight-hour demand in their educational
and organizational work. In January a *Cigarmakers' Official
Journal* editorial told in good Marxian form of how capitalists were coercing their workers to produce more for less
wages: they simply increased the hours of labor of some,
leaving no work for others, and creating competition among
workers, which drove wages down. In New York City the
Workingmen's Party American Section, led by Kronburg
and McDonnell, played a prominent role in an eight-hour
campaign, which culminated in the founding of a new city
trade council apart from the political party activists in the
city labor movement. The need of the hour was for a *"bona
fide"* or *"genuine"* council to further the organization and
amalgamation of trade unions, the founding conference
decided. For "only then could the Unions act effectively in

an effort to establish an eight hour workday." In the meantime, McDonnell warned editorially, the delegates must
"guard against political tricksters." They agreed, resolving
that, as members of the new Amalgamated Trade and
Labor Union, they might support Workingmen's Party
activities only *"as individuals."*[10] The Amalgamated was to
become the bastion of those city workers who preferred for
the time to promote issues rather than party in their politics.

Whether the trade unionists would seek to develop from
their outside bases of support a national movement fully
separate from the party depended upon the degree to
which the party itself could compromise or at least tolerate
the existing differences. As 1877 began the spokesmen of
the respective factions seemed, if anything, to have moved
further from reconciliation. At times each side dismissed its
opponent's position as not only erroneous but regressive.
McGuire abhorred the trade unions' attempt to tamper with
the expansion of wage slavery: "Let it go on! The sooner
that wages slavery has expanded so far as to leave [the
wealth] to only two or three capitalists out of the millions
of workers the better it will be for the movement, and the
speedier the labor questions will be settled." He accused the
majority of the unions of holding the "indefensible conservative position" that bettering the condition of the working
class would encourage the workingmen to change the system. The truth was that "if we could possibly make better
times under the present system," the workingmen would
become satisfied enough with their situation and "could
. . . be moved further only by slow, snail-like steps."[11]

McDonnell was certain that McGuire misread the American experience. In a manner reminiscent of Sorge's letters
to Marx, McDonnell turned to the basics of the American
environment. The United States had far too long been por-

trayed as a workingman's paradise. American workers were usually expectant capitalists who fully intended through diligence and economy to become, in time, small or even great entrepreneurs. This imposed requirements upon American socialists much different from those of Europe:

> To annihilate the power of capitalism in Europe, [is] a comparatively easy thing, because the disinherited class cannot hope to rise beyond their [*sic*] accustomed level, and capitalism is hateful to them from times immemorial; in the United States our capitalist enemy resides in the breast of almost everybody.

For the American movement to be politically effective, McDonnell contended, the great majority of the workers of the country must be infected by the "moral spirit of the party." Promoting the economic advantage of the working class on the basis of socialist principles would build a faithful following among the mass of workers who ordinarily "toil on in the beaten path, and care only for economical questions." Premature political action was dangerously regressive because it would always exhibit the socialists' practical failure, and "most men are apt to value actions according to their success."[12]

It might be noted that McDonnell, in one argument, used the anti-Chinese imagery popular among American labor leaders to make his point. In the trade unionist tradition that emerged from the First International in America the use of this imagery had ideological importance. The Chinese were an example of a civilization "reduced to the deplorable condition of pauperism" and as such stood as a warning to those who saw increasing misery and privation of the working class as the road to socialism. As McDonnell pointed out, "never yet did these famished and emaciated masses of humanity rise up in their own defense." In the *Cigarmakers' Official Journal* short warnings sometimes appeared observing that "low wages means Chinese civilization" or, by comparision, that "Trade Unions are a stepping stone to cooperation and a higher civilization." Strasser later explained that "we do not object to the Chinese because of their race or their language or their religion, but we do object to an organized effort to introduce cheap laborers into the Republic." He even argued that the term coolie applied not to the Chinese alone but to all cheap laborers who, by undercutting wages, drove their fellow workers with themselves into slavery.[13]

The Workingmen's Party could not elicit from its dissident factions the modicum of toleration needed for the coalition party to survive. McDonnell tired of McGuire's resilient defenses of political party action and announced in January 1877 that the *Labor Standard* would publish no further letters "at variance with our platform." The Corresponding Secretary of the WPUS, Philip Van Patten, promptly countermanded this policy on the grounds that political campaigns of a purely local nature, far from violating the platform, were "the very best means by which (under existing circumstances) to attract the attention and respect of our fellow-workers to our practical demands." He thought discussions on questions such as McGuire had raised were of high importance and announced in the name of the executive committee that the columns of the *Labor Standard* would remain open to a reasonable amount of this correspondence.[14]

In the next few months it became evident that the *Labor Standard*, never financially confident, was not receiving the support it needed from the party. Though its increasing identification with one of the party factions did not help its circulation among the members of the other, the growing opinion of the New York American Section attributed the decline in support to a conspiracy. In a letter to the Philadelphia section, it claimed that the executive committee continued to support the New York German party organ while unable to find the funds needed by the *Labor Standard*, and also, that the committee favored the creation of new local papers which were following a policy not consistent with the party program.[15]

By the end of May 1877 New York trade unionists had founded the *Labor Standard* Publishing Association and Adolph Strasser, as treasurer, appealed to the party sections and readers of the *Labor Standard* for financial support to run the paper on this private basis. The paper reappeared after a one-week suspension and the board of supervision acquiesced in the new arrangement. The executive committee, however, soon made it clear that it did not consider this new paper to be a party organ. Van Patten seemed interested in the new *Emancipator* of Milwaukee, a politically oriented paper, which he advised party members to purchase and which New York political socialists recommended be adopted as an English-language party organ. In return the New York American Section resolved that both Van Patten and the editor of the politically minded New York German party organ, *Arbeiter-Stimme*, be suspended. The section appointed a committee to cooperate with the publishing association in putting out the *Labor Standard* and ceased to support the *Arbeiter-Stimme*.[16]

Under these circumstances the Workingmen's Party fell apart in the second half of 1877. The executive committee suspended the board of supervision and asked New Haven to elect a new one, an action which the *Labor Standard* called unconstitutional and an usurpation of power by a subordinate body. Trade unionists called for a reorganization of the movement through "a convention of labor men from labor organizations." A convention of the party did meet in December in Newark but, dominated by the political faction, it decided to replace the *Labor Standard* and to change the name and character of the party. The organization was now to be known as the Socialistic Labor Party (SLP—soon Socialist Labor Party) with a platform favoring political action. In turn the trade unionists made plans to continue an independent pursuit of perfected labor organization. Many of them also began drifting away from formal affiliation with the party.[17]

In the latter part of 1877 the name George McNeill was often mentioned in connection with proposals for getting on with the work of nationwide labor organization along economic lines. Credited earlier by George Gunton as the man responsible for building "a labor department pure and simple" in Massachusetts, well known for his work on behalf of the eight-hour movement, he was the symbol of sorts for the economic action group. Consequently, by September, it was the opinion of the *Labor Standard* and many of its correspondents that plans should be made for "a great effort at organization for higher wages and shorter hours with Geo. E. McNeill as Chief Organizer." In December a group meeting at 10 Stanton Street claimed to be the first branch of the proposed organization. Led by John McNally, formerly of the American Section of the Workingmen's Party, the assembly defined its object as shorter hours and higher wages and pledged itself to trade union principles. In February 1878 a convention of delegates formed the Provisional Committee of the International Labor Union (ILU), including among its members J. P. McDonnell, Carl Speyer, John McNally, Otto Weydemeyer, Friedrich Sorge, George Gunton, Ira Steward, George McNeill, and others from almost a score of states.[18]

As this list of members suggests, the International Labor Union united the forces of the Boston reform labor movement and the trade union faction of the First International centered in New York City. The Boston eight-hour advocates, under George McNeill and Ira Steward, had cooperated with the political faction of the First International during the depression seventies, through the Social Democratic Workingmen's Party. In the late seventies, however, they had chosen to take their stand with the trade unionist faction of the Workingmen's Party of the United States, favoring an emphasis on the eight-hour plank of the party program and a political program that was issue-oriented rather than party-oriented for the time. This was the basis of the International Labor Union as well.

The program of the International Labor Union was limited to a series of economic measures: shorter hours and higher wages; factory, mine and workshop inspection; abolition of contract, convict and child labor; employer accident liability; and the creation of labor bureaus. To the founders, these measures were not merely ameliorative, for they would provide the basis of a labor propaganda which would work for "the final abolition of the wage system." Agitation for them would mount as the organization of the working class was perfected through the formation and unification of trades unions. A supplementary Amalgamated Trades Union with its own general fund for benefits and protection would reach the more remote elements of the working class, organized unions having no national and those in unorganized callings, i.e., the unskilled.[19]

In the next few years the ILU made its main progress among the New England textile workers where Gunton had previously done organizing work. Gompers followed the movement closely, anxious to see the unorganized brought into trade organizations in order to "prepare the way for

the national amalgamation of all organizations." In 1880 he
traveled to Cohoes, New York, on behalf of the ILU, working there as an organizer among thousands of unorganized
textile workers out of work in a spontaneous strike. Meanwhile the leaders of the ILU, viewing their activities as auxiliary to the trade unions, concentrated on organizing
among the workers to whom the trade unions were not
likely to make an appeal at the time. Thus Carl Speyer
wrote that "the object . . . is chiefly to organize the unskilled
laborers, those are often dangerous competitors to
mechanics and consequently the Trades Unions are
benefited. . . ." This placed certain natural limits on the
organization. In New York City, for instance, Speyer
admitted that the organization had made no headway
because the unskilled were scattered around in the outlying
cities and villages while the skilled could not be organized
by the ILU without interfering with the trade unions "who
regard the I.L. Un. as an associate." In addition Speyer
admitted that mistakes "which any new organization is likely
to make" had limited the ILU's success, and complained
that hard times had done the same.[20]

During the same period the ILU accomplished little
toward the unification of the trade unions, for Speyer
believed the initiative would have to come from the old,
soundly organized trade unions. When Thomas Hurdle,
secretary of the International Typographical Union,
broached the subject in 1880, Speyer warned that it would
be premature. The weaker, "superficially organized" unions
had always proven themselves eager to take "fantastical
steps," he reminded. The old unionists, on the other hand,
were found "caring for nothing but their own Trade
affairs." He urged Hurdle, therefore, to continue the inter-
union correspondence among the strong unions on the
question:

> Not only the labor question, but also the labor-
> movement, is a science, and our movement's suc-
> cess depends on the taking of the right step at the
> right time; but the propagating and agitation of
> a measure, as in this case, may harbinger the right
> time to a great extent.

Though the ILU offered encouragement, it did not provide
sponsorship and when the right time did come only a year
later, unification was the independent achievement of the
trade unions. Prominent among them was the Cigarmakers'
Union.[21]

By 1881 the Cigarmakers' International was one of the
strong old unions: in 1876 it had not been. The New York
trade report of the fall of 1876 read: "There are now more
cigars than at any time in the history of New York, yet there
is a larger number out of work and the prices paid the
employed are such that they may properly be styled *Starva-
tion wages*." Michael Raphael reported from New Haven on
his attempt to build a local there. He had formed one during the summer but so few had joined that officers could
not be elected. "Finding that it was impossible to carry on
the work with so few, the money paid was returned, and
there ended the last attempt to start a union."[22]

In assessing the "lamentable condition of our trade," the
CMIU executive council was reluctant to give the three-
year-old depression any considerable credit. In an October
communication from George Hurst, W. J. Miller, and
Strasser, president and first and second vice-presidents,
respectively, the cigarmakers were told that their troubles
could be attributed mainly to the lack of unity and "the
petty prejudices and jealousies of one portion of our trade
against the other." The cigarmakers were reminded of the
unpaid labor confiscated from them by the capitalists, and

told that only through organization could they compel the capitalists to surrender "that share of your products that he has withheld while you were in a disorganized and demoralized state." The leaders rejected the notion that "the oppressors of labor will do you justice when trade shakes off its present dullness" and contended that labor's rights could be secured only by combination, "not in separate bodies, but as a united body on this continent, and eventually an organization comprising all the toilers of the civilized world." While claiming that the eventual result of the capitalistic system was certain, they told the workers that "the circumstances and costs of the struggle are committed to our hands. We can help or hinder this march of progress."[23]

The strongest impulse for an invigorated Cigarmakers' International Union came from New York, where Strasser, Laurrell, and Gompers worked closely with their fellow Internationalists of the Economic and Sociological Club in masterminding the union's reorganization. As early as September 1876 Gompers began to urge the Cigarmakers' to build a fund for unemployment and sick benefits for members of the brotherhood. Strasser, in December 1876, echoed the call for a union of practical service to its distressed members. He wrote, "we should develop less theories, aim at practical objects, less arguments for the future and more roast-beef—for the present." To his fellow socialists he argued, "our real thoughts, even if we advocate advanced ideas, are by the force of circumstances concentrated upon work and wages." After the hard winter, Michael Raphael finally put together a local union, Number 39 of New Haven, and then joined Gompers in calling for sickness and unemployment benefits.[24]

Interest in a benefit system was not unique to Cigarmakers' leaders. William Sylvis, for instance, had promoted

many of its features in the Iron Molders' Union prior to
the interruption caused by the depression. Declining union
membership during the depression created a general interest among union leaders in a program that would have an
adhesive effect on their members. And the growing
popularity of mutual insurance companies among workers
overcame many leaders' older fears that high dues would
undermine their efforts to recruit new members. This was
the case, too, with Gompers and Strasser, the very cham-
pions of broadening the membership base in the CMIU.
Gompers again offered his proposals at the Cigarmakers'
convention in 1877, to be added to the constitution if
approved. The proposals were not accepted, and with the
next convention two years away, local 144 decided to go it
alone on the question of benefits. In April 1878 it
announced that "union 144 is reorganizing on a benevolent
and protective basis. It is proposed to introduce out of
work, sick, burial and strike benefits."[25]

If Gompers failed to gain acceptance for the benefit system at the October 1877 convention, he fought an important battle toward that goal in preventing the political activist socialists of the trade from winning support for their
approach. Having just led two victorious shop strikes in
New York City, Gompers was chosen over Strasser to represent his local at the convention, "much against my opposition," as he later recalled. At the convention his influence
proved disappointing as, one by one, the proposals he presented to strengthen the economic organization of the
union were defeated. Perhaps the membership was too
impoverished by the depression to afford the expense of
a benefit system. Indeed the convention itself was attended
by only seven delegates. Now it was the socialists' turn to
suggest a more politically oriented program. A Detroit local
had sent Frank Hirth, who a year later was to be chosen

editor of the SLP paper, the *Socialist* of Chicago. He asked
the convention to resolve that

> Whereas the trade unions are utterly incompetent
> to remove the pressure resting upon them . . . the
> delegates in convention do hereby recommend to
> and urge upon all local unions to form themselves
> into labor bodies upon the basis and platform of
> the W. P. U. S.

It may only have been Hirth's uncompromising line that
won Gompers some leverage, but the convention passed by
one vote Gompers' motion to table the resolution. The convention did vote by a strong majority, with Gompers in the
minority, to declare the cigarmakers in harmony with the
platform of the Workingmen's Party. But Gompers was able
to secure Strasser's election to the presidency, and so it
seemed certain the commitment would be to the trade
unionist interpretation of that platform.[26]

Having avoided the road to political party action, the
cigarmakers were free to perfect their organization under
the leadership of Strasser and Gompers. Basic to the fight
for a benefit system, as to the other struggles within the
CMIU in these several years, was the desire to establish the
union on a "permanent" basis. There were those, however,
who were not ready to accept the end of the old
individualistic order, to give up their role as expectant
capitalists, and to entrust their security and elevation to a
permanent class organization.

This became evident in the spring of 1878 when a controversy erupted over the admission of women workers to
the union as provided by a clause in the constitution reading, "No local shall permit the rejection of an applicant
from membership on account of sex or system of working."

A Baltimore spokesman argued that by resisting the
introduction of women laborers, his local was depriving
"odious monopolies" of their cheap labor supply. He
realized that this was only a rearguard action but believed
it was the first step in the reversal of a trend. He would
fight the introduction of women, he would fight to prevent
the spreading use of the cigar-mold, and ultimately he
hoped to campaign for the redistribution of wealth through
the destruction of monopoly. For it was his observation that

> where capital, or trade is distributed among the
> many—where small traders and employers exist
> —where any man with a small sum can establish
> a little business of his own, with perhaps, a few
> employees, *there* will be material content, and
> mutual prosperity.[27]

The idea of the redistribution of wealth in this sense was
as unacceptable to Strasser and Gompers as it had been to
Marx and, later, to McDonnell. Marx saw an irreversible
trend toward coordinated production which could be
responsibly controlled only if collectivized. As G. D. H. Cole
notes, Marx believed this trend in production deprived
individuals and small groups of "any specific product of
their own," so that labor's product was "essentially collective
in the fullest sense." To McDonnell it was obvious that
before emancipation could be achieved, "a majority of the
people must be resigning themselves to [n]ever acquire capital and its accompanying advantages." Strasser thought his
Baltimore friends, in calling for a more restricted union
membership, failed to understand that they could not
reverse the revolution in production: "Every revolution of
industry is due to material agencies and not to written

paragraphs." He called for a union of the unskilled and skilled in order to strengthen the CMIU toward the day when, sufficiently educated in their unions, the working-men would replace monopolies by "universal cooperation."[28]

Gompers discussed the nature of capital concentration in the preamble to the revised CMIU constitution of 1879. The new document was to take the first major steps toward establishing the union on a permanent basis. That the preamble represented Gompers' views seems fairly certain. He was the chairman of the committee on the constitution, the only major leader on the committee of seven that pro-duced it. It was he who moved on the convention floor that the preamble be adopted as read. And in the following decade he expressed identical views on the issue.[29]

The central idea of the preamble was that modern indus-try depended upon

> the most perfect and systematic arrangement pos-sible; to acquire such a system it requires the man-agement of business to be of one mind; thus con-centration of wealth and business tact conduce to the most perfect working of the vast business machinery of the world.

This system, it said, could be used to elevate society but in practice only reduced the masses to poverty. The lesson was that survival of the "pure and philanthropic principles" among the wealthy few could not be expected, and that the cigarmakers' independence and respectability could be achieved only through an organization "embracing every cigarmaker in the country." This organization would not only protect the workers from being further reduced but

would also "elevate them morally, socially and intellectually."[30]

"Permanency" went beyond the establishment of a benefit
system and the development of an inclusive membership.
Because the benefit system worked much as did any insurance system, its dependability could be increased by pooling
the members' payments in a common fund. An unnatural
drain in one locality could then be shared by all. It was
Gompers who first interested Strasser in the pooling
methods practiced by the British Engineers' Association,
wherein the funds held by the locals were periodically redis-
tributed among the locals in proportion to their membership. The practice, known as equalization, recommended
itself especially once the idea of a traveling benefit was
adopted by the CMIU. This benefit provided support for
members who wished to leave a locality in which trade was
poor in search of employment elsewhere. Even though the
provision was limited by a maximum annual mileage per
member, there was still a likelihood that the treasuries of
locals in distressed areas would face a heavy drain unless
the burden was distributed.[31]

When Strasser did decide to support equalization he
advocated that it "should be extended to all funds, including that for striking." But just as the general adoption of
the traveling benefit under equalization required the imposition of a mileage restriction as a means of protecting the
central fund, so too did equalization require that the freedom to strike be circumscribed. Union 144, speaking
through a committee of three, which included Gompers,
asked that the executive board and the board of appeals
of the CMIU be assigned the power "to decide whether a
strike is practicable," a considerable transfer of power from
the locals to the national union. It recommended that large
strikes be undertaken only with the approval of the mem-

bers themselves as determined through a referendum. The committee also supported an assessment measure, adopted by the union, as a means of replenishing the strike fund when it became critically low. It felt that this would have a restraining effect on the members, since they "will not readily go on strike when the funds do not warrant such action."[32]

The imposition of business-type financial considerations on the management of the union did not mean that either militancy or radicalism were necessarily on the decline in the Cigarmakers. The committee concluded its arguments by warning that no union could "shelter itself behind a theory that they [sic] are opposed to strikes and will not support them." Threatening such unions with expulsion from the CMIU, it explained that strikes were inevitable and that they should be looked upon as "the preliminary skirmishes to the great battle of labor. . . ." Though it was advisable to avoid strikes except as a last resort, the committee reminded that it was the duty of unions to render "hearty and effectual support" when strikes were necessary.[33]

By 1881, primed by trade recovery ending the devastating depression of 1873-1879, the Cigarmakers' Union had made impressive progress in membership and financial solvency. With both a benefit system carefully controlled and supported by high dues, and a broadly based membership, it was one of the most soundly organized unions in the country. In surveying the results of his and others' agitation, Gompers in 1881 expressed his satisfaction that the provisions were permanent. He predicted that though conventions would be free to improve upon them in the coming years, the provisions could never be annulled because "they have made deeper inroads into the minds of the members than the most sanguine advocates could have anticipated." The measures were progressive because they were sound:

"They are of a more decidedly protective character, more amply surrounded with efficient safeguards, than any other laws of the same nature, that have hitherto been incorporated. . . ." These were the kind of provisions which, he held, "bind the members more firmly together."[34]

6
Founding
the Federation

As the great depression of the 1870s had ground on, the political and economic factions of the First International had buried their differences in behalf of a grand common effort, the Workingmen's Party. That unity had been short-lived; the Workingmen's Party evolved into the Socialist Labor Party, which could never serve as a home for both groups. Nevertheless, some of the political activist Internationalists did make common cause with their opponents again in the later years of the 1870s, but outside the party. They joined the economic faction in working to mold the trade unions of America into an effective instrument of the working class.

Had the Socialist Labor Party itself been more effective in those years, perhaps many of the political activists could not have found the trade unions so attractive. But the SLP suffered, first, from the end of the depression, which, until 1879, had weakened the workers' traditional voting loyalties to the two established parties. At the same time the party was ravaged by internal dissension as large numbers of revolutionaries began fleeing from Germany to the United States, many joining the most violent faction of the SLP in forcing the issue of arming the proletariat.[1] Many political activists, therefore, concentrated more on their union work for the time, and, while not necessarily giving up their affiliation with the party, left an important mark on American trade unionism. Such, for instance, was the case of P. J. McGuire.

In the last years of the 1870s, McGuire began to play an important role in bringing about the trade union amalgamation which his trade unionist opponents of the Workingmen's Party had long spoken of as the route to political success. Perhaps he had become discouraged with the political scene in New Haven. Certainly his flirtation with the greenback movement there in 1877 suggests an unusual and possibly desperate political experimentation. And to some extent he had always expressed a general recognition of a role for the trade unions in emancipation. But in the spring of 1877 he excited the trade union faction by apparently moving much closer to the unionist position. In April the *Labor Standard* headlined a seemingly shocking speech by McGuire in which he stated that the Workingmen's Party was "more an educational than a political one; we do not desire to enter politics until we know what we are going to strike for." He went on to advocate concentrating on the eight-hour day, the establishment of bureaus of statistics, and the prohibition of child labor in the mills. A few days later he recommended that "instead of trusting to insurance companies, labor societies should be organized as in England, for benefit in sickness, for provision for our families after our death and ourselves in case of need."[2]

McGuire's interest was not a surrender to Marxism so

much as an ideological appropriation of the labor movement for his own Lassallean future. In the *National Socialist* of Cincinnati in June 1877 he contended that the trade unions "are indispensable under our present system" and in the future would form the intermediary link between the wage system and that of cooperation. He predicted that ultimately each trade would be self-managed, the unions assessing the market for their wares and arranging for their protection, with all labor being linked through amalgamation: "The Unions will have their own banks of credit under governmental control, and be subject to Societary regulations. Central warehouses for the deposit and storage of wares and goods will be established by the Government, which will then be the workers." Contemplating this he was willing to seek a new reconciliation of factions, observing, "we cannot afford to split on particulars so long as we agree on essentials."[3] Although he maintained his party membership, expressed a lively interest in political aspects of the labor movement, and continued to consider himself a socialist, after his move to St. Louis in 1878 he began to earn his fame more as a trade union organizer than as a party organizer.

J. P. McDonnell had long pleaded for socialists to make their home in the trade union movement. To him the members of the trade unions were the real socialists of the day: "The man who professes to be a socialist and does not work practically for its advancement is far less of a socialist than one who makes no professions and yet works for the economic interest of his class." It was a notion that especially irked the staunchest political activist socialists, particularly W. G. H. Smart, McGuire's old New Haven colleague. Smart reversed the argument on McDonnell by claiming that even the Greenback Party "with which I have not a particle of sympathy" was more socialistic "in a tenfold greater degree" than the trade unionists, "men who are trying to run an opposition to us in the shape of a labor union on a false, impracticable and utterly delusive basis." When some 10,000 New York City tenement house cigarmakers struck spontaneously in the wake of the railroad strike of 1877, Smart rejected Strasser's appeal for contributions. Writing in the *Ballot*, which he published from Boston, Smart termed the strike futile and contended that donations could be put to better use in a political campaign against the wage system. McDonnell shot back that Smart and like-thinking radicals were "PSEUDO-socialists" who misread Karl Marx because they were "conceited . . . pompous and shallow pated individuals." Had they read Marx more carefully they would have understood that without the discipline of the trade unions, "revolution—moral or physical—in this or any other country could only end in chaos or in the substitution of one set of profit mongers for another."[4]

Those of the party who were attracted to the trade union movement involved themselves just as industrial development was sweeping American trade unionism into a new stage, of which the cigarmakers' strike of 1877 had been symptomatic. A period of general labor upheaval began in the later seventies. Strasser, reflecting upon it in 1881, believed it to have begun with the "alarm bell" sounded by the great railroad strike of 1877. Gompers, looking at the period later from a longer perspective, saw the revival as a natural product of a new stage of industrial development characterized by population drift to industrial cities, importation of foreign labor, expansion of markets from a local to a national scale, and the centralization of industry under financial capitalist control.[5]

These developments excited new efforts to achieve more effective labor unity. Trade union amalgamation and unification had long been discussed outside as well as within

socialist circles. The most important initiatives for unification had always come from the solidly established unions.
It was not surprising to find, therefore, that the growth of
a strong Cigarmakers' Union, led by trade unionists of the
International tradition, now added incalculable determination to the movement.

As they had begun to rebuild their union in 1876 the
Cigarmakers' leaders had called for an organization comprehending all the world's toilers. They regularly gave their
support, thereafter, to proposals for labor unity. In 1878,
the Amalgamated Association of Iron and Steel Workers
ordered its president to call a meeting of the major unions
on the question of federation. Strasser encouraged his
union to participate, because "the want of unity among the
various labor organizations is the cause of all past defeats,
the enslavement and degradation of the working classes."
The response elsewhere, however, was generally poor. In
the next three years the call for unification became more
persistent, and the growth of the Cigarmakers' Union
became more striking. The Cigarmakers replied favorably
to each of several initiatives by the International Typographical Union in these years, though it was not until 1881
that the union actually chose a delegate to pursue the subject further.[6]

In the interim the CMIU was building and perfecting its
organization, a project hardly started in 1879 but confident-
ly and impressively underway in 1881. Strasser recalled that
after 1877 had come "a struggle for nearly two years to
maintain the organization against adversaries of all sorts, till
the fall of 1879, when unionism commenced to grow in all
directions." He claimed that the union in 1881 had six times
the number of locals it had in 1877, and attributed this
growth to the benefit system, though the general trade
recovery was no doubt of immeasurable help. Comparing

membership figures, Strasser noted that between September 1877 and September 1879, with only a strike benefit in effect, the 3,000 new members taken in were almost matched by the 2,750 members suspended. Between September 1879 and September 1880, the first year after the traveling benefit was introduced, 5,453 were initiated and only 1,853 suspended. And between September 1880 and June 1881, the first nine months under the sick benefit, the figures were 7,402 to 1,867. Equally impressive was the individual growth of Local 144, which claimed in June 1881 to be increasing at a rate of 175 members per week. The union suggested that "the introduction of the sick benefit clause has paved the way for this wonderful growth."[7]

Strasser implored his maturing union, in September 1881, to champion the more general amalgamation of labor "not only in theory, by passing the usual resolutions . . . but by taking such practical steps, as will lead to the consummation of so desireable an object." In convention the Cigarmakers responded by unanimously voting to send a delegate to Pittsburgh for a unity congress on November 15, 1881. Samuel Gompers was elected as that delegate.[8]

Perhaps as important in the consummation of the federation movement was the emergence of the United Brotherhood of Carpenters in 1881, a development in which P. J. McGuire played a large role. McGuire had moved to St. Louis in 1878 where he had become active in union affairs. A member of the St. Louis Trades and Labor Assembly, he was chosen to represent that body at a conference in Terre Haute, Indiana, in August 1881. This was the conference that issued the call for the November 15 unity congress to be held in Pittsburgh. McGuire was also instrumental in founding the United Brotherhood of Carpenters in 1881 and became its first secretary. The resolutions of the Carpenters' first annual convention committed that union to proceed by "all peaceful and lawful means to accomplish our ends before resorting to the rights guaranteed us in the constitution . . ." and called for the enactment of a variety of labor reforms, including the reduction of the hours of work. The Brotherhood convention also endorsed the Terre Haute call.[9]

In supporting trade unionism McGuire did not intend to surrender his designs for a radical alteration of society, and he went out of his way to make this point clear: "I wish it understood that when I advocate the eight-hour workday, I am none the less a Socialist." He chose to work through the trade unions because he believed that practical work toward the elimination of hunger and poverty must precede successful revolution. No longer did he see desperation as socialism's great ally, believing rather that an uprising conducted by a people "driven by hunger to attempt an unright and unprepared revolution" would lead only to disaster and a delay of emancipation. He argued that a revolution must be achieved "first in the moral, and afterward in the material sphere," and that moral education came only when facilitated by relief from poverty through higher wages, more leisure, and improved surroundings:

> If poverty alone could make converts to Socialism, then the starving millions of India . . . should be the most rabid and pronounced Socialists. . . . It is not the full or empty stomach that is condition- ary to make men a Socialist . . . it is a higher civilization.[10]

The contribution made by trade unionists of the International tradition to the movement for amalgamation went further than the support they were able to generate within their individual unions. They provided leadership for the

entire union movement, giving it definition and a sense of
independent class purpose, defending it from encroach-
ment by reform elements in American society. This placed
them, by 1881, at the heart of a more general consensus
which was developing in defense of trade unionism. Such
a defense had become necessary because the very forces of
industrialism that were moving labor toward amalgamation
had also given a new life to the American reform tradition
as represented, now, by the Knights of Labor (K. of L.).
Founded in 1869, the Knighthood began growing dramatically only in the 1880s. Here was an organization rooted
in the native American labor tradition which stretched back
to the Jacksonian period and overlapped strict class bound-
aries in its enthusiasm for reform. The Knights of Labor
was most anxious to offer itself as the vehicle for the labor
unification. It took pains to cultivate contacts with leading
labor leaders whose adherence it might gain. One Knights
of Labor leader, Charles H. Litchman, for instance, shared
his thoughts on the emancipation of labor with President
Fitzpatrick of the Iron Molders' Union in the spring of
1879. He said that he believed with Fitzpatrick that the Molders ought to improve their organization and he looked forward to the time when labor, "the great *producing* and the
great *consuming* element of the world" would form one giant
union, "which shall embrace within its ample folds all
branches of honorable toil."[11]

But many trade union leaders who had had experience
with the Knights of Labor, not the least those of IWA background, were not satisfied that an identity of principle
existed between themselves and the Knights. The leaders
of the Knights were of the workshop tradition of American
labor, seeking to subordinate the new technology to the old
master-craftsman relationships which the individual had
found manageable. They could at times sound as radical

as the Internationalists on the labor question, as when they insisted: *"The remedy must be in a change of ownership"* of machinery. But it was not social ownership that they advocated so much as cooperative shop ownership with capitalistic profit retained:

> Labor must own the machine of which it forms a part, which will be accomplished when coopera- tion, productive and distributive, is understood and practiced. . . . Then, and only then, will come the day when the laborer will receive his just reward in that proportion of the profits of the thing produced that his labor bears to the cost of production.[12]

The Knights could also sound like the Internationalists when it came to the question of a closer coordination of union activities. Terence V. Powderly, leader of the organi- zation, stressed that "isolated trades unions can accomplish nothing. One grand universal brotherhood of labor is needed." He spoke of the myriad of trade societies in the United States, "none of them . . . in a condition to accomplish that for which they were organized," and claimed that all failed for one primary reason: "that each one of these societies or trade unions was composed of men of one trade or calling. . . ." The unity that Powderly wished to construct, however, was not a trade union amalgamation but a union of all producers, including not only working- men but also farmers and entrepreneurs. In short the Knights of Labor welcomed all those who wished to pre- serve individual opportunity in a world that seemed to be succumbing to parasitic business interests and their hired manipulators, bankers and lawyers. The broad base of the Knights was a source of pride to Powderly. The Knights of Labor, he said, "has a large membership of farmers, and they are doing a world of good; it has machinists, black-smiths . . . it is ready at any time to embark in a cooperative enterprise, for it has all kinds of men to start with." And this he contrasted favorably with trade unions, which, he believed "were not aware that when one class or branch (for I hate the word 'class' and would drive it from the English language if I could) of labor was oppressed, the others suf-fered."[13]

Under Powderly's leadership the prestige and power of the ruling General Assembly of the Knights was brought to bear, down the hierarchy of district and local assemblies, against the "selfish" habits of trade unionist thinking. These assemblies received continuous advice and rulings from him calling for the avoidance of costly strikes and for careful discrimination in the selection of new members, to the end that the assemblies might have both the financial resources and the proper spirit to begin cooperatives. To one local, for instance, Powderly counseled, "Get men who . . . will resort to arbitration and cooperation as a better means than striking. . . ." He also encouraged those who wished to start an assembly and those who were attempting to expand membership to first form unions outside their assemblies into which all prospective members could be initiated and through which they could be screened to determine if they were "true" or "of the right material."[14]

When the Knights in 1880 were preparing regulations to govern disbursement of their resistance fund, Powderly worked hard to convince prospective delegates to the general assembly that this resource should be denied to strikers. To one local he wrote, "I pray to God that the G. A. will not decide that the fund is to be expended on *strikes*; if it is then the order will be destroyed for at the rate with which strikes have occurred . . . *a million dollar fund* would not last six months." From a sympathizer he solicited a letter for the official journal urging that "cooperation must come to the relief of the workers or they must *go to the wall*." He suggested that the letter be written in time to influence the general assembly. While awaiting the assembly's decision Powderly used his temporary discretionary power over the fund to encourage cooperatives and to discourage strikes. He answered the request of a striking district assembly for aid from the fund, by informing it that "for co-operative purposes alone would I touch a cent of it." On the other hand he suggested to a group requesting aid for a cooperative venture that it borrow the money from the fund subject to the decision of the forthcoming general assembly.[15]

Downward pressure within the Knights of Labor put trade unionists in the organization in a defensive posture and an irritable mood. P. J. McGuire's reaction was to use his position in the St. Louis labor movement to provoke a war of nerves with the Knights' leadership. McGuire had never been happy with Powderly's leadership of the Knights. In February 1880, Powderly had returned the bylaws of the St. Louis District Assembly, indicating that they were unsatisfactory because they did not contain a provision for arbitration as a means of avoiding strikes. Then in September the general assembly settled the matter of the resistance fund by changing the name to defense fund and allocating sixty percent for cooperative activities, thirty percent for strikes, and ten percent for education. Approval for strike support from the defense fund required that the possibilities of arbitration first be exhausted at the local level and, if necessary, at the district level. Failing arbitration, a strike could be undertaken with fund support only if approved by the officers of the general assembly.[16]

In St. Louis there was a great deal of reluctance to surrender the funds to the national organization under the terms laid down by the general assembly for their use. The members of the district assembly wished to give priority in the use of their contributions to setting up a benevolent or benefit system. It was charged that the general assembly had been corrupted, and a strong sentiment favoring secession was expressed in a motion to "start a secret labor organization with principles and name to be public and known as 'Knights of Industry.' " Although, on McGuire's recommendation, secession was deferred until all constitutional means of redress could be exhausted, the men voted in the meantime to create an auxiliary benevolent association known as the "Knights of Industry."[17]

While McGuire seemed conciliatory to the extent of not wishing to bolt the Knights immediately, he made it clear that his grievance with the general assembly could only be satisfied by dramatically reducing the powers of the national leadership, a proposal not likely to be accepted. He told Philip Van Patten that in speaking to the St. Louis Assembly

> I took advantage of the occasion to show the dangerous powers of the Grand officers of the G. A. and also the helplessness of the members unless a special G. A. was called wherein constitutional changes could be made holding the Grand Officers to a more rigid account and also giving to the members the Referendum on the acts of all representative bodies of the order.

The St. Louis District Assembly unanimously endorsed these sentiments and resolved to prevail upon other assemblies to join in a call for a special general assembly in which these issues could be settled. McGuire also took his St. Louis carpenters' union out on strike and announced in April that it had been "a glorious success."[18]

When no reconciliation was achieved by the summer of 1881, McGuire and other disgruntled trade unionist Knights became an important component of the forces backing the call of August 2, 1881, for a trade union congress. The call reflected an attitude toward trade unions that was markedly different from that of the Knights. Unity of trade unions, assemblies, and councils was needed, it suggested, because "great as has been the work done by these bodies, there is vastly more that can be done, by . . . a federation of trades." In December a preamble to the declaration of principles of the new Federation of Organized Trades and Labor Unions of the United States and Canada (FOTLU) repeated that "the past history of trade unions proves that small organizations, well conducted, have accomplished great good" and called for unifying all industrial workers on the basis of protection and benefits in order to insure that such good work might be of a "lasting character."[19]

Samuel Gompers emerged from this founding congress with the feeling that he had helped to create a new independent movement of great strength. He reported to the CMIU that

> I came there not to build a bubble, but to lay the foundation for a superstructure that will be solid and that would be a true federation of the trades and labor unions. I was in favor of progressing slowly, if working too fast was dangerous, and was strongly in favor of making the movement emphatically a working-class organization, one that would not be defiled by money improperly obtained; that would contain within itself all the elements of strength, through the combined efforts of the Federated Trades Unions of our

> common country. To say that I took an active part
> in the Proceedings is perhaps superfluous.

Gompers felt that the preamble captured the mood of the
new movement "being so deftly set forth, that it would
almost amount to neglect, not to give it in full." Aside from
the passages which described the multiplication of advantages that unity could achieve, the preamble concentrated
on creating an historical perspective. It told of a struggle
going on in the civilized nations of the world, "a struggle
between capital and labor which must grow in intensity
from year to year." This intensification must either be met
by unity or "work disastrous results for the toiling millions
of all nations." And the unity called for was a unity "for
all time to come," a permanent organization which would
"secure the recognition of the rights to which they [wage
workers] are justly entitled."[20]
    Not long after the founding of the Federation, Gompers
was called upon to give public testimony as to its meaning
before the United States Senate Committee on Education
and Labor. Gompers' testimony was memorable both for
the clarity with which he defined the independent class position of the Federation, and for the insight he offered concerning the Internationalists' rationale for working within
the organization. He presented four basic arguments. First,
he held that trade unions had evolved naturally from modern industrial conditions. Under these conditions the spirit
of cordiality and friendship between the wage receivers and
the wage payers had broken down, and class interests had
become ever more distinct, class resentments intensified.
Gompers' picture of the capitalistic wage system was reminiscent of Marx:

> There are two classes in society, one incessantly
> striving to obtain the labor of the other class for

as little as possible, and to obtain the largest
amount or number of hours of labor; and the
members of the other class being, as individuals,
utterly helpless in a contest with their employers,
naturally resort to combinations to improve their
condition, and in fact, they are forced by the conditions which surround them to organize for self-
protection.[21]

Gompers laid before the committee the Federation's preamble, feeling it set forth this principal justification for the
existence of labor unions most succinctly. He might just as
well have chosen the earlier Cigarmakers' preamble of
1879.

Second, Gompers saw in the appearance of FOTLU a
general recognition by the trade unions that the process of
the concentration of wealth within the modern industrial
system was irreversible. He had also spoken to this question
in the Cigarmakers' preamble of 1879, but now he proposed that the trade unions themselves were instruments
of the inevitable concentration of wealth. Their characteristic demands for a reduction in hours and a living wage, he
explained, provided both opportunities for the large pro-
ducer and hazards for the small. Borrowing from Ira Steward, he suggested that when workingmen worked less hours
at fair pay, they consumed more commodities, not simply
because they had more time in which to consume but
because their customs and habits were altered. They had
more leisure time for their moral, intellectual, and social
improvement.[22] Gompers, it will be seen in Chapter IX,
tried to incorporate such aspects of Steward's eight-hour
theory into an overall Marxian analysis of capital accumulation.

Employers who could afford to do so, Gompers
explained, yielded to the workers' demands and compen-

sated by more thoroughly rationalizing the production line. They more efficiently divided and subdivided each task with the help of new, expensive machinery, and then took advantage of the increasing market for their products to make up the expense. For employers less fortunate in financial resources or business skill, Gompers had little sympathy. The trade unions must contribute to their demise:

> I believe that in modern society and so long as the competitive system lasts . . . the employer is entitled to a return. That is, if he is willing to pay living wages. And if he does not do that, then I say that . . . between the consumer and the workingman he ought to be crushed out as a manufacturer and forced to take the field as a laborer.[23]

Gompers' third point was that, in facing the modern industrial system as controlled by concentrated wealth, labor's only hope of achieving emancipation lay in marshaling its own resources in its own behalf. Having discounted in 1879 the probability of entrepreneurial philanthropy curing the labor problem, Gompers now described entrepreneurial decision-making as a calculation generally made only with consideration to income and expenditures. "I do not believe that the question of feeling enters into the matter at all."

> Q. Can that absence of feeling that you speak of be well avoided under the competitive method of doing business which prevails in our day?
>
> A. I doubt it, sir.

Gompers also doubted that government could play any considerable role in labor's emancipation. A Senator wished to know, concerning the eight-hour reform, "Can any such law be properly enforced so as to reach the great mass of laborers or wage workers of the country in private employ?" Gompers did not think it could "under our present competitive system." Questioned further on the operation of government under the present system and its competence to deal with such matters, Gompers observed that

> we know very well that the Government of the United States and the legislative power cannot be more probably than a step in advance of the people. If they go much further they are apt to have the platform pulled away from under them, leaving them floating in the air without any support.

Therefore even the achievement of the popular eight-hour reform for private employment must, he argued, be left to the trade unions. And he predicted that

> regulation of that would easily evolve out of the organized efforts of labor and the means that would be taken to agitate the question and educate the workers to understand that it would be to their benefit, to their lasting benefit, to abstain from more than eight hours' work.[24]

Fourth, Gompers spoke of the Federation in terms of a recognition that the trade unions could begin to cope with the problems created by the modern industrial system only when they assumed those elements of "perfection" that assured their "permanence" in that system. One of the most important elements of "perfection" was the adoption of benefit features in each trade similar to those of the Cigarmakers, not just for humanitarian reasons but so that it would be in the mutual interest of all workers in the union to continue their organization despite such setbacks as might be experienced during strikes and other industrial struggles. Another element of perfection was the equalization of funds, which enabled an organization, if necessary, to place at the disposal of a union in trouble the entire treasury of all the unions affiliated with the organization. Relating to the Senate committee the Cigarmakers' experience with these features, Gompers recalled that between 1873 and 1878 the workers of the trade had to face systematic reductions in wages every spring and fall. "What I wish to show is the condition of the cigar-makers at that period when there was no organization." The reorganization of the union had given the Cigarmakers a treasury of between $130,000 and $150,000 in only five years, "ready to be concentrated within five days at any time at any given point."[25]

Further amalgamation, the blooming of the Federation itself, were extensions of the concept of concentration of resources, further steps as Gompers saw them in the perfection of the union movement. In fact, as the Cigarmakers' Union had gone through its reorganization and growth in the late seventies, the idea of a greater labor movement to generalize the elements of perfection the union was developing had never been far from the thoughts of its new leaders. In May 1877, for instance, the *Labor Standard* received a report on the organizational activities of Cigarmakers' Local 144 which noted, "Experience has proven that single trade unions cannot resist the power of united capitalists, therefore it shall be the constant aim of this organization to unite the whole working class in one central organization." As to how far the unification as an element of perfection should be carried, it seems clear that at this date Gompers was thinking of efforts that would reach all the wage laborers of the system. He conveyed to the Senate committee, for instance, his growing interest in the organization of farm laborers, remarking upon reports of the good work among these workers done by English organizers after some Englishmen had written off these laborers as beyond help.[26]

The natural evolution of trade unions from modern industrial conditions, their confrontation of an irreversible concentration of wealth, the necessity of proceeding independently as a class toward a perfected organization of the workers—with these Gompers explained the Federation to the Senate. Called upon, finally, to explain the relationship between socialism and the new organization to the representatives of a worried and suspicious public, Gompers came to grips with the Internationalist presence in the new Federation. There were in the movement, he admitted, a large number of good and able men who "have convictions that the state of society under which we live, the competitive system, is not one that ought to last as the highest system of civilization that we can arrive at. . . ." These men, he noted, proposed to supplant the competitive system with a universal cooperative system. In terms of goals for the future, they held "perhaps equally as strong" the convictions associated with "the more radical elements in society. . . ."[27]

Nevertheless, he said, these men refused to allow the trade unions to be used as instruments for the propagation of socialistic views. They stood in the forefront in thwarting attempts to capture the movement for precipitate action. They spoke in terms of the relegation of theoretical speculation to the background, and the subordination of convictions concerning the future to the work at hand.[28]

As if in testimony to this feature of the new movement, Gompers resisted attempts by his questioners to lead him into speculation on the capitalistic system and the future. When he testified on the lack of feeling on the part of the entrepreneurs, he was asked if the employers were not in reality victims of the system just as the workers were. Was Gompers not condemning the whole system? Gompers answered: "Well, that would be driving me into the theoretical sphere which for the present at least I would like to avoid." At another point Gompers, commenting on the function of the trade unions within the present competitive system, would not speculate on the possibility that the system itself might be terminated. "I do not know when it will end, and do not desire to prophesy on the subject either."[29]

If he did not allow himself to be drawn into speculation, Gompers did offer some insight on the prospective rewards he discerned in the subordination of conviction to the work of the movement. While the unions worked for obtaining reforms by gradual means, they were instilling in their members, at the same time, a "higher motive power." Successful practical work was generating among the workers "the spirit and demand for reform." He trusted that the future could be safely staked on the unions' ability to awaken the workers by giving them "the hope that is too frequently deadened in their breasts when unorganized."[30]

The strategy of Gompers' testimony presaged the public stance to be taken by the AFL. It reflected, on the one hand, a judgment Gompers had made as early as the Tompkins Square riot of 1874. He saw then "how professions of radicalism and sensationalism concentrated all the forces of organized society against a labor movement and nullified in advance normal, necessary activity." But it also indicated that the Internationalist experience had produced many labor leaders who were secure enough in their insight into the economic basis of power to prefer their identification with trade unionism to the more controversial socialist tag. They perceived their role as supplying guidance and definition to the Federation at a time when, as Gompers later recalled, the fundamental concept of trade union federation was "not formulated in men's minds." Gompers remembered that in the early days "not more than half a dozen people had grasped the concept that economic organization and control over economic power were the fulcrum which made possible influence and power in all other fields." It was this concept, with the priorities that it suggested, that was to stoke the next decade of struggle between Gompers and the party socialists. As Gompers summarized at the AFL convention of 1890:

> I say to you, friends and delegates, that the man who would accuse me or charge me with being an anti-Socialist says what he don't know anything about, he does not know Sam Gompers. I say here broadly and openly that there is not a noble hope that a Socialist may have that I do not hold as my ideal. There is not an inspiring and ennobling end that they are striving for that my heart does not beat in response to. But our methods are different. The Socialist Party and Trade Unions are different; inherently do they differ in their methods.[31]

7
The Early Federation: Ideologies and Conflict in New York

Although the record of Gompers' thought in the early 1880s is sparse, the ideological challenges that would draw him out in the succeeding decade, and, more especially, the terms on which those issues would be joined were in large part a product of this period. Surprisingly enough, the issues did not evolve from some massive confrontation between the Knights of Labor and the new Federation of Organized Trades and Labor Unions, for both the initial nature of the Federation and the mood of the Knighthood leadership dictated the marking of time.

For the first few years of its existence, the Federation operated primarily as a lobby, promoting the legislative demands of the trade union movement. The annual British Trades Unions Congress had been operating along these lines for some years by then, and its success commended imitation. In addition, the involvement of many unions in legislative battle, not the least being the Cigarmakers' struggle against tenement house production and Chinese immigration, made cooperation on legislative goals very natural. The political activity of the Federation was issue-oriented rather than party-oriented. The FOTLU confined its politics to lobbying in behalf of a list of reforms which J. P. McDonnell would have termed the "necessities of the hour." One of the first resolutions of the Legislative Committee of the FOTLU restrained its members from "publicly advocating the claims of any of the political parties." Although the last plank in the Federation platform recommended that trade unions "secure proper representation in all law-making bodies by means of the ballot," the FOTLU's sole instrument for making its demands felt was to be a legislative committee, charged "to watch legislative measures directly affecting the question of labor; to initiate, whenever necessary, such legislative action as the Congress may direct, or as the exigencies of the time and circumstances may demand."[1]

Outside of the general admonition on securing labor's proper representation, a series of legislative demands constituted the entire Federation program. It called for the prohibition of child labor under age fourteen and of the importation of cheap foreign labor, the abolition of the contract system for hiring temporary foreign workers or prison laborers for private domestic production, the abolition of the truck system of wage payment in kind rather than cash and of conspiracy laws as applied to labor organization activities, the incorporation of trade unions as a form of equal protection under the law, state education of children, uniform apprentice laws to protect trade standards, the enforcement of the National Eight Hours Law, the guarantee of wages earned through a lien upon the product of labor, and the establishment of a National Bureau of Labor Statistics for procuring information for the country's legislators. These measures were not designed to give over to the government the job of emancipating labor. At the most, men like Gompers simply hoped to prevail upon the legislators of the country "to assist those who are working in this cause to mount a step higher."[2]

Gompers' vigorous advocacy of legislative concessions to the workers was faithful to the spirit of his intellectual forebears. Marx in the 1850s had been led by his fear of premature revolution to reemphasize the value of immediate proletarian demands, especially legislative demands upon the government. The process of pursuing such demands would teach the workers their power as a class, bringing them substantial tangible benefits, strengthening their loyalty to their class organizations, and sharpening class antagonisms. David Kronburg and J. P. McDonnell had later sought immediate legislative amelioration, contending that the first successes would educate the workers as to their power while it freed them enough from drudgery to allow them to perfect their organization and make their class program irresistible. So, too, Gompers placed great weight on the legislative battles ahead of labor in the eighties. He told the cigarmakers that the redemption of their trade through the abolition of tenement house cigar production was only the first step in making them fit "to take up the gauntlet with concentrated capital." He feared that postponing this battle against the tenements would only allow time for another panic to set in and that "when that event comes, it will find us all in these houses." Pressure politics, or "trade union" politics as he referred to it, would allow labor to exercise the strength it currently commanded, before it atrophied. For this reason, he said, "any politics that is inconsistent with the politics of Trades Unions, is capitalistic." As an afterthought he added, "middle class."[3] Gompers was also closely connected with New York City's

Amalgamated union which was oriented toward issues in its politics.

Legislative goals comprised only half of the rationale behind the formation of the Federation. As the call for the founding congress had stated and the declaration of principles reiterated, the new organization was to encourage the formation and amalgamation of labor organizations, the long-envisioned perfection of the labor movement. That this function of the Federation was especially important to those trade unionists of the First International tradition is suggested by the letter sent to the Federation founding congress by Carl Speyer, general secretary of the International Labor Union. The minutes of the congress report that Speyer "gave advice as to the best plan to perfecting and perpetuating a Federation of Trades." A number of delegates took the opportunity of the congress to present resolutions calling for the use of the good offices of the FOTLU to encourage the organizational efforts of their respective trades, as well as generally to aid in the formation of local, national and international labor bodies. But clearly this work was to be secondary to the legislative struggle. The annual congresses of the FOTLU were, by standing order, restrained from hearing papers that did not deal with the Federation's legislative activities, and the only permanent machinery of the organization, the legislative committee, was limited by its meager resources and legislative duties from accomplishing much along organizational lines.[4]

As might have been expected, the Knights of Labor resisted the new organization, but relations between the two organizations remained outwardly peaceful after some initial hostilities. Powderly had at first believed he could control the founding congress and for a time engaged in a vigorous correspondence urging Knights to "capture the *Inter-*

national Trades Congress . . . have as many members in that body as possible. . . ." Afterwards, Powderly issued a decision that it was unlawful for a member of the Knights "to organize or assist in organizing an association having in view similar aims and objects." He held that such activity would be a violation of a member's obligation to the Knights, requiring that he be "tried for his offense on that charge."[5]

But in the main Powderly concentrated on the positive aspects of the competition, attempting to appeal for trade union loyalty by emphasizing the important role of the trade unions within the Knights. In the fall of 1882 the Knights of Labor convention demarcated a special place for the large trade unions in its organizational structure, authorizing their incorporation as district trade assemblies alongside the mixed district assemblies, long the sole district level bodies. Powderly also ruled that local trade assemblies within mixed district assemblies would have an exclusive right to the membership of applicants of their trade within that district. He was therefore able to assure J. P. McDonnell in the fall of 1882 that McDonnell himself would find a comfortable place in the Knights, urging him to form an assembly with the understanding that

> the K. of L. makes no attempt on trade unions
> . . . on the contrary they try to show the folly of
> separate action and endeavor to bring all working-
> men into one organization, we have several
> assemblies, composed wholly of trades unions that
> came in in a body.[6]

Nor did the Knights take issue with what Gompers described as trade union politics, for Powderly too preferred issue-oriented to party politics. He typically warned correspondents to "by no means allow any one electioneer in the meeting room," reminding them that "our order is above politics, it teaches man his duty by educating him on the great question of labor. . . ." The Knights and the Federation would have agreed during these years that, in the words of Knights leader Charles Litchman, "that man has not learned the first principles of Labor Reform who does not know that political action is absolutely necessary to secure legislation in the interest of labor."[7]

The Knights of Labor participated in lobbying efforts and was also no less anxious than the FOTLU to see that labor made itself felt at the polls in a nonpartisan manner. Powderly himself was an active politician, serving three terms as mayor of Scranton, Pennsylvania. As late as the summer of 1884 he showed interest in running for Congress, foregoing the nomination because he had no money to run a campaign. When not working for his own election he was an active political strategist and observer, cheering the victories of local labor movements in capturing "one or the other of the old parties" and in electing "a man well known to be a friend to labor or else . . . a man of their own."[8]

With a national confrontation with the Knights seemingly postponed, Gompers found, for the moment, his gravest challenge in New York City. There he was in the first echelon of the labor "establishment" in the 1880s, a time when trade unionism in the city was undergoing a fresh critical assessment by immigrant Marxists looking for a home. "Designing and evil disposed" was Strasser's reaction to the socialist dissenters among the hundreds of new members he estimated had joined local 144 in the first years of the new decade. They had been increasingly thwarting his leadership.[9]

These newcomers first riled the union establishment by violating the solidarity of the campaign in New York City to reelect State Assemblyman Edward Gross. Gross was a "friend of labor," a man who had introduced legislation to abolish tenement house production of cigars, as well as advocating the establishment of a bureau of labor statistics, a mechanics' lien law, and the reduction of fares on the elevated railroad. New York's Amalgamated Trade and Labor Association, one with the Cigarmakers in backing Gross, saw such measures as smoothing the unions' path to permanence and power. The Amalgamated opposed nominating a separate ticket of labor candidates "before our trades are sufficiently consolidated, and have reached a certain degree of permanency."[10]

Much to the dismay of Gompers and Strasser, the new group of socialists in their union termed the entire legislative campaign useless and accused the Cigarmakers' leadership of selling out to capitalistic politicians. They demanded that workingmen abstain from voting until they were presented with labor candidates running on a Workingmen's Party ticket, a development which in fact materialized before the end of 1882. Gompers wrote in February 1882 that the opposition was caused by certain cigarmakers who, "within the last few months . . . arriving from Europe, have joined our Union (no. 144), without waiting to become informed as to the practical operations of our Unions, both International and Local." Early in April 1882 their numbers told in the election of their candidates to most of the commanding positions in Local 144, including the presidency.[11]

Because the trade unionist faction in the CMIU had effective control of the higher union machinery, the socialist effort to gain control of Local 144 failed, despite the electoral victory of that faction. Gompers and the older leadership of the local prepared an appeal to the International president based on the fact that the socialist elected to the local's presidency, Samuel Schimkowitz, was a manufacturer. Cigarmakers' International President Strasser suspended Schimkowitz pending investigation, and authorized a committee of the local, on which Gompers served, to investigate the charges. When the charges were substantiated by the committee in May, the socialists appealed the president's decision to the Executive Board of the International. On June 2 the board reinstated Schimkowitz pending a more thorough investigation by Union 144; on June 15 the result of that investigation in effect sustained Strasser's original judgment. The trade union faction therefore retained control of Local 144, although, by the time the final investigation had been completed, the socialist cigarmakers were already operating as a separate union and lacked only a formal declaration to constitute a secessionist movement. On July 17, 1882, they officially formed the rival Cigarmakers' Progressive Union in combination with a smaller group, the American Tobacco Workers' Association, which had seceded the previous year.[12]

By the time the cigarmakers split in mid-1882, the secessionists did not have to stand alone. Backing the Progressive Cigarmakers was a newly formed workers' organization in the city, the Central Labor Union (CLU). The Central had been formed in February 1882 among workers who looked favorably on the launching of an independent labor party. Its program stressed the need for immediate political party action on the part of the city's workers to secure labor reforms, especially the nationalization of the land. Its rapid success stood as a rebuke to the old Amalgamated Trade and Labor Association of the city, which had dismissed as premature the idea of nominating independent labor candidates for city offices. The Amalgamated leaders continued to argue that, because the trade unions were still in their infancy, they would "need fostering and developing before they enter into an open conflict with oppression." While the Amalgamated left open the possibility of such

party action once the unions "have developed their
strength, and have reached a permanent stage" it also held
that, for the time being, the unions "need to be trained to
act together and for a single aim," the strengthening of
their organizations' power and influence.[13]

Despite pleas by the Amalgamated against dual unionism,
the Central Labor Union proceeded with its plans to
organize independently. Gompers served on a committee of
the Amalgamated which tried in vain to reach some adjust-
ment. One of the people with whom Gompers was contending in this affair was P. J. McGuire. While McGuire had
shed his hostility toward trade unionism after the depression crisis of the 1870s and since that time had been active
and effective in the work of trade union organization and
amalgamation, he had not given up his interest in working
through electoral campaigns where circumstances looked
promising to build a labor party. He still retained his membership in the Socialist Labor Party and attended the party
congress in Europe in 1881 as his party's elected delegate.
Now both SLP President Philip Van Patten and McGuire
gave their blessings to the CLU by speaking at its founding
convention. McGuire also took part in the preparation of
the CLU program.[14]

The older trade union leadership seems to have made the
judgment that the talent and support which the Central
Labor Union was able to attract precluded its destruction
for the time being. The Amalgamated continued to work
actively for its legislative goals, but many trade unions
joined the CLU, and only a few of those retained membership in the older organization. Some of the trade unions
which joined the CLU did, however, form an economic
action faction from within. Though they could not sidetrack
plans for a CLU electoral campaign in 1882, they were able
to bring the action up for a serious questioning. As early

as September 1882, McGuire admitted that the question of the mission of the CLU was still not settled and asked for further discussion on "Shall the Central Labor Union be political or industrial," which he interpreted to mean "shall it organize a political movement of its own or shall it abstain from all forms of political action?"[15]

After a disappointing showing in the election of 1882, the Central Labor Union reverted more and more to economic action, concentrating on developing the boycott as a means of coercion. Within six months of the election, a much larger number of trade unions were attracted to the CLU, and although many, like the Progressive Cigarmakers, favored political party action in principle, the business of considering the economic grievances in the various trades took up an ever-increasing amount of the union's time. Nevertheless the Progressives, rather than the Cigarmakers' International, represented the city's cigarmakers in the CLU and, assured of support from this organization, launched an offensive against the CMIU. For this purpose it founded an official journal called *Progress*, which appeared in 1882.[16]

In part, *Progress* devoted itself to demonstrating the existence of a Strasser dictatorship in the Cigarmakers' International, and of a "Strasser clique" in the Trade Assembly of New York State and the FOTLU. In February 1883 it summarized the recent conventions of the latter two organizations with the observation that the clique had been "the loudest and most vicious in attacking resolutions opposing land monopoly, and in defeating all of the other progressive declarations."[17] But *Progress* also had a role to play in developing a case against the CMIU in ideological terms. Over the next several years it undertook to sponsor a thorough critique, in a Marxian context, of trade unionism in the United States.

At the heart of this critique was the contention that trade

unionism as practiced in the United States was not indigenous to the country but rather an imitation of the English
form and highly out of place in its new environment. Marx,
it was argued, had never recommended the English form
of trade union as the one approved form of that institution:
"During the debates of the Congresses of the International
Workingmen's Association, trades unionism was certainly
commended as necessary for emancipation, but no particular form and activity of the same was commended. . . ."
The reason Marx settled upon no particular form of trade
union for every country, it was explained, was that he
understood "that what is in one country a *natural growth*
from real causes in the system of production, cannot on that
account be an *ideal* for other populations living under other
real conditions."[18]

The Progressives held, therefore, that trade unions in the
United States could only be instruments of emancipation
insofar as they served as the means of seeking out and supporting the natural and indigenous working class movement
in the United States environment. In this search the working class of the United States had only certain general
guidelines set out by Marx, the charges of the *Manifesto* that
"the laboring classes must emancipate themselves through
their own exertions" and that the efforts of the workers in
their separate nations must lead toward the international
political organization of labor. The result of the search in
the United States, the Progressives reasoned, was bound to
be different from that in England. Political organization
could not have been a first step for the English workers
since they had no franchise and "had to lean on one or the
other (alternately) of the old parties to carry on 'tail politics'
in order to obtain any rights at all." In the United States,
on the other hand, the large agricultural base had been conducive to an extensive enjoyment of the franchise. This

right to vote had itself been an obstacle to the organizing of trade unions, but insofar as trade unions had grown up in the United States, the Progressives believed it was now their duty to support the workers' movements adapted to an atmosphere of political freedom. More specifically the unions were asked to support the "independent political organization of workingmen, such as the Greenbackers, Grangers, the Socialistic Labor Party and the Knights of Labor are trying to establish."[19]

Strasser in turn accused the Progressives of not understanding the American environment. It was they who were misapplying European methods to the American scene. He believed that the method of political agitation which the socialists practiced had been developed in the struggle to establish republican governments in Europe. As such it was useless in a country which already had such a form of government. The American working class, on the other hand, had developed, in the trade union movement, an instrument suited to the actual conditions in the United States. In joining the trade unions the socialists intended, according to their own frequently repeated statements, "to propagate the principles of socialism—i.e., to turn the same into a socialistic political club." They were attempting to force upon the unions methods which were not consonant with the environment, and their campaign could only lead to the retardation of the movement.[20]

The use of these tactics by the Progressives reminded Strasser of the sectarians who had plagued Marx and the First International in Europe during the previous decade. Claiming to have watched the labor movement of the civilized world for a long time, taking care to distinguish the various movements and their members, Strasser blamed the New York conflict on the same individuals "who attempted to destroy a powerful organization about thirteen years ago in another part of the globe." Strangely enough, he continued, "they resorted to the same methods here as they did there."[21]

The challenge of the Progressives also reminded Strasser that even before the recent immigration of German exiles, smaller numbers of like-thinking socialists had weighed down the efforts of the trade union leadership, wrecking many a trade union in the process. He recalled that within the CMIU, such men had first assumed "an aggressive attitude" in the convention of 1877, referring to Frank Hirth's resolution on political action, ". . . the main idea of which is that—trades unions are useless and should therefore be turned into political clubs." And in New York City the local cigarmakers' unions had been harassed by semi-annual assaults aimed at their capture "in the interest of the Socialistic Party," each attempt followed by a cycle of secession and subsequent grudging return to the fold by the "truants."[22]

Gompers was insistent, many years later, in making a distinction between the German socialists from whom he had received his education in trade unionism, and the latter-day German exiles from Bismarckian Germany who formed the Progressive movement. The Germans he had first met in Hirsh's shop in the early seventies were "men of keener mentality and wider thought than any I had met before." Even from the little English that was spoken in that shop, Gompers was able to gain an understanding that the trade union movement "meant to those men something vastly bigger than anything I had ever conceived." They were "genuine revolutionaries in thought and in deed."[23]

The Progressive socialists whom he confronted in the early eighties, on the other hand, were "zealots and impractical visionaries," men who paid little heed to Marx.

They were fanatics who believed in partisan political methods exclusively, for German Socialism was under the spell of Lassalle despite the counsel of Karl Marx. They preferred to see evils continue rather than see remedies from any other agencies than those prescribed by Socialism. The "party" was a fetish.

It was that ideological issue between party and trade union methodology that motivated the disruptive struggles in which Gompers was involved in New York City. That the issue did not resolve itself so much as become institutionalized within the trade union movement was due to two factors: an attitude of cautious reconciliation by the trade union leadership, Gompers included, toward the politically oriented component of the movement; and the pressure of increasing outside interference by the Knights of Labor.[24]

A period of stalemate between the two cigarmakers' organizations followed the split in mid-1882, during which their struggle occupied the attention of the FOTLU. Though standing officially behind the CMIU in the dispute, the Federation continuously provided encouragement for the pursuit of a policy of reconciliation within the trade. In 1884, for instance, the credentials committee of the FOTLU convention refused to seat Jacob Selig, a delegate from the Progressive Cigarmakers of Chicago, much to the delight of the New York State Trades Assembly which telegraphed its approval to the convention. But at the same time the committee asked that the convention instruct the members of the legislative committee "to use their best efforts to adjust the unhappy difficulties between the contending bodies."[25]

Part of the explanation for the Federation's careful hand-
ling of the dispute lies in the presence within the FOTLU
of an important contingent of delegates whose political
views were similar to the Progressives and whose sympathies
were with them. Many party socialists had preferred, it is
true, to work within the Knights of Labor, whose regional
mixed assemblies might more easily have been converted
into party cadres than could the trade unions. In New York
City, for instance, some socialists helped form a small disciplined inner group of Knights, known as the Home Club,
which achieved considerable power within the K. of L.
nationally.[26] But others of the party socialists had, like
McGuire, become active in their respective trade unions,
and some had helped create a political mindedness among
their unions' membership. When some of these unions fell
into line behind the new Federation, these party socialists
found themselves in a position from which potentially they
might powerfully influence the nature of the amalgamated
movement.

Henry Emrich was one of the most vocal of this group.
A socialist tailor and member of the New York CLU, he
avidly supported the Federation's eight-hour campaign in
the belief "that the workmen must rely upon themselves
and their own power exclusively." By the same reasoning
he also felt that the workingmen should support only candidates from a strictly workingmen's party and in an unsuc-
cessful challenge to established FOTLU policy in 1885
asked the convention to agree that

> it is unworthy of an intelligent working class
> whose constituting elements know what is neces-
> sary for their own well-being to elect legislators
> who may pledge themselves to support a few of
> the demands of labor and even keep such pledges,

but by supporting, on the other hand, measures intended for the sole benefit of capitalists and monopolists, to whom they are likewise under obligations, again destroy the little good created by their action in favoring labor legislation. . . .[27]

Emrich kept close watch on the actions of the Federation in the cigarmakers' dispute, and when, in 1885, the convention endorsed the CMIU union label, he informed the convention that his union "took sides" with the Progressives. His union preferred the Progressive label to that of the CMIU, Emrich said, and it believed that the Progressive union had been shabbily treated in the negotiations underway with the CMIU for the purpose of consolidation. He made it clear that his union would support the CMIU label only "with the full expectation that the proposed consolidation of the two Unions of cigarmakers would, in the near future, be an accomplished fact." Emrich was regarded as important enough in the Federation to be nominated and unanimously elected for one of the vice-presidential positions at the convention.[28]

The manner in which the cigarmakers' dispute was ultimately resolved, insofar as it actually was, is more than just an intricate episode in the history of a trade. The nature of the movement over which Gompers would preside in the next decade was both presaged in and influenced by the confrontation and its settlement. Believing that the cigarmakers' dispute had to be solved by the return of the Progressives to the fold once again, Strasser quickly found a way to make an impressive demonstration of the Cigarmakers' International's power within the trade. An incident arose in New York City concerning a year-old boycott of the firm of Straiton and Storm. In February 1884 the Progressive Union had struck against the firm, resisting a reduction in wages. Three months later the Progressives returned to work in defeat. During the strike, however, the Central Labor Union had declared a boycott of Straiton and Storm cigars, and the Knights of Labor had added its adherence, giving it a national following. The next year a committee of CMIU Local 144 traveled through a number of eastern cities and reported that, inexplicably, the boycott had never been lifted by the Knights.[29]

The CMIU now offered to help Straiton and Storm shake the boycott. Straiton and Storm locked out its 2,300 Progressive cigarmakers, declared itself a CMIU union shop, was given the CMIU blue label to use on its cigars, and waited for Strasser to convince the workers to join the International Union and gain reemployment with the firm. As justification for his actions Strasser claimed that only the International Union had the power to break this unjust boycott, and that it had the responsibility to do it. He argued that the CLU "has not enough influence to do much" while the CMIU "has a better and larger following." The Knights of Labor was embarrassed by the whole affair and attempted to extricate itself at the last moment by sending its executive board to New York City for a well-publicized investigation. But by the time the Knights, as a result of the investigation, announced the raising of the boycott in late December, the CLU and Progressive Cigarmakers had agreed to retain the boycott during the new crisis.[30]

The boycott controversy went no further because the Cigar Manufacturers' Association chose this moment to announce a new bill of prices in the trade, sharply reducing wages. One reporter noted that the manufacturers

> had the subject under consideration for some
> time, and if the unification of the cigarmakers had

been perfected it is hardly probable that the
reduction would have been sought. Knowing of
the bitter strife, they took advantage of the situation. . . .

The five CMIU locals of New York gained permission to
strike, and the manufacturers' association, following a
prearranged agreement among its members, instituted a
general lockout in response. Then the association moved to
take advantage of the split in the cigarmakers' organizations. Since the Progressives' strength lay mainly among the
lowest paid workers in the trade, the manufacturers offered
to make a new price list for the entire trade which would
be an average of the lowest and highest rates paid in New
York City shops previous to January 1. At the same time
the manufacturers attempted to ward off the effects of an
expected CMIU boycott by arranging through District
Assembly 49 of the K. of L. to have the use of the Knights'
label for their cigars. The Knights agreed to supply these
labels with the understanding that the Progressive Cigarmakers would be organized into the Order. A committee
appointed by the Central Labor Union to assist the Progressives favored this settlement, and before the end of February 1886, the Progressives returned to work.[31]
    Before the CLU endorsed the agreement, the CMIU had
attempted to curry its favor. During January, four of the
five CMIU locals of the city attempted to join the CLU to
bolster support for the Cigarmakers' International from
within. The Progressives and their supporters in the CLU
effectively barred the CMIU locals from membership, however, by making their admittance contingent upon their
acceptance of the Progressives as a bona fide union. By
January 1886, therefore, the Progressives had managed to
preempt the CMIU in both the local central union of the

city and in District Assembly 49 of the Knights of Labor, whose jurisdiction included the city.[32]

Ultimately, the success of the Cigarmakers' International rested upon its own strength in the trade, the incompatibility of the Progressives and the Knights of Labor, the flexibility of the CMIU leaders in accommodating themselves to the Progressives' political aspirations, and the ability of the Federation to tolerate a socialist presence. The CMIU maintained its strike and continued to boycott all Manufacturers' Association shops, some of which reopened with the aid of K. of L. Progressive workers. By the first week in March, however, many other local manufacturers had found it impossible to procure an adequate labor force without the International. Four decided to reopen as CMIU blue label shops, and the press reported that other manufacturers were preparing to make similar arrangements. As the trade returned to its normal status, the Progressives began to renege on the understanding they had reached that in return for the use of the K. of L. label, the union should join District Assembly 49 and give up its autonomy. An ultimatum from D. A. 49 either to surrender that autonomy or leave the Knights nudged the Progressives closer to the CMIU once again. By August 1886, the Progressives had met in convention and resolved to dissolve their union and amalgamate with the International.[33]

Politically the rapprochement between the two unions was probably encouraged by the willingness of the CMIU leadership to help contest the November elections. The mood of the city's workers was strongly political during 1886 and was reflected in a major reorganization of the Central Labor Union in the first half of the year. Before the reorganization, it had been complained that the quantity of trade business being considered at meetings precluded political discussion on the land and greenback questions and relegated independent politics to the future. Therefore the CLU organized trade sections, which, meeting separately, considered all grievances peculiar to the particular trades, leaving the general body's meetings free for the consideration of "such questions as occupied the attention of the Union in its callow days."[34]

By the summer, the reorganized CLU was deeply involved in a coalition of labor parties and organizations seeking to elect a labor candidate to the New York mayoralty. The candidate was Henry George, whose widely read *Progress and Poverty* (1880) offered to make America a land of opportunity once again. George held that wages had been high and opportunities rich for workers in America before speculative interests had acquired the land and its resources. Now productive people had to pay a premium for developing those resources and for living convenient to their work. Labor's exploitation and unemployment were both caused by land monopoly. During 1886 George unsuccessfully pursued the city mayoralty in behalf of his solution to that evil, the single tax on windfall profits from speculative investment in land. He sought to place all men "on an equality with regard to the use of the earth and the enjoyment of the bounty of their Creator."[35]

Samuel Gompers, far from resisting the movement, emerged as one of George's leading advocates. Five years previously he had made the mistake of taking his stand with the old Amalgamated Trade and Labor Union of the city against the political inclinations of the city workers, only to watch the Central Labor Union's political appeal allow it to quickly outstrip the Amalgamated in membership. Now in 1886 Gompers began to appreciate the importance of staying attuned to the periodic waves of political interest which

swept the workers. He headed the city organization of
Henry George Clubs and ran the Henry George Speakers'
Bureau, telling his fellow tradesmen,

> I have been working for organized labor for
> twenty-five years and have never declared myself
> a politician. Now I come out for George as a trade
> unionist and intend to support him with all my
> might.[36]

It is important here to understand that Gompers supported George "as a trade unionist." To him George was
merely one candidate who deserved support as a promising
friend of labor. Trade unionists should support him
enthusiastically, but without submerging the independent
identity of their unions to the new independent labor party
whose ticket George headed. At the same time there were
other friends of labor running on major party tickets for
state legislative posts who equally deserved labor's support.
Meeting at the end of October, Gompers and the six other
New York City members of the State Workingmen's Assembly executive council gave their endorsement to nine candidates for the legislature. They also urged the defeat of
one candidate who was "a pronounced enemy of labor."
Finally, in the same vein, they urged support of Henry
George in accordance with the resolutions of the state convention of the Assembly.[37]

Thus the political activity of Gompers in 1886 was a continuation of the approach he had taken earlier in his support of Edward Gross. It was based on the assumption that
the development of an actual party of the workers must follow upon the "perfected" organization of the workers,
rather than preceding it. It was the old Amalgamated Trade
and Labor Union's philosophy of seeking through friends

in politics to enact measures that would foster the development of labor's economic power and organization. Ironically, it was now brought to bear in the context of a campaign led by the Central Labor Union which had won dominance in the city on the claim that the Amalgamated's approach must give way to independent labor party politics. And in the course of this campaign leaders of the formerly feuding wings of the cigarmakers' movement outdid each other in burying the hatchet amid a common aspiration for New York's mayoralty.[38]

Because the FOTLU had handled the entire Cigarmakers' dispute very carefully, the CMIU's affiliation with the Federation presented no obstacles to trade unity. The example of Henry Emrich and other political activists demonstrated to the Progressives that there was room for men of their point of view to operate within the FOTLU. This assumption would have seemed even more justified when the Federation met in convention toward the end of the year and heard the legislative committee report its approval of the political activity in the campaigns of 1886:

> We regard with pleasure the recent political action of the organized workingmen of the country, and by which they have demonstrated that they are determined to exhibit their political power. We in full accord therewith, recommend to organized labor throughout the country that they persist in their recent efforts to the end that labor may achieve its just rights through the exercise of its political powers.[39]

The struggle within the cigarmaker's trade continued even after the merger of the two unions. It now became a battle between the refurbished International and those of the former Progressive union who chose to remain within District Assembly 49. The district assembly convinced some of the manufacturers of New York City to lock out the Progressives who had returned to the CMIU and replace them with K. of L. workers. The CMIU in turn voted $20,000 to sustain the Progressive locals affected by the lockout. With the lines of battle thus redrawn, both the CMIU locals, and the K. of L. cigarmakers working through a "Progressive Labor Club," sought the right of representing the local trade in the Central Labor Union.[40]

Since the CLU, after its reorganization, was no longer willing to consider disputes within a particular trade at its general meetings, the applications were referred to its newly created Tobacco Trades Section. There the CMIU locals finally gained admittance to the CLU, the credentials of the "Progressive Labor Club" being laid on the table. Efforts by the K. of L. sympathizers to appeal this action at the general meeting were defeated, but not always peacefully. One observer gave an account of the meeting of Sunday, August 8, in which District Assembly 49 was accused of trying to pack the hall:

> After the first blow was struck, at least 200 beligerants rushed upon each other pell-mell, and fought till the whole was in a wriggling pyramid of shrieking and infuriated combatants. Many men were severely hurt, and appeared on the street soon after with bruised faces and torn clothes. . . . It is the most disgraceful and disastrous incident that ever took place in the ranks of labor in the United States. . . .

Finally in 1887 Samuel Gompers had the pleasure of presiding over a meeting of the CLU which endorsed the CMIU label.[41]

As president of the State Workingmen's Assembly during 1886-1887, Gompers also presided over a rabid struggle between the CMIU and D. A. 49 at the state level. Powderly himself had shown intense interest in the assembly, urging that "we must control that body if it is possible, put your irons in the fire at once." In January 1887 D. A. 49's delegates attempted to take from the assembly president the power to appoint the committee on credentials. An observer reported the subsequent struggle:

> The scenes in both open and executive session were . . . such as to make the cooler heads ashamed. . . . There were threats of violence, and one delegate to whom objection was made rushed to the platform and drew a pistol, which, however, was taken from him.

Gompers' own description adds some detail. According to him the man

> rushed from the rear of the room, scaled the bar, and jumped upon the platform where I was standing. He pointed a revolver at my breast . . . I caught the lapel of his coat and . . . in as emphatic a tone as I could command said: "Give me that pistol!" He did not give it to me, and still louder . . . I repeated my demand. At the third repetition he dropped the pistol in my hand, and then bedlam broke loose.

The convention eventually sustained the president in his right to appoint the committee.[42]

The absorption of the Progressives into the CMIU and hence into the Federation had two important effects. First, absorbed along with the members of the Progressive union were the questions they had raised concerning the nature of the trade union movement. These questions were internalized but not digested, and the cause of the many politically minded socialists already active in the federated labor movement was invigorated by the infusion of new blood. Second, the problem of the presence of the Knighthood in the cigar trade could now quickly escalate into a national struggle. Should the local Knights demand recourse at the national level, the dispute was bound to involve the heretofore mild-mannered Federation in defense of the unions of the trade. For, having absorbed the Progressive union, the CMIU was for the first time assured of a more than qualified support from the FOTLU.

8
Gompers and the Use
of Economic Power

The mid-1880s marked Gompers' accession to the leading
place in American trade unionism. As a member of the
FOTLU's legislative committee, he strove to make over the
Federation in his image, and in the process helped to dif-
ferentiate it more sharply ideologically from the Knights of
Labor. In this period Gompers was still involved with the
radical trade unionist concerns of McDonnell, Kronburg,
and the Bolte group of the International: the historical
process of evolving class consciousness, the economic basis
of political power, the electricity and momentum of the
workers' practical demands, the abolition of the wage system. In the next decade he would elaborate considerably
on these themes.

The Federation of Trades and Labor Unions was mod-
eled after the British Trades Union Council, lobbying on
behalf of labor's immediate legislative demands. But what
of the solid superstructure Samuel Gompers envisioned to

perfect the organization of America's workers? Gompers, P. J. McGuire, and Frank K. Foster became the leading spokesmen in the FOTLU for welding the trade unions together into a powerful national movement. These three men each came from different ideological groups within the labor movement and together they symbolize the coalition which produced the American Federation of Labor in 1886.

P. J. McGuire, one of the party socialists to take a leading role in the labor federation, told the FOTLU's second convention that a federation of labor's forces was "the most natural and assimilative" form of bringing the trade and labor unions together: "It preserves the industrial autonomy and distinctive character of each trade and labor union, and without doing violence to their feelings or traditions, blends them all in one harmonious whole. . . ." He urged upon the delegates that "not political but industrial unity" be the first aim of the Federation. He wanted a structure formidable enough not only to give moral and financial aid to striking workers but also to cow employers from engaging in industrial conflict by teaching them the habit of hesitation. He hoped to see a systematic plan of trade union propaganda "strengthen and enliven all the unions" and in an obvious comparison with the Knights of Labor, preferred the federation form because it proceeded

> not by prescribing a stereotyped, uniform plan of organization for all, regardless of their experience or necessities, nor by antagonizing or aiming to destroy existing organization, but by preserving all that is integral in them and widening their scope so that each, without submerging its individuality, may act with the others in all that concerns them.[1]

When McGuire offered these ideas in 1882, most FOTLU delegates still hoped the federation could work alongside the Knights of Labor in benefiting the workers. They allowed the district assemblies of the Knights to send representatives to FOTLU conventions despite the warning of some of the delegates, as Gompers reported to his union, that "it seemed to be the policy of that organization to increase its membership and influence, even if by so doing it had *to tear down* Trades. Unions" by admitting into its ranks *"dissatisfied and insubordinate elements"* of other unions. The cigarmakers hastened to concur in this judgment, recalling that members suspended from the CMIU for not paying their dues had been initiated by cigarmakers' local assemblies of the Knights. Ominously they referred to the practice as one of making war on trade unions. Despite such accusations, the FOTLU convention of the following year again committed the Federation to working for unification with other labor societies in the country. It only refrained from mentioning the K. of L. by name after Gompers offered a more generally worded substitute.[2]

It was not until 1884 that the idea of working in solidarity with the Knights seemed to be dying. Frank K. Foster, a Boston printer, was secretary of the legislative committee that year. Foster was one of the line of Boston labor reformers who had collaborated with Gompers and the New York City Internationalists in the Workingmen's Party of the United States and in the International Labor Union. This group included Ira Steward, George McNeill, and George Gunton. In the early 1880s, McNeill and Foster were both officers in District Assembly 30 of the Knights of Labor in Boston. Foster became editor of the Knights of Labor's official journal in Massachusetts in 1884, the very year he held the leading position in the FOTLU. But while McNeill worked desperately trying to reconcile the Knights and the new labor federation in the middle of the decade, Foster somewhat earlier reconciled himself to the need for an independent trade union movement. Speaking to the FOTLU convention in 1884 he observed:

> It appears to me that the radical difference in the views of different societies preclude [sic] the idea of unification excepting among the genuine unions. Progressive trades unionism will furnish a broad and enduring basis for societies desiring practical leaguing together. The onward movement must of necessity follow the trade line, both on account of its greater feasibility and the economic soundness of the course.

Foster confessed, however, that the Federation of Trades was in trouble. During the year poor organization and the lack of funds had "seriously crippled" its work. Where was the resolve to "initiate such a movement as will be productive of incalculable good to the working people not only of America but of the Civilized world"? He asked the delegates to watch for a key resolution which would be offered the convention toward this end.[3]

This vital proposal, as it turned out, had first appeared at the Cigarmakers' convention that year. In its original form it had been offered by Gompers and Fred Blend, in answer to the 1883 FOTLU consensus that "a system by which one trade can assist another in time of trouble, financially as well as morally" was "an essential to the permanent organization of this Federation." Gompers and Blend had asked the CMIU to pledge to the Federation in 1884, "any amount not to exceed ten (10) percent of the income of our organization" to make the FOTLU "protective in its mission." Protection was bound to be attractive to workers facing strikes and lockouts over wage reductions induced by the depression of 1883-1885. The Cigarmakers modified the pledge, reducing it to two percent and requiring that it go into effect only if all the other trades of the Federation took the same action. In this form it was now presented to the Federation. Due to serious family illness, Gompers himself did not attend the convention in 1884.[4]

The desire to make the FOTLU protective was part of Frank Foster's greater design for taking the organization beyond lobbying and toward a greater reliance upon the combined economic power of the workers for the achievement of the goals of the labor movement. He believed that protective and permanent organization gave organized labor an alternative to lobbying in seeking its ends. This was also true of his approach to the demand for the eight-hour day. The FOTLU had, until this time, preferred to rely upon lobbying strength to achieve legislation of the eight-hour day, but as early as 1882 P. J. McGuire indicated that if the Federation were transformed into an "industrial unity" it might quickly move to confront the employers directly with the demand, backed by the combined economic strength of the united trade unions. Now in 1884 Foster rejected the lobbying approach to the eight-hour day, contending,

> this much has been determined by the history of the eight-hour law—it is useless to wait for legislation in this matter. In the world of economic reform the working classes must depend upon themselves for the enforcement of measures as well as for their conception.

He promised that if the delegates would give their careful

consideration to making the organization protective, they
would be taking the first step toward a "universal, centrally
directed advance" for the eight-hour day. And he argued
that

> a united demand for a shorter working day,
> backed by thorough organization, will prove vastly
> more effective than the enactment of a thousand
> laws depending for enforcement upon the
> pleasure of aspiring politicians of [or] sycophantic
> department officials.[5]

If the Federation did give indication of a new tendency
in 1884, its meager income of $336.22 for the year, its lack
of authority and as yet limited prestige within the labor
movement, and the preoccupation of labor with the problems of another depression, limited the degree to which it
could be translated into an effective program. Yet the
imperatives for pushing forth the program existed, for
there had been much talk preceding the convention of 1884
that the FOTLU would have to be replaced with a more
solid organization of the trades. The Haverhill *Laborer* even
contended that because the FOTLU had originally been
conceived on the example of the English trades congresses,
it was hopelessly bound to the task of securing legislation.
Despite the usefulness of such work, the editorialist held,
"the need of a closer practical union of trades has become
evident." He assessed that "it is not improbable that some
means may be devised so that issues and treasuries may be
pooled by the great Trade Unions of the country whenever
it becomes necessary to engage in a contest with capital."[6]
Ambitious plans were made, therefore, to redirect the
efforts of the FOTLU. The Gompers-Blend proposal asked
the national unions to surrender a part of their control over

the power of the purse to a federated strike fund. The transfer of power that this would effect, if enacted, was comparable only to the transfer of sovereignty which the national unions themselves achieved over their locals when consolidated trade benefit systems and strike funds had begun to appear. The welding together of so powerful a new institution in the union hierarchy obviously required a major amendment to the FOTLU constitution. The convention asked the nationals to give special study during the year to "the best method to secure the organization and unification of labor on a sound financial basis" and looked to the 1885 convention for a decision. On the question of the eight-hour day, the same convention went out on a limb by stating that on and after May 1, 1886, "eight hours shall constitute a day's labor" and recommending that labor organizations make the appropriate changes in their laws to conform to this decision by that date. The legislative committee was instructed to invite the Knights of Labor to join in this movement.[7]

Participation by the Knights was unlikely, however, for as the FOTLU turned in 1884 to the development of the power potentialities of the trade unions' economic resources, the Knights of Labor was changing too. By 1884 the Knights' leadership tended to recognize the practical failure of the cooperative movement through which it had intended to develop the economic power of the Knighthood. Powderly admitted in January that he could not recall the names of any of the assemblies that were engaged in cooperative enterprises and that insofar as they existed in several localities, they were on a small scale. He complained that "to be successful in co-operation *capital* is necessary. The workingmen who have a little capital cling to it, and hold aloof from co-operation, those who have no capital cannot embark in it. . . ." Because of this failure, interest

in the possibilities of reform politics had been growing in
Powderly's mind for some time, stimulated by the numerous
schemes of land nationalization and by none more than that
of Henry George. As early as August 1882 Powderly had
taken issue with an editor who did not seem impressed by
George's ideas: "I believe that Henry George is right in the
main. I may be wrong but it will take *argument* to convince
me of it." In his annual message as mayor of Scranton, Powderly proposed to the city council that city tax assessments
distinguish between speculative and improved property.[8]

Henry George soon became aware of Powderly's advocacy
of ideas similar to his own and for some time the two men
engaged in a correspondence. In April 1883 George
offered Powderly a prescription for the success of the
Knights of Labor. He had been prompted to write by reading a portion of an address by Powderly dealing with the
land question and noticing "how thoroughly it accords with
my own earnest belief." George thought the Knights' official
journal seemed to reflect "a lack of definite purpose" and
warned that an enthusiastic membership and great organization could not be built upon the advocation of "small
measures."

> There is a wide-spread consciousness among the
> masses that there is something *radically* wrong in
> the present social organization. All that is needed
> to weld this feeling into a power which will at
> length become irresistible, is concentration and
> enlightenment. The failure of all previous labor
> organizations to accomplish much, or to force
> their issues into politics seems to me to have been
> due to their failure to urge anything radical
> enough and large enough within to satisfy this
> feeling or to arouse opposition.

He urged that Powderly's own solution of the land problem become the program of the Knights of Labor.[9]

Powderly agreed with George and did his best to make land reform the standard of the Knights. During the summer of 1883, however, the Telegraphers National District No. 45 went on strike against Western Union seeking a wage increase and a settlement of grievances, and Powderly felt constrained by this event to postpone proselytizing the loftier reform: ". . . at such a time as that you could preach 'land reform' till hoarse and instead of securing a listener you would drive men from you. Men will not listen to *reason* while in the heat of battle. . . ." But in private he revealed that his next annual address to the general assembly would demonstrate that he had "not taken one backward step" from his previous position on land reform but had "gone still farther" in support of it. He confided that his new address would strike "the key note that will reach the American heart," by which he meant his attack on

> the alien land lord who first drives his victims
> from Irish soil and heads them off in this land
> by buying (stealing) up the land and compels his
> slave to go up into an eight story tenement in a
> large city and live on a crust or pay an exorbitant
> price for land which God made for all honest men
> instead of for thieves.

Land reform continued during the next decade to be one of Powderly's main interests.[10]

For trade unionists intent upon the cultivation of labor's concentrated economic power for ameliorative gains, a niche in the political reform-minded Knights of Labor was bound to become progressively more uncomfortable. One indication of the growing ideological distance between the

Knights and the Federation was the fact that Gompers had
rejected land reform in favor of the demand for higher
wages at about the same time that Powderly was becoming
a supporter of the nationalization of land. During the
FOTLU convention of 1882 Gompers argued against a
proposal for land nationalization, contending that in the
system of private ownership labor's real battle with the
employers lay in the confrontation over the division of
labor's product. Ultimately, he believed, labor would find
that land monopoly did not determine wages, but "that
wages controlled land and everything else."[11]

On the Knights of Labor side, Powderly, by 1885, was
making little effort to hide his opinion that the trade district
assemblies with which the Knights had sought to accommodate the trade unions were "a step backward." By the
beginning of the following year the Knights' official journal
was publishing such opinions as that of H. E. Burton, District Master Workman of Assembly 104 of Troy, stating that

> we have a great many among us who still adhere
> to their old trade-union principles, and join our
> Order for nothing more than to assist them in
> their trade-union ideas, and, if called upon to
> sever their connection with either, would drop the
> Knights of Labor.

Burton contended that this type of man was attempting the
impossibility of serving two masters. "If his mind is nar-
rowed down to old trade-unionism, then he cannot be a
good Knight, and no body of men should work under the
two charters."[12]

As a result of this growing divergence, the FOTLU never
achieved the labor unity it sought for its eight-hour cam-

paign. On its last day the 1884 convention of the Federation instructed the legislative committee to seek the cooperation of the Knights of Labor in the campaign. Gabriel Edmonston, co-sponsor of the resolution and secretary of the incoming legislative committee, passed the proposal on to Fred Turner, secretary of the Knights, but received no answer. Powderly meanwhile made every effort to publicly declare his sympathy with the goal of eight hours while emphasizing the impracticality of the FOTLU's proposal for the use of massive economic coercion. His theme throughout 1885 and in a secret circular to the Knights on March 13, 1886, was that the labor organizations ought to concentrate on cultivating a healthy public opinion in favor of shorter hours and that education along these lines was necessary for the workers as much as for the employers.[13]

A second result of the divergence of views was the growing sensitivity among trade unionists to the everyday irritations caused by the existence of dual unions. The Knights' policy toward local affiliates did not require their membership in the national and international union of their trade. As a consequence many local trade assemblies shared geographical jurisdiction with corresponding locals of the national or international union of their trade and consequently competed with that union for members. Complaints about this situation were heard with increasing frequency after 1884. The Iron Molders' statement in the spring of 1885 was typical: "We can not approve of the action of some of the Assemblies who are admitting to membership suspended or expelled members of our local Unions." Other complaints included proselytizing by K. of L. organizers among members of locals affiliated with the national unions and boycotting by the K. of L. of goods of employers hiring members of such locals. These irritations were widespread by the time of the FOTLU convention in

December 1885 and a special committee of the Federation communicated the unions' displeasure to the Knights.[14]

Powderly replied promptly to the complaints. When annoyances of this sort occurred, he assured the Federation, they were more often than not due to carelessness. Expelled members would not have been admitted to the K. of L. had the assemblies been given a list of those they should watch out for. The Knights had often boycotted employers upon the request of, and alongside, local unions but had sometimes not been informed of a settlement and of the workers' return to the job; the boycott therefore continued to the detriment of the shop at which they worked. Finally, if organizers had gone beyond their jurisdiction and meddled in the affairs of local unions, it had not been with Powderly's encouragement. He urged that specific complaints of this kind be called to his attention and promised to investigate and properly adjust these situations when they occurred. In commenting on Powderly's attitude at the FOTLU convention the following year, the legislative committee praised his "tone of fairness," regretting only that the continuation of K. of L. hostility toward trade unions in the interim meant either that Powderly had no real power in the Knights or that he was a liar.[15]

As labor leaders looked at the chasm developing between the Knights of Labor and the FOTLU, some began to speak of developing a formula by which separate spheres of action could be delineated for each and the services of both be retained for the greater labor movement. As early as 1883 Edward King, New York labor organizer, socialist, and Central Labor Union member, believed he discerned a clear understanding working itself out among the various labor organizations in the field, "not by any direct effort, but spontaneously." Speaking to the U.S. Senate Committee on Education and Labor he claimed that so far as the work

of unifying the labor movement was concerned, "The idea
of the division of the work is generally entertained by the
workingmen." He noted three "departments" into which
the various organizations were channeling their major
energies—education, organization, and agitation. The
Knights of Labor he relegated to the first, praising the organization for introducing methods

> which will make it imperative that the members
> shall have the opportunity of forming their opin-
> ions into logical groups and sharing their minds
> and their thoughts so that there shall be some real
> unity or sympathy of thought and feeling on the
> labor question as a condition of united action.

Such a project, he pointed out, was "not strictly connected
with the trades unionism [*sic*]." Nor did King believe the
agitational organizations, such as the Socialist Labor Party,
interfered with the work of trade union organization. Political agitation was needed among the so-called unskilled, he
said, because in this group "the political concept is subject
to a great deal of fluctuation," yet in this group "the hope
of obtaining some amelioration by politics" was spreading.
Here too it was possible to carry out activity without intrud-
ing upon the realm of the trade unions, for "it is now almost
universally recognized that you must not mix up politics
with trade unions."[16]

The trade unions took up the idea of spheres of action
three years later in a conference held in Philadelphia, May
18, 1886. Here twenty-two delegates representing twenty
unions came together to consider ways of preventing
encroachments "by overzealous organizers" of the Knights
upon the trade unions, "and to prepare a plan to secure
harmony." The conference produced a treaty to be offered

to the Knights of Labor. If accepted, it would have ended
the K. of L.'s jurisdiction over the organized trades. The
agreement provided that national and international trades
unions would have the exclusive right within their trade to
control the organization of workers, to affiliate local unions,
to manage strikes or deal with lockouts, and to regulate the
use of the trade label. No restriction was placed on the continued membership of trade workers in mixed K. of L.
assemblies, though such bodies could not accept the membership of those excluded from the union of their trade
because of scabbing, informing, or embezzlement. But
organizers of the Knights were to have their commissions
revoked if they endeavored "to induce trades unions to dis-
band" or if they tampered with the "growth or privileges"
of the trades unions.[17]

For Powderly, who considered even the existence of trade
assemblies within the Knights to be a step backward, the
attempt to reserve trade jurisdiction to the autonomous
trade unions seemed nothing less than reactionary. Embit-
tered, he wondered if it might not be wise to make Adolph
Strasser General Master Workman of the Order: ". . . then
we will have all the other unions fighting Strasser . . . so
that they won't lose their AUTONOMY." To the Knights'
legislative committee chairman, Ralph Beaumont, he suggested that the crisis might be overcome by bringing large
numbers of farmers into the Knights of Labor, contending
that "if that is done the *aristocracy* of labor will have to follow
in order to get under a wing big enough to shelter them."
Nor was the Knights without its attraction for farmers.
There had already been serious cooperation at the local and
state level between farm groups and K. of L. assemblies.
Texas, which led in such activity, had by late 1885 seen the
beginnings of coordinated farmer and K. of L. activities "in
commercial co-operation and all such social measures as will

tend to give assistance to the laboring classes." There were indications of similar developments in New Jersey, Illinois, Iowa, Kansas, and Nebraska. And toward the end of the following year the Knights organized their first "straight out-and-out Farmers Assembly" in Carmagro, Illinois, with the justification that "the toilers on the farm must be organized and combined with the wage workers of the cities and towns before the forces of labor can be victorious."[18]

The Knights of Labor, then, was far from ready to relinquish its jurisdiction over the trades. In reply to the treaty the Knights claimed "the propositions contained therein are inconsistent with our duty to our members. . . ." The special general assembly, which began May 25 in Cleveland, proposed a meeting of committees to reach some accommodation, but the summer passed without the appointment of a committee of Knights by Powderly, and the trade unionists grew impatient. The *Carpenter* wished to know "why has not that committee of five been appointed by Mr. Powderly. . . . It was so ordered by the Special General Assembly. . . ."[19]

In the meantime reports were appearing from conventions of various national trade unions that the Knights of Labor was actively seeking the affiliation of those bodies. In New York City alarm spread over the Home Club's efforts to capture the trade unions for the K. of L., the *Carpenter* reporting that "the recent actions of a mischievous element of the K. of L. in New York, demand the interference of Mr. Powderly if open and fratricidal war is to be avoided." But since it was precisely this group of Knights that had obtained control of the executive board at the special general assembly, it was well to wonder how much freedom of action Powderly had in this regard.[20]

Even assuming that Powderly retained considerable influence, the summer and fall of 1886 found him distinctly hostile to certain leaders in the trade union movement. Throughout the crisis, he contended, the Order stood on the defensive, warfare being made against it "not by the trade unions but by a few men at the head of the International Cigarmakers' union." He insisted he had tried before to negotiate with these men but found them impossible to deal with:

> Whenever the officers of the International Union came to call on us one or more of them was so drunk that they could not transact business. I will speak plainly, Mr. Gompers never came near me only when he was drunk and *I will not transact business with a drunkard at any time or place*.

Others had called for compromise with these leaders, said Powderly, not understanding the scorn in which such men held the Order. "In the face of this to have our own Assemblies pass resolutions asking of us to sacrifice every principle and kneel at the feet of Socialistic fanatics seemed to be too bad."[21]

When finally in late September a trade union committee met with leading Knights in Philadelphia, Powderly claimed he was bound by the special general assembly's instructions to deal only with specific grievances. The consideration of the more general settlement represented by the treaty, he claimed, would have to be the task of the annual general assembly to meet in Richmond in October. The conference adjourned with professions of good faith on both sides, but the trade union committee did not intend to sustain its hopes on faith alone. An address drafted to the trade unions of the country expressed the committee's hope that the Richmond assembly would "outline a policy whereby all phases of the labor movement may work together side by side." But the same address issued a call for a national labor congress, to be held at Columbus, Ohio, on December 8, to establish an American federation of labor. The purpose of the new federation would be the encouragement of trade union organization at all levels, and "the federative unity of all branches of labor."[22]

In Columbus in December the trade union movement formally broke with the Knights of Labor. The convention delegates declared that the failure of the eight-hour movement was "chargeable to the expressions of hostility coming from the leading members of the Knights of Labor." They characterized as "scabbing" the activities of the Knighthood in the battle for jurisdiction over the trades. The Knights were condemned and the new American Federation of Labor refused to admit K. of L. assemblies to membership, as the Federation of Organized Trades and Labor Unions, now dissolved, had done for half a decade.[23]

The meeting proceeded in the flush of political excitement following a year of election campaigning by labor. Happily and optimistically the delegates, including many socialists, joined in claiming that political action, once "a prolific source of dissension and trouble in the ranks of the workingmen," was now a source of unity:

> The revolution recently witnessed in the election contests in several states, notably, the remarkable and extraordinary demonstration made by the workingmen of New York, Milwaukee, Chicago, and other places, shows us the time has now arrived when the working people should decide upon the necessity of united action, as citizens at the ballot box.

The convention urged continued support for the independent political movement of the workers.[24]

Samuel Gompers in 1886 was a natural choice to fill the office of president of the new American Federation of Labor. He had been a major participant in the project to instill the Cigarmakers' International Union with the elements of "perfection," and a principal spokesman for a new direction to bring those elements to the Federation of Organized Trades and Labor Unions in 1884. The battle between the Cigarmakers' local and the Knights had become a *cause célèbre* at the founding convention of the AFL because of a K. of L. resolution adopted at Richmond in October demanding all members of the CMIU choose between membership in that union and membership in the Knights. He was also a leading labor leader in New York City, the movement's Apollo according to *John Swinton's Paper*. And New York housed by far the largest trade union movement among the country's urban centers. What is more, Gompers was able to remain on top of the city movement during 1886 despite its enthusiastic dash into independent party politics on behalf of Henry George.[25]

Closely attuned to the spirit of the workers he led, acknowledged as a dominant labor leader in New York City and New York State, Gompers had also held the leading post on the legislative committee of the FOTLU during the year preceding the AFL's founding, and for four years in all. At the same time he did not hesitate to give the full support of the FOTLU to the work of the national convention called to create the AFL. He led the legislative committee of the FOTLU in transferring the site of the annual convention of 1886 from St. Louis to Columbus where the national convention of trades unions would be held, announcing to the membership that this was done to take advantage of the opportunity thus presented of "forming a thorough and permanent Federation—a unity of all the forces of labor into a solid phalanx, yet each Trade Union to preserve its own identity and autonomy." In the preamble to the Cigarmakers' constitution seven years earlier Gompers had endorsed the idea of capital as a social product entrusted to the employing class as a public trust and implying grave responsibilities on that class's part. Now he led the FOTLU into the new movement to combat in unity the breaking of that trust,

> the tendency of the employing class to not only refuse the just demands of labor, but to use the power of their possessions to coerce labor into more degrading conditions and wrest from the toilers the rights which are considered sacred and achieved.[26]

As Gompers moved from his period of intensive campaigning for Henry George to the presidency of the new federation of labor, the election coalition began to dissolve on the city scene. Ideological conflict between single-taxers and socialists was particularly disruptive and the future of New York's Labor Party was in some doubt. Amid this breakdown, Gompers was interviewed concerning new directions for the party.[27]

He made clear, to begin with, that he had little enchantment with the program Henry George had bequeathed the party, holding that "the mere taxation of land values cannot settle the questions between capital and labor arising from the wage system and the progress of machinery. . . ." Claiming to "believe with the most advanced thinkers as to the ultimate ends, including the abolition of the wage system," he nevertheless argued that the party must join the federation in working at the practical level, pacing itself to the aspirations of the workers at their present stage of consciousness. For the party this would mean supporting such measures as the reduction of hours, the prohibition of child labor, and the restriction and regulation of female labor.

If Gompers demanded attention to practical issues, he did so with the same justification J. P. McDonnell had offered in speaking of the "Necessities of the Hour" and that David Kronburg had reiterated in discussing "Labor from the Real and Ideal Standpoint." This was that no attempt to emancipate the workers could be successful if it did not begin with the workers' present conditions. The goal of the trade union movement encompassed both "immediate relief" and "further aims." From success in a few practical measures the workers would derive "an immediate and substantial improvement" which alone would enable them to "advance further in economic and moral education, and in their perception of ultimate ends. . . ." "Continual improvement," Gompers explained, "by opening new vistas, creates new desires and develops legitimate aspirations. It makes men more dissatisfied with unjust conditions and readier to battle for the right."

Gompers saw class spirit and discipline as deriving from a chain reaction inaugurated by immediate improvements:

> Organization, the requisite of progress, is more readily effected as the first object in view is more clearly perceived. This object once attained, others are seen which previously lay beyond the ordinary range of vision. It is, therefore, of the utmost importance to have a well-defined object in view from the start—something that everybody can see—because the hope of reaching it facilitates organization, through which the final aim, however dim to the perception of many, is steadily advanced.

Reducing this insight to very tangible terms, Gompers recounted a recent experience:

> Some time ago I heard a mother say she wished her sick child were dead. She lived in a pestilential tenement house, and her misery was such that this was, indeed, the most merciful wish her circumstances could inspire. But give this mother a ray of hope, improve her condition ever so little, and mark the change in her speech! Yes, I believe in immediate relief. It is not in degradation that men aspire most to get out of it.

Here Gompers stood at the inception of the AFL, attuned to the practical necessities of the hour, talking economic issues to reform-minded Knights and political activists alike. "The poor, the hungry, have not the strength to engage in a conflict even when life is at stake." "The great political ourburst of last fall was the result of previous organization in the economic field. The same thing will be true of all future movements." The working-class movement must be allowed to work along these "natural lines" toward "its own logical outcome." The movement, though anchored in practical measures, was "not a narrow one, for we can see from it that nothing is impossible." "No intelligent observer can fail to perceive its natural tendency." Yet many an intelligent observer, bourgeois and socialist, did fail to perceive its natural tendency in the AFL's formative decade.

9
Gompers and the Challenge of Bourgeois America

In his first years as president of the American Federation of Labor, Gompers moved eagerly to place his ideological stamp on American trade unionism. As his voluminous correspondence soon made clear, his overriding concern was to mold a purely wage-worker movement based upon "the identity of interests of all wage-workers." If he relied upon the trade union as the basic building block of the Federation, it was not with any intention of excluding workers not yet organized by trades. Gompers was determined to follow the natural or historical patterns of organization of the American workingmen toward the end of some thoroughgoing unity.[1]

Clearly from the beginning Gompers regarded the existing trade unions as only a starting point for linking all the workers of the continent "in one solid phalanx powerful [*enough*] to resist the aggressions of the opponents of the emancipation of our class." A network of organizations known as federal labor unions, councils, or assemblies, was provided for at the first AFL convention, giving workers in jobs not immediately conducive to trade organization an avenue to affiliation with the greater movement of labor. Through this mechanism, Gompers believed, the door would be opened "to an immense number who previously could not identify themselves with the labor movement proper." He also insisted that the use of the trade organization approach did not restrict the Federation's scope to a skilled aristocracy of tradesmen. The Federation was for him an organization

> not necessarily of skilled labor as many seem to think but of all wage-workers who organize Unions of their trades or callings, skilled or unskilled, to protect and advance their interests in their particular trades or callings first and as a wage-earning *class* next.[2]

Thus Gompers found himself the leader of what he believed was a genuine mass movement. Although he insisted upon an understanding of "first principles" by the masses prior to taking "another step in the right direction," he believed as well that the movement's goals encompassed the full range of human improvement for the masses, "materially, morally, politically, and socially." The effort of a "bona fide" labor movement to ameliorate the conditions of the workers would raise the "manhood" of the masses "to a higher level" enabling labor to "finally achieve its emancipation from the thraldom of injustice and wrong."[3]

Despite his many executive responsibilities in these years, Gompers still found time to discuss his views on the modern industrial system. Fundamental was his belief that capital was a social product. Society, he explained, had achieved

its considerable development in industry and science by
accumulating past labor in the form of capital:

> At the outset of industrial life when each man
> worked his little bit of land with the rudest tools
> and lived in the most complete isolation possible,
> even then, when industry was most exclusively
> personal . . . each stroke of work that he per-
> formed was laying the foundation of that impor-
> tant instrument called capital. Thus capital is the
> product of the whole past industrial efforts of the
> human race.[4]

Gompers saw profound implications for his contemporary world in these origins of industrial wealth. It meant
particularly that

> capital, by common consent, is concentrated in
> individual hands in order the better to develop its
> efficiency as an industrial instrument. The capital-
> ist therefore stands in the dignified position of a
> trustee of the capital placed in his hands.

Responsible use of the common heritage required the payment of a decent wage to the wage workers, but it included
a great deal beyond this:

> It is a great mistake made by many of our public
> men when they suppose that it is a mere question
> of wages, of dollars and cents, that is now convuls-
> ing every country of the civilized world. . . . There
> is a deeper trouble, and a nobler aspiration agitat-
> ing the working class. . . . They feel that Capital
> has its duties no less than its rights. . . .[5]

Gompers' understanding of the "duties of capital" derived from his theory of wages. Like Marx, he believed that "the wages of the workers can never be considered as a payment of the value of the work performed." Labor was responsible for its total product. The Federation's task was to see that this product was used in a socially responsible way, "first of all to maintain and conserve, and in some degree develop the indispensable instrument, capital; and then to provide for all the other needs of society." The daily requirements of every family must be supplied whether or not the breadwinner is able to work or find employment: "The capitalist does not starve when business is slack nor even when it is totally suspended; and the capital which furnishes subsistence to the one must do the same for the others." Finally, severe retribution was due the trustees if they violated the trust of their charge:

> When the capitalist diverts any portion of this common heritage from its destined purpose and uses it for selfish purposes, whether in ostentatious luxury or in the payment of armed police he commits the most flagrant crime the mind of man can conceive.[6]

But the appearance of the American Federation of Labor, the quickening growth of national and international trade unions, the establishment of city trade and labor councils, and the numerical increase of labor organizations all along the line, already testified to the betrayal by the capitalists of their trust. The crimes of the capitalists were forcing "upon the consciousness of the wage workers" the understanding that "they are a distinct and practically permanent class in modern society" with "distinct and permanently common interests." Nor, in Gompers' analytical understand-

ing, could it have been any other way. Far from advocating
a doctrine of stewardship, Gompers set up the capitalist as
a trustee only to prove his impossibility in that capacity.
This was the very justification for the trade union movement. The larger forces of capitalistic development, as
Gompers understood them, worked inexorably and imper-
sonally against the survival of the nobler sentiments in the
capitalist class. Like Marx, Gompers saw the competitive
process driving industry toward large-scale production,
activated by capital drawn together in partnerships, corpo-
rations, and trusts, sustained by the "diminution of the profit of the capitalist per dollar" as mechanization increased.
The businessman was confronted with "a constant increasing necessity for a large share of production to be stored
in order that future production may be successfully carried
on, on a still greater scale." Mechanization, then, was a
traumatic rather than peaceful development in capitalistic
society. The instincts of the trustee had to be buried in the
struggle to sustain residue profit over and above the other
mounting demands upon the product of industry. For
Gompers, as for Marx, unemployment, increased velocity
of work, and the exploitation of woman and child labor
were all organic to this stage of development.[7]

It appeared to Gompers, therefore, that the organization
of laborers into a permanent class under capitalism was historically "inevitable." The trade union movement represented the attempt by the workers to establish "normal
permanent relations between capitalists and laborers" which
would assure the responsible use of the "common heritage."
But the very process of attempting to achieve a responsible
use of the common heritage would take place in an
atmosphere of "ever-recurring disputes destined to become
more and more gigantic." The vision of the swelling of
labor's ranks stoking more bitter class confrontation and

further accelerating working class organization led Gompers to contemplate the achievement of a completely unified working class. Once that stage was reached, he said, "a successful attempt made [may] be made to eliminate the evils of which we, as a class, so bitterly and justly complain." A drive begun to achieve a responsible trust, developed in the context of a continuing class conflict, "cannot cease until the laborers shall be the capitalists, i.e., the capitalists shall be the laborers. In other words they shall be one and the same."[8]

Did Gompers in fact believe, as he said, that the day was not far distant when his class could make an attempt to eliminate the evils of which he spoke? Was it mere rhetoric that led him to agree with a correspondent that "we are on the eve of an important crisis in the fortune of our class" and that it was therefore urgent to educate the workers "to the important requirement of the age," i.e., unity? In terms of the ideology of the Internationalist tradition, which the previous chapters have traced through a quarter century, Gompers appears to have approached the leadership of the AFL in its first decade with a considerably more radical intent than scholars have heretofore supposed.[9]

Within this tradition, the successful beginning of an organization such as the AFL could easily excite a leader of labor with a sense of imminent class power and change. The communications of Gompers in the first decade exude such excitement, often coupled with a repetition of the same arguments used by earlier Internationalist leaders of this tradition to justify their choice of amalgamation and the perfection of the labor movement as the route to emancipation. Gompers, for instance, talked again of the submissiveness of Chinese civilization as a continuing refutation of the argument of some that destitution was sufficient of itself to initiate radical change. The workers, he proposed, must

first be prepared for emancipation through organization
and the witnessing of a gradual "evolution" of material
improvement through concessions forced from the employing class. This was essential to the workers' education.

> The more the improved conditions prevail, the
> greater discontent prevails with any wrongs that
> may exist. It is only through the enlightenment
> begotten from material prosperity that makes it
> at all possible for mental advancement.

Gompers envisioned the workers' education as a compound
of contradictions, of improvements conceded but not sustained, of material prosperity without material well-being.
Even the term evolution used in this context referred only
to reaching a takeoff point, for the improvement involved
could not be sustained without radical change. "Mark me
well I do not pretend to say that the time for other action
is not coming," Gompers lectured. "I only deprecate an
immature action." He saw the evolution of amelioration as
facilitating an acceleration of the work of "organizing, disci-
plining, and educating the vast hosts of labor" and in turn
infusing the movement with the confidence that

> in a few short years we shall have the satisfaction
> of witnessing the grand economic and social trans-
> formation for which the whole past history of our
> race has been one long, gradual preparation.[10]

Nor did Gompers always appear confident that the grand
transformation toward which the movement was proceeding
would be achieved without bloody resistance. He seems to
have been torn at times between the hope that the employing class would recognize its own advantage in conceding

to "the growing demands of the people" and a more gloomy recognition that "if capitalism in its mad rush for gains regardless of consequences will not heed the conscious deliberation of the workers in their trade unions," then "the industrial struggle between the capitalists and laborers will continue to grow on a larger scale and become intensified in feeling and action." This foreboding grew at times of grave crisis, as when, in observation of the bloodshed at Homestead during the steel strike of the summer of 1892, Gompers regretfully pronounced it a "premonition of what is yet to come." And he confessed, "Sometimes my heart almost sinks at the thought of what we in our day may yet witness as the results of the overweaning greed of the corporate and capitalist class."[11]

The sense of excitement and immediacy that the vision of trade union unity brought to Gompers helps to explain his impatient reaction to organizations with alternative programs for labor. They were outsiders who posed stumbling blocks to the working-class unity he sensed was within the grasp of the Federation. The emancipation of the working class had to be achieved by the workers themselves. This at base was the issue between the Federation and the Knights of Labor. From the beginning the greatest danger to the AFL appeared to Gompers to be "the unnecessary desire of persons thrusting their individual opinions upon the organized workers." This defect, he believed, had been built into all previous labor organizations, including the Knights of Labor. While the workers had historically developed the autonomous trade unions as a natural response to modern industrial conditions, previous national organizations had been based upon the "non-recognition of the principle of autonomy, or the right of self-government" of the trades in trade matters. This was blatantly true of the Knights of Labor, Gompers claimed, for the Knights "fight labor unions with much more vigor and bitterness than they do unscrupulous employers." In fact, he argued, those who postulated the destruction of trade unions as a first step toward a unified labor movement were as dangerous to the masses as the employing class itself. They were, in his words, "false friends" or "pseudo-leaders" and he read them out of the working class.[12]

Key to the working-class unity which Gompers hoped to achieve was the pursuit of the eight-hour day by the AFL. Boston labor reformers and trade unionists of the International tradition had long worked together for this goal. Politically minded socialists in the federation, such as Henry Emrich and P. J. McGuire, were enthusiastic about the demand. Gompers felt the issue had the virtue of appealing to all who were interested in building a working-class unity, "however much they may differ upon other matters," and he worked to convince key members in the Federation that postponement of more far-reaching programs in its behalf represented strategy rather than a retreat in principle. He advised an AFL organizer, for instance, that "many of our fellow workers who are not advanced as far as we" would merely be antagonized by the promulgation of divisive principles at this stage.[13]

Continually Gompers spoke of the eight-hour day as a rallying cry for a working class temporarily experiencing a general malaise in spirit. "Eight hours," he contended, "is the cry which can unite all forces at least for the present and will check the indifference and want of confidence too prevalent today." The issue was, for him, an exercise in the concentration and crystallization of proletarian thought on a single issue calculated to stress the identity of interests of all workers. The value lay not merely in tangible gain but in the intellectual processes of the workers which the issue would engage. It was "a question that gives a man time and an opportunity to investigate for himself, the underlying principles. . . ." It was more than a material issue because it was designed to raise the worker "not only materially, but morally and socially to higher appreciation of his duties as a man."[14]

Materially, in fact, Gompers believed the demand for a reduction of hours of work was more a reaction to deteriorating working conditions than a genuine advance by the workers. Mechanization of industry under capitalism oppressed the workers. Though it raised productivity and hence, wages, and though it lowered prices, it also reduced profit per dollar of investment and forced employers to try to squeeze more profit out of its labor force. Workers were subjected, therefore, to the "enervating influence" of "close application and working the nerves up to the fullest tension to keep [up] with the ever increasing velocity of labor by machinery." They needed reduced hours.

Gompers' view of the eight-hour demand was very different from that of the Boston reformer, Ira Steward. Steward believed the rise in wages and lowering of prices attending the mechanization of industry would facilitate accumulation of capital by the workers, driving down interest rates, enabling laborers to set themselves up in business through cooperative enterprise, depriving capitalists of a labor force willing to hire out. For Gompers, there was a joker in all this: the "vast army of unemployed."

Mechanization under capitalism, in Gompers' mind, sustained a large pool of technologically unemployed workers, always ready to take the jobs of striking workers, making it impossible to sustain concessions wrung from the employers. Even where Gompers agreed with Steward, that shorter hours and more leisure did alter the workers' standard of living, raise their consumption, and so stimulate the capitalistic economy, he knew this would only further encourage mechanization. Under capitalism this was the problem in the first place. The eight-hour reform was a temporary palliative. What was needed was a powerful union movement composed of grand organizations of all workers by industrial groups that could negotiate with industrial associations of employers. Only such a labor movement could force employers to accede to that amount of reduction in hours necessary to eliminate the industrial unemployed army and, hence, all profit on labor. Far from the optimism of Steward's conclusion, Gompers freely warned that forceful conflict was a lesser evil than the continued existence of a million unemployed.[15]

Thus, for Gompers, the eight-hour demand was only an instance of worker resistance to a constant tendency in competitive capitalism toward the reduction of wages ensuing upon the division and subdivision of labor in the continuing mechanical revolution. He returned, in the last analysis, to his belief that the major benefit of the eight-hour movement for labor lay not in the material but in the moral-intellectual sphere. The achievement of the eight-hour day, he predicted, "will not be the end of the efforts of the working people for economic and social improvements and reform." Rather it would help "clear the path and prepare the working people to see the wrongs and injustices practiced upon them in subtle and ingenious ways." The movement would give the wage earner the time and opportunity "to learn his iron strength, to husband his own resources, to organize his own faculties, and to widen his own horizons." By this process the wage earner was forced by the maturation of the capitalistic system to pursue, in defense, a demand which was the source of his social education, and he "is thereby furnished with the weapons which shall secure for him industrial emancipation."[16]

Mobilization of the AFL for the eight-hour campaign

began with the resolutions of the St. Louis convention in December 1888. The convention chose the target date of May 1, 1890, and called upon all working people of America to agitate and organize toward being fully prepared to enforce the measure on that day. The Federation proposed a "defense" fund, whereby the unions might fill a campaign chest for the defensive eight-hour campaign. A call went out for mass meetings in 1889, to be held on Washington's Birthday, Independence Day, and Labor Day, and the labor movements of hundreds of cities and towns responded with meetings on those dates. The AFL organizers for various localities presented the demand in their local addresses to labor groups, while special AFL organizers and lecturers took the question on the road with them and the national officers continually brought the issue up for public discussion. Authorities on the question compiled pamphlets for Federation distribution, and some 50,000 of these together with more than a quarter of a million shorter circulars went out at AFL expense that year. Finally, the AFL made a direct appeal to the Knights of Labor to cooperate in the eight-hour movement.[17]

More clearly than before, the Knights of Labor in 1889 bore the stamp of Terence V. Powderly. At the time the AFL was founded, Powderly's power had been seriously circumscribed by the entrenchment of the members of the Home Club of District Assembly 49 on the general executive board. The founding of the Federation helped jolt Powderly free of their embrace, for in their uncompromising anti-unionism they bore the brunt of the blame for the division of the labor movement. By the spring of 1887 the labor press, and Gompers as well, took note of the Powderly style. Trade assemblies simply no longer appeared to have second-class citizenship in the Knighthood. *John Swinton's Paper* reported in April on the unprecedented freedom with

which the K. of L. Executive Board was issuing charters to
trade districts. Gompers also wondered at the obvious contrast between the antagonism of the Knights toward trade
bodies preceding December 1886 and the apparent
"forebearance" of the authorities in the Knighthood since
then.[18]

The reversal of policy, however, was in degree rather
than in kind. Powderly scolded "Brothers Bailey, Barry and
McGuire" of the Home Club for their bitter opposition to
the trade unions but he continued his personal vendetta
against the Cigarmakers' leadership. He also ventured the
belief that "trade matters exist, they will continue to exist,"
such an admission leading him virtually to a recognition of
the autonomy of the trades "so long as the Constitution of
the General Assembly is not violated." But trade affairs
remained an uncomfortable presence for him. He believed
the virtue of the multiplication of trade assemblies lay precisely in the possibility that through them the tradesmen
might be educated to look beyond these dry matters, to
"grapple with the disease itself."[19]

For the education of the tradesmen, Powderly still looked
beyond simple working-class measures to the solidarity of
interests he believed existed among all producers, whether
in factory or on farm. Under him the Knights became self-
consciously pragmatic in its search for a specific reform
program which would draw these interests together. The
Knighthood made clear its rejection of reforms derived
from foreign ideologies, such as anarchism, socialism, and
communism. At the same time it began to sample reforms
"indigenous to our soil," including the nearly two dozen in
the K. of L. preamble. And the official journal of the
Knights of Labor defended this sampling process by arguing that

All life is an experiment. It is with governments
as much as the individual. The present and the
past alone furnish that experience from which
springs abiding change. Theories cannot become
crystallized into principles before they are given
the test of trial. There can be no sudden overturn-
ing of existing conditions. Whatever may be the
established estimate of the value of the ore it is
useless until it has passed the test of the crucible
and is separated from the slag.

Ideologically, the Knights under Powderly had the better
claim on pragmatism in these years than did the AFL under
Gompers, with whom, in a more popular sense, it is usually
associated.[20]

It became apparent early in 1888 that the education of
the K. of L. tradesmen was to be administered sternly. In
March, Powderly asked that all members be taxed fifteen
cents to finance the sending out of competent lecturers to
wage "the fight against trusts and monopolies on the educational plan." He coupled this with an appeal for power to
enforce "discipline" upon the assemblies, meaning the pre-
rogative, within the context of the K. of L. constitution, to
prohibit assembly strikes. This was in keeping with Powderly's concept of education, which demanded a recognition of
the hopelessness of matching in battle a "combination of
hungry men" with a "combination of dollars." Under the
Knights' tutelage, the workers would learn that it was their
primary duty to use the vote for legislation to "control the
dollar, curb the power of money and kill the trusts."[21]

Later in 1888, Powderly decided to focus the educational
efforts of the Knights on three reforms in the preamble,
which he summarized as finance (currency reform), trans-

portation (governmental control of railroad and telegraph systems), and land (government taxation and management of the land). He hoped through this approach to "paralyze the country in an educational way" within four years, forcing all political parties to place these issues on their platform in 1892. To implement this campaign he solicited additional authority within the Knights, arguing that

> those who control the land, the railways and the issuing of the currency are more thoroughly organized than we; they realize the necessity for an adherence to the principles of unity. . . . They yield obedience to the one-man power after they have conferred it themselves. . . .

The general assembly of 1888 responded by granting Powderly the right to name his own executive board, subject only to assembly approval.[22]

While the Knights of Labor was tightening its control over its trade assemblies in the interest of education, the organizational work of the Knights in the trades was earning it the growing animosity of the competing AFL unions. After the founding of the Federation, Gompers regularly shared his observations of K. of L. competition with union leaders engaged in struggles with the Knights. He found its leaders to be "usurpers," their organization an "incoherent mess." He scorned their methods, particularly the practice of initiating "a few simpletons" in order to stake a claim to jurisdiction in their trade. And he encouraged a spirited resistance to the Knighthood: ". . . they will give us no quarter and I would give them their own medicine in return."[23]

Consequently the shift of the Knights toward a program of education was not bound to receive a friendly appraisal from the Federation. Gompers greeted the news of the Knights' attempt to raise a $75,000 education fund with sarcasm and scepticism:

> I am wont [to] do anything to prevent their "education." There is no doubt *they sorely need it*. The only question that seems to me to deserve consideration is that their teachers themselves lack knowledge except in their experimental attempts to disrupt Trades Unions.

The AFL and its affiliates continued to regard the Knights as a dual union threat rather than as a supplementary educational organization. Offers from the K. of L. for the reciprocal recognition of working cards were rejected down the line.[24]

Despite this continued hostility, the year 1889 found the AFL making overtures of unity toward the K. of L. in the interest of promoting the eight-hour movement. In February a harmony conference convened in Philadelphia and the two organizations joined each other in recognizing the trivial nature of their differences and hoping for the alliance of all labor societies in the near future. Gompers, however, withheld his signature from the joint harmony address of this conference for several months, claiming bad faith on the part of the Knights in continuing to interfere with the trade unions. Subsequent conferences in August and October resulted only in mutual accusations and the presentation of each side's characteristic solution. The Knights suggested the mutual exchange of working cards. The AFL offered instead to give up its federal labor unions, which functioned in competition with the mixed assemblies of the Knights, if the Knights would cease operating trade assemblies. Since the K. of L. leadership was determined not to surrender its dual organizations and its authority over the trades, Gompers concluded by December that "a conflict is inevitable and can only end disastrously to all interests."[25]

Once again then conciliation had broken down and, perhaps more obviously than ever, for reasons essentially ideological in nature. Gompers had hoped to achieve a harmony which would gain K. of L. support for the eight-hour movement. Yet Powderly was distinctly hostile toward the AFL drive for eight hours for two principal reasons. First, the whole issue was simply too peripheral to the important questions of the day as he saw them, those questions embodied in the Knights' demands concerning land, transportation, and finance. Second, the AFL's pursuit of the demand was based on the assumption that the use or potential use of economic force by the workers would compel its achievement. Powderly, however, claimed that the eight-hour day would materialize through education. The Knighthood would nurse the employers toward an understanding that pressures on them from unjust taxes, interest rates, and freight rates could only be relieved through the K. of L. reform program, that the success of the reform program depended on indoctrinating the masses on its behalf, and that long hours of work retarded the education of the masses and ran counter to the employers' interests.[26]

Powderly pressed in this period for the inauguration of a grand national coalition which would cross class lines in the interest of broad reform. This was as unacceptable ideologically to Gompers as the AFL's eight-hour movement was to Powderly. Powderly's strategy in the late 1880s was to attract rural reformers to the land, finance, and transportation program of the Knighthood. In order to accommodate the farmers, who he thought were suspicious that land taxation would shift the tax burden to the rural tax-payer, he reduced Henry George's land tax proposal to one in favor of "fair" taxation, a move that sorely disillu-sioned George. He also set about writing a book to replace George's *Progress and Poverty* as a basic document of the re-form movement. This he believed he had done with *Thirty Years of Labor, 1859 to 1889*, which stressed that the roots of the Knights' program lay in Greenback-Laborism.[27]

During 1889 it was Powderly's growing conviction that coordinated activities between the Knights and the Farmers' Alliance or populist movement could free the legislative bodies of the country from the control of "the sharp, shrewd and cunning of the race." Such a development began to materialize in December 1889 when Powderly led a K. of L. contingent to St. Louis to attend an Alliance con-vention. He returned excited with the potential for an alliance and more confident that he had handled the AFL correctly:

> We met the Farmers and we are theirs, or they are ours, and for the purposes of our organization it is much better to have co-operation with the Farmers than that of "sawed off Sam and forked tongued Pete [Gompers and AFL Vice-President P. J. McGuire].[28]

The 1889 conventions of the AFL and the K. of L. each proved unsympathetic to the fundamental approach of the other to the labor problem. The K. of L. General Assembly statement on the eight-hour campaign was not a forthright rejection of the AFL eight-hour movement, but this, Pow-derly indicated, was a well-designed caution: ". . . we are courting the Farmers now and must engage in no unseemly wrangles. . . ." The assembly mustered only a statement giving moral support to the eight-hour campaign, one which Powderly privately admitted was designed to ward off publicity among the workers. Gompers later summarized it as "a number of platitudes" and "a generalization."[29]

Shortly afterward, the AFL convention heard Gompers give what would be his consistent position on collaboration with the Farmers' Alliance. Reporting on letters he had received from farmer organizations, he questioned the wisdom of accepting their proffered cooperation. Like Marx, Gompers saw in agriculture both a growing proletariat of farm laborers and a declining petite bourgeoisie of smaller farmers. Admittedly, there was much in the small farmers' suffering that deserved notice, but it was his opinion that "our purpose should be to organize and ally ourselves with the farm laborers whose condition is so wretched and whose living so precarious."[30]

To sustain his rejection of the K. of L. and populism in the 1890s, Gompers felt compelled to devote a good deal of attention in that decade to the definition of his ideological position in relation to both. The growing cooperation of the Knights with populism at the local as well as the national level was matched by Gompers' increasing identification of both as bourgeois movements. The cooperation tendered the workingmen by the farmers was, in his eyes, a desperate attempt "to prevent the men who have a little property from becoming wage-earners." To Gompers the farmers' position was untenable:

> . . . it seems to me inevitable by the operations of concentrated wealth that they will soon be forced into either one of the two classes of society, the large employers and possessors of wealth or else the great army of wage workers.

Similarly the K. of L. was no longer regarded by Gompers as a legitimate labor organization:

> For a long time I have not even deigned to notice them for I believed that the time would soon come to pass when they would disappear entirely from the field of labor and join either the Bourgeoisie or Kleinburglichen. They are drifting in this direction already and I am sure my judgment in this matter will not prove incorrect.[31]

With the depression in 1893 Gompers became increasingly worried that the pattern of partisan political involvement being followed by local populist and K. of L. groups would be followed by AFL locals. When a printing pressmen's union in Portland, Oregon, became involved in partisan politics during that year to such an extent that the neglect of ordinary union organizational work threatened its very existence, Gompers blamed the situation on "a hodgepodge of Knights of Labor, Farmers' Alliance, Populists etc.," who had been permitted representation in the union. Later in the year Gompers warned the secretary of the Dallas Federation of Labor not to allow members of the Knights or of the Farmers' Alliance to affiliate: "You will find it safest and most advantageous to permit representation only from wage-workers. . . ."[32]

In keeping with his original contention that the main rural interest of the AFL was the farm laborers, Gompers alertly encouraged the few weak strands of organization of which he was aware in the rural proletariat of these years. He had long been impressed with the work done among the farm laborers by English unions, saying in February 1892 that until the advent of unions among these workers the greatest problem of the ruling class had been "how to have sufficient prisons to keep them in." Since then, he observed, "wages were increased, the home of the farm laborer was made permanent and the prisons were emptied and transformed into school houses and meeting rooms." In August 1892, consequently, he wrote encouragingly to a nascent farm laborer movement in Ohio, the Farm Hands Labor Union, suggesting it affiliate with the AFL. He spoke of giving "tangible assistance" to the union if it affiliated with the Federation, and when in a short time he received the union's application for a charter he repeated his desire to "go a great way to further organization among the farm laborers of the country." Gompers also received a personal visit from one of the union's officers, and at the 1892 convention in December asked for a definite Federation action to aid in furthering farm labor organization.[33]

The hostility of the farmers to the organization of the farm laborers confirmed Gompers' impression of the Alliance movement as one representing the employing class. The new farm laborers' affiliate was quickly met with what Gompers characterized as "the stubborn and selfish opposition of the wealthy farmers and Alliance men throughout the country." He complained in a letter to John McBride of the Mine Workers that farmers were blacklisting the union's members and denying it the use of schoolhouses for union meetings: "I find that the opinion I always held in reference to the Farmers' Alliance and kindred organizations of the farmers, is more than verified." Hoping to bolster the union, he offered financial assistance toward the support of an organizer. Nothing came of this, however, the union apparently dissolving under farmer pressure. Several years later Gompers attempted to encourage a Kansas farm laborer union, but this group seems to have faded even more quickly than the first.[34]

Gompers' continued rejection of the K. of L. and the

populist movement in the 1890s had involved for him a relatively easy ideological stance on the traditional question of class collaboration with the bourgeoisie. Much more rigorous arguments were required of him in the defense of trade union tactics against the socialist purveyors of an alternative but equally independent working-class program.

10
Gompers and the Socialists

During the AFL's first decade, a refurbished Socialist Labor Party provided a center for an independent Marxist critique of the American trade union movement. The party's impact was closely related to the arrival of Lucien Saniel, an immigrant French journalist who became editor of the socialist English-language *Workingman's Advocate*. Saniel's appearance was central to the new American look of the party, abashed by disapproval from such theoretical heights as Friedrich Engels himself. "The Germans have not understood how to use their theory as a lever which could set the American masses in motion," Engels had challenged, accusing the German-American leaders of being doctrinaire, and suggesting that they actually refused to learn English "on principle." He advised, in 1886, that they

> act up to their own theory—if they understand it,
> as we did in 1845 and 1848—to go in for any real

> general working-class movement, accept its actual
> starting points as such and work it gradually up
> to the theoretical views in the original pro-
> gramme; they ought, in the words of *The Commun-
> ist Manifesto*, to represent the movement of the
> future in the movement of the present.

Enjoying a new strength and searching out a new relevance
to the American scene, the party engaged trade unionism
of the Internationalist tradition ideologically in a way in
which it had not been confronted since the late seventies.
The significance of the challenge in terms of this study is
that it evoked from Gompers much the same ideological
response as the earlier challenge had from McDonnell and
Kronburg a decade and more before.[1]

As in the 1870s the intensity of disagreement was a function of the closeness of the two positions, which was
reflected in the similarity in party and AFL assessments of
populism. Saniel, like Gompers, was basically concerned
with the relation of populism to the farm laborers. He
found they were absent from the Farmers' Alliance, the
bulk of the membership being composed of small farmers
and tenants led by wealthy farmers. The motives of the latter, he believed, were either political ambition or a desire
to seek railroad rebates on their freight "and such other
favors as may enable them to crush out the small farmers
and tenants." And the little hope he saw for populism
involved the possibility that the small farmers and tenants
would grow dissatisfied with the spreading farm and railroad monopolies, fall back upon their instincts for independent political action as reflected in the Greenback tradition,
and thence "use their influence over the farm laborers and
array them against their wealthy employers."[2]

Similar to the Federation's, too, was Saniel's assessment

of the Knights of Labor. The Knights' shortcomings in the economic realm, he suggested, reflected a more basic failure to comprehend the law of evolution. Like Gompers, Saniel believed the organization of the workers by trades, and their federation, was the first natural tendency of the labor movement. Having failed to organize along these lines the Knights were left with only one line of further advance, in the field of unskilled and unorganized labor, by far the largest portion of which consisted of agricultural labor. Work in this direction depended, he felt, on Powderly's adopting "far-reaching" views. But discussions within Saniel's New York American Section of the party were marked by doubt that Powderly was moving in that direction.[3]

Impressed, on the other hand, by the comparative economic soundness of the AFL, socialists, especially of Saniel's section, had been probing within Gompers' organization as the promise of New York City labor politics dimmed for their party in the late eighties. The composition of the Federation recommended itself to the socialists, including as it did a strong component of unions in which the socialists were either dominant or influential. Socialists within the AFL, in the interest of establishing class independence, had been leading supporters of the eight-hour movement, to which Gompers was more fully than ever committed. And official convention resolutions had in the past put the AFL on record as favoring, much as the socialists did, independent political action by labor.[4]

As opposed to these attractions for the socialists, there was the enigma of Samuel Gompers, who tended to halt adamantly, tantalizingly short of the "correct" socialist position on politics. Independent or third-party politics, Gompers told the AFL convention of 1888, would be extremely unwise "for the present at least." Yet the eight-hour cam-

paign and the perfected organization of the trade unions,
he told the same convention, would have important results
"both political as well as economical." Similarly, at the 1889
convention of the Cigarmakers, Gompers joined Strasser in
opposing the adoption of an openly socialist preamble for
the union's constitution. Yet Gompers opposed the measure
only on the grounds of the discord it would create and
claimed he had nothing to say against the arguments presented in favor of the motion. This caused one socialist
delegate to denounce Gompers in frustration:

> You, Mr. Gompers . . . you cannot any longer
> smile with one eye upon the socialists and upon
> their opponents with the other. What is your
> remedy for existing abuses? What do you pro-
> pose? Tell us! Whoever has become convinced of
> a truth acknowledges it if he has any courage. Are
> we not cowardly to conceal our honest convic-
> tion?[5]

The New York party socialists came gradually to the decision that they must advocate a new departure in American
trade unionism. Their turn in this direction was in good
part a reflection of their lack of political success in New
York City after a half decade of trying to galvanize the
Central Labor Union for their own purposes. Within the
CLU they achieved only a standoff in battling for political
support against followers of Henry George, the Knights of
Labor, and an assortment of other politicians. Despite two
dramatic secessions by socialist unions from the CLU, the
first with the support of Gompers, who opposed the anti-
eight-hour influence of the Knights, the second alone and
for good, factionalism rather than unanimity continued to
mark the Central's political character. Since the success of

any city labor party depended upon a much broader coalition than the socialists could command alone, the Central Labor Federation (CLF) which they formed and reformed after each secession proved inadequate for party purposes.[6]

By mid-1890, therefore, the party socialists effected a fundamental shift in tactics, beginning to explore avenues to power within the AFL and the K. of L. Their Central Labor Federation jockeyed for AFL favor by denouncing the CLU for treating the eight-hour movement with "utmost contempt." The CLF also immediately made application to the AFL for the return of the charter Gompers had once issued to it after its earlier secession. At the same time the CLF, after lengthy discussion, voted to include K. of L. city locals among its affiliates, Adolph Jablonowski arguing that their admission "would make it easier to permeate that organization with advanced ideas."[7]

While the new CLF was attempting, through formalized connections, to open channels of influence within the national labor organizations, it also moved to give the Socialist Labor Party of New York direct access to those channels. On July 5 a delegation of the New York American Section of the party was admitted to the CLF by a unanimous vote. The delegates included Lucien Saniel and Hugo Vogt. Gompers believed this was a departure from tradition, noted the inclusion of the SLP on the list of affiliates sent him by the CLF and wrote: "I cannot bring myself to understand how a political party as such can be represented in a central trade union organization." He ruled that SLP membership in an AFL affiliate was not permissible, and the CLF was denied an AFL charter. The socialists were rebuffed in attempting to have the decision overruled at the AFL convention of 1890.[8]

Defeated at the convention, the SLP launched a new drive at the New York City level to bolster its strength. In the

months after that convention the party inaugurated two
new socialist labor federations in the New York City area,
one for Brooklyn and one for New Jersey. Both competed
with central labor unions already operating in those sections. Gompers wrote P. J. McGuire:

> I cannot begin to tell you in a letter of all the
> intrigues and wirepulling that has been going on
> among these people. They represent so few that
> they really amount to nothing in the labor move-
> ment, except that some people are frightened
> . . . they are not sincere socialists in best
> acceptance of that term. They are partisans as dis-
> honest as any of the old corrupt political par-
> ties. . . .

To him it was clear in retrospect that the socialists by their
manipulations at the New York City level, "intended to
extend their control from the CLF to the national movement, as represented by American Federation of Labor."[9]
By 1891 the party socialists, as the key point of their new
departure, were propagandizing for the merger of the
political and economic movements as represented by the
proposed affiliation of the SLP with the AFL. Saniel spoke
of this as the "new unionism" and Hugo Vogt saw in this
a parallel with the First International, which also had
embraced trade unions and political labor organizations.
Vogt reminded the socialists that "Samuel Gompers himself
and his friend Strasser belonged to a branch of that politico-
economical organization." Yet the socialists realized in
invoking the imagery of the First International that there
was no more unity on the question of tactics in the 1870s
than there was in the 1890s and that Gompers and Strasser
were, in the earlier decade, members of the "famous 10

Stanton Street combination" which had even then stood for the primacy of trade union work.[10]

Demanding a return to the concept of the First International as they interpreted it, the socialists launched a critique of pure and simple unionism. Lucien Saniel contended that this philosophy accepted "the fundamentals of our present social state" and sought "merely to better the wage and time conditions, now of this, then of that particular craft" through the boycott and strike and other economic weapons. Given the power of "combined capital," Saniel believed pure and simple unionism was "utterly futile."[11] At this point the rise of the energetic Daniel DeLeon in the ranks of the New York SLP presented the AFL with an even more resourceful socialist adversary.

DeLeon was a lawyer, German educated prior to his Columbia Law School training. A well-known Marxist lecturer, he was finally given the editorship of the party's English-language paper, now to be known as *People*, in August 1891, after Saniel's eyesight began failing. At the same time he also led a small contingent of socialists in capturing District Assembly 49 of the Knights of Labor. From this base he expanded his influence in the Knights and was elected to the general executive board. He was instrumental in forming a coalition on the board which deposed Terence Powderly in 1893 and prevented his comeback in 1894, but he was unable to cultivate his power there, after the breakup of the coalition in 1895. In that year, therefore, DeLeon led in the founding of a new radical national labor organization, the Socialist Trade and Labor Alliance. Founded in December, it frankly avowed a policy of warfare against the older unions. It was to be the economic wing of the SLP.[12]

In treating the "new unionism" forces under Saniel and DeLeon, Gompers chose to emphasize what he believed was the common tradition of the two movements. "What you term new trade unionism" he told the secretary of the SLP American Section of New York in June 1892, "is naught but what thoughtful and consistent union men have for years hoped and struggled for." To Henry Demarest Lloyd, the midwestern fabian socialist, he wrote two years later, insisting that all that divided him from the socialists was "a difference of opinion as to the most practical methods to be employed in securing to the laborer his just rights." He scorned DeLeon, contending that socialists had always recognized their differences with the AFL as tactical until his advent.[13]

Gompers believed that within the context of the common tradition of the two movements, the AFL took the sounder position on the question of political action. The Federation did not reject independent political action by labor, he insisted, but neither would it equate independent action with socialist party action. Rather, the AFL recognized that political success was economically determined and that political gains made previous to the organization of the wage workers in trade unions were not defensible. In political action, therefore, the AFL chose to govern itself by the maxim that "our political action should always be a lever to strengthen our economic position." In tangible form the AFL political program in the mid-1890s embodied some dozen legislative demands officially adopted by the Federation in convention and promulgated through AFL lobbying activities. If this program of political action was "not exactly in line as we hope for," Gompers said, "yet intelligent men must feel convinced it is but a forerunner of what is to come." The Federation did not give up the hope of achieving labor's ultimate ends, Gompers contended, so much as it sought to meet the prerequisites for their achievement: "I am sure when the time is ripe an effective blow will be struck at the ballot box. . . . At present we are ourselves in a course of evolution."[14]

The evolution of which Gompers spoke was a moral and intellectual development toward an appreciation of the action necessary for emancipation. Distraught at the contention of one labor leader that the existing labor organizations lacked progressive leadership, Gompers argued forcefully for the Federation's approach.

> I believe I know the ultimate ends and aims as well as result of present struggles and I have never failed to give expression to and avow them, but I have always been impressed with the belief that it was our duty to arouse a spirit of independence, to instill in the hearts and minds of the toilers that it was essential to promote and protect their class interests in order to reach and elevate the entire human family, and that any tangible action that will lead them to take the aggressive in the contest to solidify their ranks, to crystalize their thoughts and to concentrate their efforts was a "progressive movement."

Such tactics would create the conditions that would enable workers to "find the full means of emancipation." Not only would the organized pursuit of tangible goals focus the workers' attention and increase their aggressiveness, but it would also give them the administrative ability to function in the future under altered social conditions:

> To become possessed of these qualifications necessitates the experience which can and will only come to them from the management of their own organizations of their own class—the trade unions

—the germ of any future state of society into which the present may merge or develop.[15]

In outlining this process of evolution, Gompers, in opposition to the socialists, argued that the AFL approach was radical. He believed that the "apparent slowness" of the AFL tactics had confused his "fellow 'radicals,'" adding parenthetically, "I count myself among the radicals willing to take second place with no one as to the views of the ultimate change of our social and economic condition." To his way of thinking the slowness of the movement was "upon the surface" and this very apparent slowness served to pacify the forces of reaction while fundamental change was taking place. What was transpiring was the acceleration of labor's organization and consciousness:

> As the workers are weaned from the political parties and are more staunch and true to the interests of their class movement, the trade union movement, the more distinct will the line of interest become and the advances of labor accelerated, gathering strength as they go, and growing until final emancipation is achieved eliminating class interests in the interest and disenthrallment of all from false economic, social and political conditions.

As he reiterated in 1896, the end result of this process was the abolition of "all classes based upon wealth or possessions."[16]

Yet despite his appeals to the socialists, Gompers must have realized that his style of leadership, which he in one instance referred to as "passive resistance," suggested that anything but a true radical lurked beneath. It will be remembered that Gompers faced the possibility of a violent revolution in labor's future with foreboding, not exultation. This posture was ideologically significant. It was based upon his belief that although history was moving capitalism inexorably toward revolution, it left room for a peaceful revolution.[17]

Gompers believed that the aggressive, warlike stand was historically incompatible with industrialism. This type of militancy had been characteristic of feudalism, he argued, the means by which the feudal barons forced their subjects to accept the inherited prerogatives of the lords. The development of industrial crafts, the defense of a nascent capitalism by artisans within the shelter of the fortified cities, and the subsequent desire of the feudal barons for the industrial luxuries which only the artisans could supply, compelled acquiescence in a spirit of peace under which industrialism could operate; "hence arose that change which insensibly transformed all activity from aggressive to defensive warfare. . . ."[18]

The capitalists, Gompers believed, were the modern industrial world's counterparts of the feudal barons. With decreasing opportunity for new markets, employers formed combinations to sustain their profits, forcing weaker competitors down "to swell the labor ranks already crowded by reason of restrictions upon ability to consume." Again, for considerations of profitability, the employers maintained long hours of work for their employees. New workers became an unemployed "surplus force," wages declining because "more men are seeking employment than the market demands." Projecting these tendencies forward, Gompers saw them as self-destructive to the "regime of status" they were designed to maintain. "Where the conditions are universally such that work does not seek workmen," he suggested, "the present status cannot be an enduring one."[19]

For Gompers, the question at this point reduced itself to ascertaining the means by which the system would be replaced. The capitalists had resorted to the anachronistic weapons of aggression, the weapons of a past age, to maintain the prerogatives of their status:

> Against us we find arrayed a host guarded by special privilege, buttressed by legalized trusts, fed by streams of legalized monopolists, picketed by gangs of legalized Pinkertons, and having in reserve thousands of embryo employers who, under the name of militia, are organized, uniformed, and armed for the sole purpose of holding the discontented in subservient bondage to iniquitous conditions.

But labor could not use similarly aggressive means successfully because they were incompatible with the *zeitgeist* of the industrial age. Like the artisans under feudalism, Gompers believed, the workingmen had to seek their emancipation through instruments of defense.[20]

At the root of Gompers' differences with the socialists was his faith in the ability of an essentially peaceful institution of defense to organize the workers for radical change. "Wherever a union of the toilers has come into existence," Gompers told the American Social Science Congress in 1891, "it has arisen from a necessity to combat oppression." He saw the development of class aspirations for complete emancipation as an unconscious development derived from a maturing of feelings of class solidarity within the framework of a defensive federation of unions. He believed that the defensive weapons of the unions were bound to become more powerful, despite the power of united capital, because modern industry was vulnerable to defensive strikes of gigantic proportions which made them too costly to endure. Amid growing pressure from the capitalists and growing power and determination on the part of the workers, he discerned that the inevitable invocation of "the valiant spirit of the industrial army" could be accomplished in a spirit of peace, "a spirit born of everlasting Zeitgeist."[21]

While speaking of the work of the AFL in radical terms, Gompers also tended to discount the radicalism of his socialist opponents, i.e., those socialists who rejected the Federation movement: "They are not sincere socialists in the best acceptance of that term," he insisted in 1891. In keeping with this contention he made a point of referring to them as "so-called socialists" or as those "who call themselves socialists." He felt that the basic shortcoming of these theoreticians "who are supposed to possess scientific information" was their inability to comprehend the "social economics" of the trade union movement, and particularly the proposition that it was those workers who "deal with the conditions as they exist" who were fighting "the real battle in the struggle for economic, social and political emancipation." He urged that it was therefore the duty of those "who may be possessed of high conceptions, noble thoughts, and the ability to make timely and practical suggestions" to join the movement and "by their honesty of purpose, earnestness and zeal help raise the material, social, moral and intellectual standard of all." This led him to conclude that "the terms radical and conservative, as generally used, are at best relative," and that the "so-called radical declaration of purposes" was often little more than an attempt to hide weakness and impotence.[22]

In seeking to bolster his position on the correctness of the AFL's position in the dispute with the SLP, Gompers wrote in January 1891 to Friedrich Engels himself. He wrote as "a student of your writings and those of Marx and others in the same line," and pointed out that "some of our best men and staunchest in holding as I do are well-known and avowed socialists." He hoped, he said, that by providing an account of the AFL-SLP dispute, he could prevent Engels from drawing conclusions based upon "erroneous information." Disappointed by his failure to receive a reply from Engels he wrote to Friedrich Sorge in November:

> For years and years I have honored the man and know his devotion to the cause of labor. An opinion from him would have had large weight with me and an expression of it would no doubt have had some influence in determining the action of the Socialist Party, particularly in New York.[23]

Sorge volunteered to write Engels concerning the failure to answer Gompers' letter. Engels replied in January 1892, describing intervening circumstances and considerations which had occupied his time and then indicating that he wished to decline the role of arbiter in the heated dispute. Engels' private correspondence of a year earlier reveals, however, that he was not unsympathetic to the AFL position after reading Gompers' letter. Though accepting the SLP assessment of the Federation as an organization motivated by what he termed a "narrow-minded trade union standpoint," he noted in one letter that as "an association of trade unions and nothing but trade unions" the AFL had a formal right to reject delegates from any other type of organization. The rejection of the SLP "had to come," he believed, "and I, for one, cannot blame Gompers for it." Further, Engels saw in the AFL a much more fertile field for socialist influence, and attributed to its leaders a much greater possibility for radical growth, than did the SLP in New York. Speaking of the forthcoming Brussels international labor congress, Engels thought

> it would have been well to keep on good terms with Gompers, who has more workers behind him, at any rate than the S.L.P., and to ensure as big a delegation from America as possible there, including his people. They would see many things there that would disconcert them. . . .

Besides, he added, "where do you want to find a recruiting ground if not in the trade unions?"[24]

In rejecting SLP membership in the AFL, Gompers had been certain that his position was "logically and scientifically correct in the labor movement." In fact on all questions of organizational form and content Gompers showed great concern that the AFL remain sensitive to what he considered the natural requirements which developing industrial conditions imposed logically upon it. In 1888, for instance, he presented the St. Louis convention of the Federation with suggestions for organizing the AFL by industrial divisions, each composed of the trades common to a particular industry, for the purpose of considering aside from the general Federation convention those issues of particular interest to a single industry. Organization by industries dictated itself at this time because the common sense of industrial conditions always imposed its most "scientific form of organization" upon the working people. Even after the Federation resisted active promulgation of the plan, Gompers remained convinced that it was inevitable. He noted in 1891 how the Amalgamated Association of Iron and Steel Workers already included twenty or more branches connected with the iron and steel "trade," how the International Typographical Union included not only compositors but pressmen, bookbinders and others, and how his own Cigarmakers had under its jurisdiction as well cigar packers and cigar strippers. In an editorial in the *American Federationist* in 1894 he continued to contend that the idea of organizing the "grand and resistless army of labor" into industrial divisions was "the basis of the scientific organization of the labor movement of the near future" and predicted that the division would evolve "probably before we are fully aware of its growth."[25]

Gompers also expected that more economic power would be transferred from the national unions to the labor federation as industrial conditions forced those unions to recognize the identity of interests of all workers, regardless of craft. In 1884 he and Fred Blend had developed a proposal for an independent strike fund under FOTLU control. It created hardly a ripple of interest among the big nationals, who themselves had gained ascendancy over their locals in large part because of their control of strike funds. In the next decades Gompers continually pressed for some system of mutual financial assistance, supported by regular dues and assessments, under Federation control. In 1889 the Federation hesitantly created a small strike fund in preparation for the drive in 1890 to obtain the eight-hour day. It was surrounded by safeguards to protect the autonomy of the national unions. In 1892 the AFL convention was willing to allow an increase in the fund through a series of small assessments. During the depression years of the mid-nineties, Gompers thought it best not to pursue the issue, but thereafter he continued to jockey with the national unions for financial power. In 1901, chiding the convention delegates for their continued reluctance to approve compulsory, rather than voluntary, contributions to the fund, he warned that the labor organization could not survive without a recognition of the unity and solidarity of all workers. Without a mutual assistance system "under one administration or direction" he saw only division, dissension, and diffusion of labor's efforts. And, he warned, if the AFL did not meet this challenge, it would be left to "another organization or federation, perhaps in rivalry and antagonism to the American Federation of Labor."[26]

Gompers was aware of how easily the scientific integrity of a working-class movement could be compromised by misguided leadership. The inclusion of employers in the membership of the Knights of Labor, he held, had violated what for the AFL was a maxim, that "the emancipation of the working classes must be achieved by the working classes themselves." Fearing lest they offend their employers, Gompers believed, workers in the Knighthood had not always been free to pursue their true class interests. If the inclusion of non-workers was destructive to the integrity of the movement, the non-inclusion of any class of workers was equally as dangerous scientifically. "I regret very much to learn that any of the unions are following the false course of 'exclusiveness,' " Gompers wrote in December 1891, "for I know that that must inevitably lead to conflicts and disorganization and defeat." Deploring the concept of an "Aristocracy of labor," Gompers pointed out that "it is not a 'feature' of the trade union movement, but rather an 'abortive phenomenon' that will take place in it. It is in fact the very antithesis of the fundamental principle of trade unionism."[27]

As he had defended the place of women in the cigarmakers' union, so now did Gompers extend the logic of his principles to the black man. In certain instances he could be adamant on the question, as in his five-year resistance to the admission of the Machinists to the AFL because of the use of the word "white" in the membership section of the union constitution. The social problem was economically determined; unionists had to "recognize the mechanical abilities of the black man, let their social conditions take care of themselves." Facing considerable resistance in attempting to overcome racial prejudice, he consoled himself with the observation that modern industrial conditions would here, as in the case of industrial divisions, eventually impose their logic upon the movement. He saw in the beginning of trade organization in any trade, even if that organization was through separate unions according to race, the first step to the end of prejudice among the workers of that trade: "It is only when men begin to organize that they also begin to realize that their interests are much more closely allied regardless of color, nationality, religion, or other prejudices."[28]

Gompers' certainty of the existence of a "natural course of proper and healthy development" from which the labor movement could not deviate without compromising its integrity also governed his attitude toward organization among the railroad workers. He disliked having separate organizations for engineers, firemen, conductors, and switchmen plus a brotherhood for "trainmen" and prodded the workers of the industry to consolidate. The natural tendency of the day was toward federation, he lectured the railroad union leaders,

> hence, I believe the primary consideration with you should be the federation of all the railroad trade unions. What the ultimate tendency of federation with the organized trade unions of other callings may develop the common sense of the wage-workers and the future will decide.[29]

At the same time, Gompers continuously discounted sug-

gestions that some new organization was needed among the
railroad workers. There were already all the organizations
"that are necessary and which can be of any benefit" to the
railroad workers. Further organizations "can only result to
the detriment of all concerned." Most notably Gompers
resisted the organization of the American Railway Union
(ARU) under Eugene Debs. Though sympathizing with the
union in the death struggle which it entered into in the Pullman strike of 1894, Gompers had to characterize Debs as
"sincere and honest, but an enthusiast and mistaken." The
ARU was based on an unsound principle: "It was instituted
not for the purpose of consolidating the existing railroad
organizations, but to supplant them."[30]

By far the greatest threat to the integrity of the AFL in
its first decade was, for Gompers, the socialist attempt to
take over the ideological leadership of the Federation. The
failure of the American Section of the SLP in New York
to gain affiliation with the AFL via the Central Labor Federation, coupled with the rise of Daniel DeLeon and the
Socialist Trade and Labor Alliance, discouraged the eastern
socialist movement's interest in the AFL. But within the
AFL there had always been an important contingent of
socialists whose evaluation of the Federation was made independently of the SLP. Particularly important among them
were those from the urban areas of the midwest who, after
the shock of the depression which began in 1893, took stock
anew of the possibilities of radical political action through
the AFL in conjunction with the populist movement.

The eastern socialists under DeLeon, after a brief interest
in western populism in the early nineties, had come to
regard a merger with that movement as potentially the
greatest of misfortunes for socialism. DeLeon's initial interest during his trip through the country in the spring of
1891 was based upon the hope that the socialists could cap-

ture the populist organizations of the midwestern states for their own purposes. SLP members, he reported from Minnesota, had infiltrated all the city branches of the Farmers' Alliance "and will forthwith, in fact, have a perfect plan of operation to build up Socialist sections throughout the state." A year later, however, it had become clear that the revolutionary appearances of the populist movement could easily lead to the absorption of the socialist movement rather than the capture of populism for socialism. Thereafter DeLeon's efforts were in the direction of repudiating western populism:

> Far from being a revolutionary movement, it is one of the most conservative and even retrograde attempts ever recorded in the history of economic evolution. Its object is to perpetuate a class that modern progress has doomed. . . .[31]

The midwestern socialists, unlike the DeLeon forces, wrote off neither the AFL nor the populist movement. At the Chicago convention of the AFL in 1893 the leading figure in the Chicago SLP and founder of the Chicago Trades and Labor Assembly, Thomas J. Morgan, introduced his controversial "program and basis of a political labor movement." Of the eleven planks in the program, ten could be embodied in a conventional legislative program for the Federation. Plank ten, however, called for "the collective ownership by the people of all means of production and distribution." With this plank retained, the convention submitted the entire program to the AFL affiliates to be considered in time for the next annual convention.[32]

Before the AFL's verdict was in, these socialists also served up plank ten to the farmers and workers of Illinois. The time was ripe for a farm-labor movement in that state.

The dramatic failure of an Illinois coal strike and the beginning of the Pullman strike brought the state's reform forces together in July 1894, at an industrial conference in Springfield sponsored by the Illinois State Federation of Labor. Although the socialists' plank ten was not acceptable to the populists or the conservative trade unionists who together controlled a bare majority, the influential Henry Demarest Lloyd proposed an acceptable compromise. The conference resolved to take independent political action through a new national coalition party. Until it could be organized, all were to support those candidates of the Populist or People's Party who accepted "the principle of the collective ownership by the people of all such means of production and distribution as the people elect to operate for the commonwealth."[33]

Lloyd also attempted to serve as the intermediary between the proposed national party and the AFL. The 1893 Federation convention had resolved that the executive council make every possible effort "to effect and perfect an alliance between the trade and labor unions and the farmers' organizations," and in July Lloyd wrote to Gompers to suggest the means of doing so. He asked that Gompers join in the calling of "a national conference of all reformers," arguing:

> This crisis is greater than that of 1776 and 1861. You have in your place at the head of the workingmen the key to the immediate future. You can write your name by the side of our greatest patriots. What is done needs to be done quickly. . . .

In August he urged that the conference meet no later than

September to seek unity among the People's Party, the Socialist Labor Party, the Single Taxers and the workingmen in general.[34]

Gompers opposed both the midwestern socialists' declaration for collective ownership and Lloyd's appeal for political action. Promulgation of plank ten presented the Federation with "a very crucial test." It was a misconceived attempt by "those who do not understand our movement" to "divert it from its proper channels." Adopting a "decidedly theoretical" plank, which "even if founded upon economic truth, is not demonstrable," would alienate many important national trade unions "from joining our ranks to do battle with us to attain first things first." He believed its passage at the 1894 Denver convention in December would put the proper work of the trade unions in the shade for a decade and lead to a general deterioration in the condition of the workers.[35]

Gompers was not so much opposed to Lloyd's call for a political movement as he was convinced that it would grow organically out of the economic movement. He had long held that

> There can scarcely be a division of opinion that
> when the economic movement has sufficiently
> developed so as to produce a unity of thought on
> all essentials, that a political Labor Movement will
> be the result.

But he also believed that political liberty without sufficient economic organization "is but a phantasy and a delusion." Until the natural evolution of the political labor movement from the economic had taken place, he held, labor must be satisfied to understand that there "cannot be any

economic action taken by organized labor unless it has its
political and social influence." He appealed to the
December convention:

> It is ridiculous to imagine that the wage-workers
> can be slaves in employment and yet achieve con-
> trol of the polls. There never yet existed coinci-
> dent with each other autocracy in the shop and
> democracy in political life.

Here again there was the danger of sidetracking the unions'
proper work, he reminded the delegates, pointing to the
division and disruption of those unions which had entered
into local elections the previous month.[36]

Gompers won his points at the convention but suffered
the loss of the presidency in retaliation. Yet he remained
satisfied that he had been mowed down in defense of principle by disgruntled socialists. After regaining the presidency the following year he continued to defend his position on politics as essential to preserving the integrity of the
class movement. Concerning the Populist Party, he wrote
preceding the election of 1896: "Because a party takes up
one of these demands of organized labor, is no reason why
the labor movement should lose its distinctive character and
become the adjunct of any political party." And he maintained the same stance in respect to the SLP, which claimed
to be the political arm of the class movement.[37] In a manner
reminiscent of Marx's treatment of socialist sectarians, Gompers drew an inverse ratio between the growth of the party
movement and the growth of the true working class movement:

> The trade union movement is the only working
> class movement in the country or in the world.

> The movement often called a class movement is often nothing more than a party movement, and in the same degree as this party movement increases, in the same ratio does it lose its working class character.[38]

By 1896 Gompers had established the integrity of the AFL as a class movement seeking tangible gains in a maturing capitalist society. His judgments tempered by twenty-five years of reading history according to an ideology whose roots were in the First International of Karl Marx, he had rejected with remarkable consistency and self-confidence proffered cooperation of other movements. The independent path he had chosen for the American Federation of Labor secure, he had now to await the somber responsibilities which the AFL would assume for society, providing his reading of history was correct.

11
Gompers and the Origins of the AFL in Perspective

In 1848, Marx and Engels had written in the *Manifesto* that in preparation for the revolution the Communists "fight for the attainment of the immediate aims, for the enforcement of the momentary interests of the working class; but in the movement of the present, they also represent and take care of the future of that movement." As late as 1886 Engels had urged the German-American leadership of the Socialist Labor Party to "represent the movement of the future in the movement of the present." It was a lesson that Samuel Gompers had already learned well.[1]

Gompers had received the *Manifesto* as part of the inheritance of the First International, that is, after it had been reread in the light of the subsiding imminence of revolution. Political power in 1848 would have proven illusory for the workingmen, it was now conceded. Political power could only be revolutionary when built upon the foundation of a previous organization of the working class, designed to achieve a sense of identity of class interests, growing class consciousness, expanding conceptions of justice, invigorated confidence in class power.

Yet though the revolution was now somewhat more remote, that basic tactical insight of the *Manifesto*, that "the present encloses the germ of the future" (in David Kronburg's words), remained a Marxist hallmark. As to whether the prerequisite class organization should be a party or a labor federation or some combination of both, the heirs of the Internationalist tradition could not agree. But within the trade union branch of the Internationalist heritage, Samuel Gompers helped mold a federation out of the trade union movement of the present, with a radically different future very much in mind.

It is not necessary here to argue that Gompers was a Marxist. He did not attempt to articulate an organically complete economic theory.[2] He sometimes borrowed ideas from sources not thoroughly consistent with an orthodox Marxist position. Certainly his acceptance of aspects of Ira Steward's philosophy suggests that his debt to Marx, though substantial, was not total. What is more, in the wake of the First International, he and his Marxist associates seemed to become more concerned with the special case of America than with the subsequent course of Continental Marxism in the German heartland. In fact, Gompers may have developed his mode of thinking as much by discussing labor matters with Marxist trade unionists or by reading the *Labor Standard* as from his reading of Marx, Ferdinand Lassalle, and others.

Nevertheless, Gompers was a serious thinker, his entire orientation in the late nineteenth century relying on a rugged integrity of intellect which precluded mere opportunism. He projected a growing influence for his movement based upon its "scientific" development as the form of class

organization prescribed by the historical development of
American capitalism. He intended to base this class movement upon the practical demands of the workers, demands
that would swell in scope as the movement became larger
and stronger. He saw his movement as directed toward the
achievement of class power, inseparably political and
economic, but scorned the notion that political power could
be achieved prior to the previous economic organization of
his class. He believed that American conditions required an
approach different from that being urged upon Germany
by Marx and Engels, and only regretted that this was not
understood by latter-day Marxists and by Engels himself
during the AFL's formative decade.

It may be agreed that the vagueness of Gompers' elabora-
tion of the future is not very satisfying, but this was, in
effect, the logical result of his conception of future as present. The emancipation of the working classes economically,
politically, socially, morally, and intellectually "from its
dependence on the capitalist" was a process of history that
was already operative, with history rather than men in
charge. Resolutions and speculation were irrelevant and at
times self-defeating in the face of the "natural" evolution
of trade unions within the context of the historical development of industry under capitalism. The perfection of a
class-wide unity was inevitable. With that would come power
and responsibility. Good leadership included the focusing
of proletarian attention on tangible first goals and first principles of organization toward the acceleration of that
process. And in the process, "the emancipation of the working classes must be achieved by the working classes themselves."[3]

Admittedly, the sincerity of Gompers' radical posture is,
in the last analysis, unprovable. It is apparent that Gompers
struggled to place his actions in a context with which he

could live and within which he could present them to others. But the credibility of his justification relies not only upon the consistency of his argument but also upon the degree to which it reflected an operating motivation rather than a rationalization for his actions. Making the latter distinction is a tenuous business at best, complicated by the nature of the documentation of Gompers' ideas for this period. For the earlier decades, before he had achieved an important stature in the labor world, there remains only an occasional record of Gompers' position in the dialogue over Marxist tactics, coupled with the implication suggested by his choice of Marxist trade unionists as his closest teachers and associates. Only for the last decade of this study is the existing correspondence and journalism substantial enough on its own to establish Gompers' apparent Marxian orientation, and for much of this decade he was attempting to bolster his national leadership in the face of intense criticism by more politically oriented Marxist leaders.

In the perspective of a history of ideas approach to Gompers, however, it is possible to accept the tentativeness imposed by such limitations and still offer a number of persuasive considerations which suggest a man motivated by a deeply held commitment to radical change. Beyond Gompers' efforts to give systematic presentation to his view of labor in the capitalistic world, there appears to lie a pattern of intellectual loyalty. He maintained an allegiance to a set of concepts over a prolonged period of time, both in continuity with a previously rationalized system of thought and in proximity to associates schooled in, and dedicated to, that system of thought. The concepts involved the historical process of revolution inherent in the capitalistic system; the necessity of achieving economic class power through trade organization prior to acquiring political class power; the dependence of effective trade organization on the confrontation of practical working class problems; the catalyzing of workers' class consciousness through the medium of a movement for the unionization of all workers; the inevitable emancipation of the workers, by their own efforts, from the wage system.

These were the core of Marx's message to the First International as they were the basis of his letters to his lieutenants in America in the early seventies. To a small coterie of Internationalists who continued to meet in New York City following the International's demise, a group which included Gompers and to which he referred as the Economic and Sociological Club, these concepts became the "fundamentals" upon which policy was to be grounded. In loyalty to them, members of the group insistently approached the workingmen in the seventies through consecutively improvised organizations: the United Workers of America, the International Labor Union, the Amalgamated Trade and Labor Union of New York City, the New York American Section of the Workingmen's Party of the United States; and through a journal, the *Labor Standard*. In a direct line from the old Bolte group of the First International, through these organizations, to the AFL, the basic strategy called for the amalgamation of existing unions and the organization of the unorganized toward the creation of a proletarian phalanx with a radical function in the classical Marxian sense.

Amalgamation was consistently a central concern of the Cigarmakers' International Union, whose reorganization was being masterminded by Strasser, Laurrell, and Gompers in the late 1870s. This was no mere coincidence, for the headquarters of the Cigarmakers' presidency at 75 Chatham Street was constantly being nurtured by an interchange of ideas with the larger Internationalist group at 10 Stanton Street, the so-called Economic and Sociological Club. The Cigarmakers' office was a substation for the larger group, and many of the most active of the Cigarmakers' reorganizers, including Gompers, were active at Stanton Street as well. The heavy borrowing of *Labor Standard* editorials by the *Cigarmakers' Official Journal* during this period made the intimacy of the relationship obvious. At both locations the recommendations to be made at Cigarmakers conventions were discussed and measured against the broader experience and general philosophy of the Internationalists.

There seems little reason to suspect that the attempt to ground a radical philosophy upon a strategy of trade union organization and federation and attention to practical labor issues—the approach enunciated in the Stanton Street discussions and the *Labor Standard* editorials of the late seventies and early eighties—reflected an abandonment of Marxist principles. Too many fervent Internationalists of only a few years previous were involved in the new movement for it to have been a conservative sellout of radical ideals. Too often was Marx drawn upon in their arguments for there to have been intended any conscious abandonment of Marxism in the federation movement.

The more troublesome question remains of whether Gompers, as the standard bearer for the new movement, did not gradually abandon, during the next fifteen years, the radical idealism behind the federation movement. Perhaps, while continuing to utilize in debate all the nuances of the new federationism of the late 1870s, he ceased believing in it by the late eighties and early nineties, using the rhetoric to his advantage, as Marxian historians have suggested. Institutional forms, after all, survive their original substance, and perhaps can do so with all their original ideological trappings intact, under the leadership of a superb debater.

In the final analysis there appear to be enough considerations weighing in the balance to make a stronger case for the radical nature of the nineteenth-century AFL leadership under Gompers. There is an intellectual stamina in the confidence and persistence of Gompers' theoretical defense of his course throughout these years which argues for his genuine commitment to the Internationalist tradition of trade unionism. Gompers remained rigorously loyal to both the architecture and the rationale envisioned in the deliberations of the late seventies, accepting the trade unions as building blocks and working inexhaustibly toward what he still predicted in the nineties would be the acceleration of economic organization and the abolition of the wage system. Had he first begun to speak of trade unionism in radical terms only after the socialists began to attack his leadership in the nineties, it might be possible to dismiss his public posture as a maliciously cynical ploy behind which to build a bureaucratic political machine. But as it was, the arguments he presented for the radical nature of his movement were applied consistently in the face of diverse tides of organizational and political crisis through this period. The justification he gave for his movement in 1887, before the dissolution of the socialist-trade union rapprochement which had attended the George mayoralty campaign, was in all essentials the defense he subsequently used against the socialists when they challenged his leadership in the nineties. In the face of his tenacity, there seems to be no good reason to assume his arguments became less sincere simply because the opposition was now more orthodox.

All of which is to say that in Gompers American labor was witnessing a new type of leader, one whose very energy stemmed from a doctrinal commitment to trade unionism. Jonathan Grossman's observation that William Sylvis of the Iron Molders preceded Gompers in developing the features of modern union administration only serves to emphasize the basic difference between the two men. It could not be said of Gompers, as Grossman says of Sylvis, that "he had not the body of tradition to guide him," that he allowed himself "to be swayed by varying doctrines."[4] If Gompers' determined commitment to pure trade unionism is to be understood and his half century of perpetual drive for its perfection explained, they must be seen as a product of the assimilation of a Marxian tradition to the American circumstance.

In closing it might be well to ask what difference Gompers' vision of a radically altered future made in view of the fact that pure and simple unionism was the means to its achievement. The answer is that neither the means themselves, nor their longevity, can be understood outside the ideological context. The Marxists from whom Gompers learned were studious environmentalists. Their attention to "live" issues on the American scene gave them a following which was the envy and frustration of other socialists. But much of the evaluation of the American environment that went into the development of their master plan was predetermined, by the assumptions of their analysis, to yield a purist, self-confident, and single-minded approach.[5] If this dictated that they remain aloof from the potentially massive reform effort of the day, it also explains why they were imbued with the fervor of visionaries in the work they did pursue. But for the schooling in Marxian analysis, would Gompers have had his sense of historical moment and fundamental relevance to society as a whole?

The more delicate suspicion will remain that, by the late eighties and early nineties, the radical substance may have drained from Gompers' still doctrinally consistent polemic, and that a brave enthusiasm may have replaced what had once been a firmer conviction that a new order would soon be at hand. As seen from the perspective of a much less radical contemporary American labor movement, the first decade of the AFL might appear to have signaled the rise of a merely progressive rather than revolutionary force. But Gompers in 1896 did not have the advantage of such a perspective. The federation movement had only been institutionalized for fifteen years, ten as the AFL, and its inner strength had just been dramatized by its survival of a major depression—no small achievement. The Gompers of the nineties, therefore, appears to require a reading from the perspective of the First International forward, one that makes it much more reasonable to accept his words as sincerely rather than rhetorically intended and to see both the man and the experiment that was the Federation as they there appear, in the context of a Marxian tradition.

Notes

Introduction

[1] Selig Perlman, "Upheaval and Reconstruction," in John R. Commons, et al., *History of Labour in the United States*, 4 vols. (New York, 1918-1935), 2: 308; Louis S. Reed, *The Labor Philosophy of Samuel Gompers* (New York, 1930), 75.

[2] Bernard Mandel, *Samuel Gompers: A Biography* (Yellow Springs, Ohio, 1963), 65; Philip S. Foner, *History of the Labor Movement in the United States*, 4 vols. (New York, 1947-1965), 2: 186-87.

[3] Robert H. Wiebe, *The Search for Order, 1877-1920* (New York, 1967), xiii, 124-25.

Chapter 1

[1] Samuel Gompers, *Seventy Years of Life and Labour: An Autobiography* (New York, 1925), 1: 17-18.

[2] Henry Collins and Chimen Abramsky, *Karl Marx and the British Labour Movement: Years of the First International* (London, 1965), 18-22.

[3]Letter from John P. Walker, Secretary of the Cigarmakers Mutual Association, London, in *Cigarmakers' Official Journal*, November 11, 1878, 1; Gompers, *Life*, 1: 19-22.

[4]Royden Harrison, "Professor Beesly and the Working-Class Movement," in Asa Briggs and John Saville, eds., *Essays in Labour History* (London, 1960), 215.

[5]G. D. H. Cole, *A History of Socialist Thought* (London, 1954) 2: 6-7.

[6]Karl Marx and Friedrich Engels, "Manifesto of the Communist Party," in C. P. Dutt, ed., *Karl Marx: Selected Works* (New York, 1958), 1: 206-16, 220.

[7]Ibid., 1: 214-15, 218.

[8]Ibid., 1: 207, 215, 218.

[9]George Lichtheim, *Marxism: An Historical and Critical Study* (New York, 1961), 56.

[10]Ibid., 58, 79; Marx and Engels, "Manifesto," in Dutt, ed., *Marx*, 1: 228.

[11]Cited in Shlomo Avineri, "Marx and the Intellectuals," *Journal of the History of Ideas* 28 (1967), 271.

[12]Marx and Engels, "Manifesto," in Dutt, ed., *Marx*, 1: 216, 219.

[13]Bertram D. Wolfe, *Marxism: One Hundred Years in the Life of a Doctrine* (New York, 1965), 199-200; Cole, *Socialist Thought*, 2: 92, 150; Avineri, "Marx and the Intellectuals," 272, 274.

[14]Lichtheim, *Marxism*, 139.

[15]Ibid., 139 f.

[16]Collins and Abramsky, *Marx and British Labour*, 37-38, 44; Cole, *Socialist Thought*, 2: 92.

[17]Harrison, "Professor Beesly and the Working Class Movement," 209-12; Royden Harrison, *Before the Socialists: Studies in Labour and Politics, 1861-1881* (London, 1965), 16, 58-70, 254-74; Stephen Coltham, "The *BeeHive* Newspaper: Its Origin and Early Struggles," in Briggs and Saville, eds., *Essays in Labour History*, 174-80; E. P. Thompson, *The Making of the English Working Class* (New York, 1964), 806, 829; Collins and Abramsky, *Marx and British Labour*, 15-17, 20-28, 40.

[18]Cole, *Socialist Thought*, 2: 88-90.

[19]Collins and Abramsky, *Marx and British Labour*, 22-23.

[20]Cole, *Socialist Thought*, 2: 98.

[21]Marx, "Address and Provisional Rules of the Working Men's International Association," in Dutt, ed., *Marx*, 2: 441-42.

[22]Marx and Engels, "Manifesto," in Ibid., 1: 215; Marx, "Address and Provisional Rules," in Ibid., 2: 437, 439.

[23]Ibid., 2: 439-40.

[24]Ibid., 2: 442-44.

[25] Cole, *Socialist Thought*, 2: Chapters 6-7.

[26]Collins and Abramsky, *Marx and British Labour*, 38.

[27]Marx, "Value, Price and Profit," in Dutt, ed., *Marx*, 1: 305, 308, 317-19, 325-34; Karl Marx, *Capital: A Critique of Political Economy*, 1 (New York, 1906), 114, 189-90.

[28]Marx, "Value, Price and Profit," in Dutt, ed., *Marx*, 1: 334-36; *Capital*, 1: 686-711.

[29]Marx, "Value, Price and Profit," in Dutt, ed., *Marx*, 1: 329; *Capital*, 1: 447-48.

[30]Ibid., 1: 456, 580-81, 701, 708.

[31]Marx, "Value, Price and Profit," in Dutt, ed., *Marx*, 1: 337; "Address and Provisional Rules," in Ibid., 2: 443; Samuel Bernstein, *The First International in America* (New York, 1962), 160.

Chapter 2

[1]Gompers, *Seventy Years of Life and Labour: An Autobiography*, 1: 33, 42; *Report of the (Education and Labor) Committee of the Senate Upon the Relations between Labor and Capital* (Washington, D. C., 1885), 1: 270; Theodore Wesley Glocker, *The Government of American Trade Unions* (Baltimore, 1913), 59. The word "white" was soon dropped.

[2]Gompers, *Life*, 1: 30-31.

[3]Ibid., 1: 29, 40-41.

[4]Ibid., 1: 46-47.

[5]*Labor Standard*, October 14, 1876, 4.

[6]Gompers, *Life*, 1: 85.

[7]Howard H. Quint, *The Forging of American Socialism: Origins of the Modern Movement* (Columbia, South Carolina, 1953), 10; Gompers, *Life*, 1: 55.

[8]Friedrich Sorge to the General Council, IWA, April 1, 1871, IWA Correspondence, State Historical Society of Wisconson; Selig Perlman, "Upheaval and Reconstruction" in Commons, et al., *History of Labour in the United States*, 2: 206-209, 217f.; Quint, *American Socialism*, 6-10.

[9]Sorge to the General Council, IWA, May 21, 1871, IWA Correspondence.

[10]Marx to Sorge, September 12, November 9, 1871, in Karl Marx and Frederick Engels, *Letters to Americans, 1848-1895: A Selection* (New York, 1953), 84-85, 86-87; Sorge to the General Council, IWA, May 21, August 20, 1871, IWA Correspondence.

[11]Marx to Siegfried Meyer and August Vogt, April 9, 1870, in Marx and Engels, *Letters*, 77-80; Marx, "Value, Price and Profit," C. P. Dutt, ed., *Karl Marx: Selected Works*, 1: 334.

[12]Although the demand for eight-hour legislation was of primary importance in the founding convention of the National Labor Union in 1866, greenbackism dominated from 1867. By 1871 the majority of the delegates consisted of agrarian reformers. Sorge's colleague, Friedrich Bolte, called for the exposure of the bourgeois nature of the farmers' movement and for attention to the organization of the agrarian proletariat, the farm laborers. See John B. Andrews, "Nationalization," in Commons, et al., *History of Labour*, 2: Chapter 6; Gerald N. Grob, *Workers and Utopia: A Study of Ideological Conflict in the American Labor Movement, 1865-1900* (Evanston, Illinois, 1961), 29; and Samuel Bernstein, *The First International, in America*, 192.

[13]Sorge to the General Council, IWA, August 20, 1871, IWA Correspondence.

[14]Sorge to the General Council, IWA, September 3, 1871, ibid.

[15]Marx to Friedrich Bolte, November 23, 1871, in Marx and Engels, *Letters*, 88-94.

[16]Marx to Bolte, November 23, 1871, ibid., 85-86.

[17]Sorge to Fr. [?] Parker, October 18, 1871, and to the General Council, IWA, November 25, 1871, IWA Correspondence. Sorge himself, having earned his living as a music teacher, had dubious credentials as a workingman. He was obviously operating in the tradition of the intellectual vanguard, much as were Marx and Engels themselves.

[18]Marx to Bolte, November 23, 1871, in Marx and Engels, *Letters*, 88-94; Sorge to the General Council, IWA, December 17, 1871, IWA Correspondence; G. D. H. Cole, *A History of Socialist Thought*, 2: 198.

[19]Sorge to the General Council, IWA, December 17, 1871, IWA Correspondence.

[20]Sorge to the General Council, IWA, December 17, 1871; Bolte, "Appeal to the Workingmen of America," May 19, 1872; and Sorge to the Congress of the British Federation, May 9, 1873; all in ibid.

[21]Marx to Bolte, November 23, 1871, in Marx and Engels, *Letters*, 88-94; Bolte, "Appeal to the Workingmen of America," May 19, 1872, IWA Correspondence. Gompers, *Life*, 1:51.

[22]Charles Praitsching to the General Council, IWA, "Monthly Report for May, 1872," June 3, 1872, IWA Correspondence; Gompers, *Life*, 1: 84-85; Andrews, "Nationalization," 151-52.

[23]Gompers, *Life*, 1: 60; Charles Praitsching to the General Council, IWA, "Special Report," June 25, 1872, IWA Correspondence.

[24]Sorge, "Circulaire Confidentielle," October 17, 1872; "Circulaire Confidentielle," February 2, 1873; au C. F. espagnol, April 11, 1873; an die Vereinigten Tischler, New York, June 6, 1873; to the British Federal Council, August 1, 1873; all in Box 2, IWA Correspondence.

[25]H. M. Gitelman, "Adolph Strasser and the Origins of Pure and Simple Unionism," *Labor History* 6 (Winter 1965): 74; Bolte to the General Council, IWA, "Report for the Months of December 1872, January and February 1873," March 1873, IWA Correspondence; Gompers, *Life*, 1: 110-11.

[26]Chicago *Workingmen's Advocate*, August 23, 1873, 2; Bolte to the General Council, IWA, "Annual Report of the Federal Council of the North American Federation," August 1873, IWA Correspondence.

[27]Gompers, *Life*, 1: 5-6, 68-71; Theodore Draper, *The Roots of American Communism* (New York, 1957), 63.

[28]Gompers, *Life*, 1: 48, 74-75, 84, 102; Sorge, "Circulaire Confidentielle," October 27, 1872, Box 2, IWA Correspondence.

[29]Gompers, *Life*, 1: 112.

[30]Ibid., 85; Bolte, two letters to the officers and members of the Workingmen's Assembly of the State of New York, dates illegible [c. January 1873]; to the General Council, "Report for the Months of December 1872, January and February 1873," March 1873; to the General Council, "Annual Report of the Federal Council of the North American Federation," August 1873; all in IWA Correspondence; Philip Taft, *The A. F. of L. in the Time of Gompers* (New York, 1957), 6.

[31]Sorge to Auguste Serreillier, "Instructions for the Delegate of the General Council to the Sixth General Congress," August 8, 1873, Box 2, IWA Correspondence.

[32]Quint, *American Socialism,* 11-13; Gitelman, "Adolph Strasser," 74f.; Bernstein, *First International,* 136; Gompers, *Life,* 1: 74-75.

Chapter 3

[1]Carl Landauer, *European Socialism: A History of Ideas and Movements from the Industrial Revolution to Hitler's Seizure of Power,* 2 vols. (Berkeley and Los Angeles, 1959), 1: 235-36.

[2]G. D. H. Cole, *A History of Socialist Thought,* 2: 80-81, 119; Landauer, *European Socialism,* 1: 240.

[3]Landauer, *European Socialism,* 1: 256-60.

[4]Cole, *Socialist Thought,* 2: 129; Landauer, *European Socialism,* 1: 256-60.

[5]Cole, *Socialist Thought,* 2: 101.

[6]This was a consistent theme for Gompers, who believed his own ideological kinship to Marx much closer than that of his socialist opponents. In August 1905, for instance, he would editorialize: "No severer critic of socialists ever lived than Karl Marx. No one more bitterly attacked them and their policy toward the trade unions than he. He knew what they had and have 'up their sleeve', and yet Socialists regard him as their 'patron saint.' " *American Federationist* 12 (August 1905): 520.

[7]Samuel Gompers, *Seventy Years of Life and Labour: An Autobiography,* 1: 51, 83-85.

[8]Samuel Bernstein, *The First International in America*, 227.

[9]Gompers, *Life*, 1: 94-97; Herbert C. Gutman, "The Tompkins Square Riot in New York City on January 13, 1874: A Reexamination of Its Causes and Its Aftermath," *Labor History* 6 (Winter 1965): 46-47.

[10]Gompers, *Life*, 1: 112-13.

[11]See Selig Perlman, "Upheaval and Reconstruction," in Commons et al., *History of Labour*, 2: 216-17; Bernstein, *First International*, 259-61; Engels to Sorge, September 12 and 17, 1874, in Karl Marx and Frederick Engels, *Letters to Americans, 1848-1895: A Selection*, 114-15.

[12]Bernstein, *First International*, 245-47; Howard H. Quint, *The Forging of American Socialism*, 12; Gutman, "The Tompkins Square Riot," 74-75, 75f.; New York *Socialist*, June 10, 1876, 2. The Boston Eight Hour League was founded in 1869 by Ira Steward and George E. McNeill. See John B. Andrews, "Nationalization," in Commons, et al., *History of Labour*, 2: 140.

[13]Marx to Bolte, November 23, 1871, in Marx and Engels, *Letters*, 88-94.

[14]Bolte, "Appeal to the Workingmen of America," May 19, 1872, IWA Correspondence.

[15]"General Rules of the United Workers of America, 1874," in John R. Commons, ed., *A Documentary History of American Industrial Society* (Cleveland, Ohio, 1910), 11: 376-78.

[16]Ibid.; Bolte to the officers and members of the Workingmen's Assembly of the State of New York, date illegible [c. January 1873], IWA Correspondence.

[17]"General Rules of the United Workers of America, 1874," in Commons, ed., *Documentary History*, 11: 376-78; Gompers, *Life*, 1: 102.

[18]Gompers, *Life*, 1: 102.

[19]"Resolutions on the Political Action of the IWA. Adopted by the Congress Held at Philadelphia," April 11-13, 1874, Box 2, IWA Correspondence.

[20]Friedrich Sorge, *Socialism and the Worker* (New York, 1876), 12-13, 19-20.

Chapter 4

¹Selig Perlman, "Upheaval and Reconstruction," in Commons et al., *History of Labour*, 2: 233-34.

²Ibid., 2: 222, 233-34; *Labor Standard*, August 12, 1876, 2; Howard H. Quint, *The Forging of American Socialism*, 13; Samuel Bernstein, *The First International in America*, 281.

³*Cigarmakers' Official Journal*, April 1876, 1; Gompers, *Seventy Years of Life and Labour: An Autobiography*, 1: 114-15.

⁴Gompers, *Life*, 1: 209.

⁵New York *Socialist*, April 15, 1876, 3; April 29, 1876, 1.

⁶*National Labor Tribune*, September 25, 1875, 3; and October 9, 1875, 4.

⁷Ibid., October 16, 1875, 4.

⁸Perlman, "Upheaval and Reconstruction," 201-2; Nathan Fine, *Labor and Farmer Parties in the United States, 1828-1928* (New York, 1961), 64; New York *Socialist*, April 29, 1876, 1, 2.

⁹New York *Socialist*, May 6, 1876, 3.

¹⁰Gompers, *Life*, 1: 128; Carl Speyer to the Board of Administration of the *Socialist*, May 26, 1876, IWA Correspondence.

¹¹Gompers, *Life*, 1: 128; "Minutes of the Philadelphia Branch, Social Democratic Workingmen's Party," Manuscripts Division, Library of Congress; New York *Socialist*, May 13, 1876, 2.

¹²McDonnell received every vote except that of P. J. McGuire of the Social Democrats, with Adolph Strasser abstaining.

¹³Conrad had recently transformed the Chicago *Vorbote* from a Lassallean to a Marxist paper. See Perlman, "Upheaval and Reconstruction," 230.

¹⁴"Proceedings of the Union Congress, Held at Philadelphia," July 19-22, Box 1, IWA Correspondence; New York *Socialist*, July 29, 1876, 4, and August 5, 1876, 1.

¹⁵New York *Socialist*, July 29, 1876, 4.

¹⁶H. M. Gitelman, "Adolph Strasser and the Origins of Pure and Simple Unionism," *Labor History* 6 (Winter 1965): 71, 78; New York *Socialist*, April 22, 1876, 1.

¹⁷For McGuire's position see New York *Socialist*, April 25, 1876, 2; *Labor Standard*, September 16, 1876, 3; September 30, 1876,

3; November 18, 1876, 4. For Smart's position, see New York *Socialist*, April 29, 1876, 2; May 20, 1876, 3; July, 8, 1876, 1; July 22, 1876, 3; and August 5, 1876, 1; *Labor Standard*, November 25, 1876, 2; and March 31, 1877, 3. For Raphael's position, see *Labor Standard*, August 26, 1876, 2. Raphael had been a member of the Boston branch of the Social Democratic Party along with Smart. See New York *Socialist*, May 6, 1876, 1.

[18]Marx to Siegfried Meyer and August Vogt, April 9, 1870, in Karl Marx and Frederick Engels, *Letters to Americans, 1848-1895: A Selection*, 77-80; *Labor Standard*, August 19, 1876, 1.

[19]See Chapter II, p. 24.

[20]*Labor Standard*, October 28, 1876, 4.

[21]Ibid., September 9, 1876, 2.

[22]Ibid.

[23]Ibid., August 19, 1876, 2.

[24]*Cigarmakers' Official Journal*, November 1876, 2; *Labor Standard*, October 28, 1876, 2.

[25]*Labor Standard*, September 9, 1876, 4.

[26]Ibid., September 30, 1876, 3; and December 30, 1876, 4.

[27]Ibid., November 4, 1876, 2; and November 25, 1876, 4.

[28]*Labor Standard*, December 2, 1876, 2; and March 24, 1877, 2.

[29]Ibid., January 6, 1877, 3.

[30]Ibid., January 6, 1887, 3; and January 27, 1877, 3.

[31]*Cigarmakers' Official Journal*, November 1876, 2.

[32]Gompers, *Life*, 1: 85; Kronburg's lecture is serialized in the *Labor Standard*, April 7, 1877, 2, 3; April 14, 1877, 2, 3; and April 21, 1877, 3.

[33]*Labor Standard*, December 9, 1876, 3.

[34]Ibid., January 6, 1877, 3.

Chapter 5

[1]*Cigarmakers' Official Journal*, June 1877, 2; *Labor Standard* June 23, 1877, 1.

[2]*Labor Standard*, January 13, 1877, 2, 3.

[3]Gompers, *Seventy Years of Life and Labour: An Autobiography*, 1: 209, 290; New York *Socialist*, June 10, 1876, 2.

[4]*Labor Standard*, October 8, 1876, 4; December 9, 1876, 4; March 24, 1877, 4.

[5]Ibid., December 23, 1876, 2; December 30, 1876, 2.

[6]Ibid., August 4, 1877, 2; August 26, 1877, 2.

[7]Ibid., March 24, 1877, 2.

[8]Ibid., March 31, 1877, 3.

[9]Ibid., August 4, 1877, 2; June 9, 1877, 1.

[10]*Cigarmakers' Official Journal*, January 1877, 1; *Labor Standard*, March 31, 1877, 1.

[11]*Labor Standard*, January 28, 1876, 3.

[12]Ibid., June 2, 1877, 2.

[13]Ibid., May 12, 1877, 2; *Cigarmakers' Official Journal*, June 10, 1878, 1; February 10, 1881, 1; July 10, 1881, 1; March 15, 1882, 1.

[14]*Labor Standard*, January 29, 1877, 2; February 24, 1877, 4.

[15]"Minutes of the Philadelphia Branch, Social Democratic Workingmen's Party," May 1, 1877, Manuscripts Division, Library of Congress.

[16]*Labor Standard*, May 12, 1877, 1; May 26, 1877, 3; June 2, 1877, 3.

[17]Ibid., October 14, 1877, 3; October 28, 1877, 3; Selig Perlman, "Upheaval and Reconstruction," in Commons et al., *History of Labour*, 2, 277-79.

[18]*Labor Standard*, August 4, 1877, 2; September 9, 1877, 3; November 11, 1877, 3; November 18, 1877, 3; December 1, 1877, 1; April 7, 1878, 5. For a time the *Labor Standard* was printed in Fall River, Mass., where followers of Ira Steward helped bring it out. The paper functioned as the organ of the ILU. See Samuel Bernstein, *The First International in America*, 292-93.

[19]*Labor Standard*, February 10, 1878, 2.

[20]Gompers, *Life*, 1: 212-14; Carl Speyer to Spinners Association, Lowell, Mass., February 29, 1880, IWA Correspondence.

[21]Speyer to Thomas Hurdle, June 6, 1880, IWA Correspondence.

[22]*Cigarmakers' Official Journal*, November 1876, 3; *Labor Standard*, November 25, 1876, 4.

[23]*Labor Standard*, September 9, 1876, 2.

[24]*Cigarmakers' Official Journal*, June 1877, 2; September 1876, 1; Gompers, *Life*, 1: 165, 214.

[25]Jonathan Grossman, *William Sylvis, Pioneer of American Labor: A Study of the Labor Movement during the Era of the Civil War* (New York, 1945), 88; Lloyd Ulman, *The Rise of the National Trade Union: The Development and Significance of its Structure, Governing Institutions, and Economic Policies* (Cambridge, Mass., 1966), 182; *Cigarmakers' Official Journal*, October 1877, 3-4; April 10, 1878, 4.

[26]Gompers, *Life*, 1: 143, 145-46; *Cigarmakers' Official Journal*, October 15, 1877, 3-4; March 10, 1878, 3.

[27]*Cigarmakers' Official Journal*, May 10, 1878, 2.

[28]Cole, *Socialist Thought*, 2: 83; *Labor Standard*, June 2, 1877, 2; *Cigarmakers' Official Journal*, May 10, 1878, 1; June 10, 1878, 1.

[29]*Cigarmakers' Official Journal*, September 15, 1879, 3-4; October 10, 1879, 2-3; Gompers to the Officers and Members of the New York Stereotypers Association, meeting February 23-27, 1888, Letterbooks of Samuel Gompers, Manuscripts Division, Library of Congress.

[30]*Cigarmakers' Official Journal*, September 15, 1879, 3-4.

[31]Gompers, *Life*, 1: 167-68; *Cigarmakers' Official Journal*, June 10, 1879, 1.

[32]*Cigarmakers' Official Journal*, April 10, 1879, 2.

[33]Ibid.

[34]Ibid., March 10, 1881, 4.

Chapter 6

[1]Howard H. Quint, *The Forging of American Socialism*, 15-25.

[2]*Labor Standard*, April 14, 1877, 3; August 11, 1877, 3; September 23, 1877, 4; December 16, 1877, 3; *National Labor Tribune*, March 11, 1876, 3.

[3]Cincinnati *National Socialist*, June 15, 1878, 2.

[4]*Labor Standard*, November 25, 1877, 2; January 20, 1878, 2; Detroit *Socialist*, March 30, 1878, 6.

[5]*Cigarmakers' Official Journal*, March 10, 1881, 1; Gompers, *Seventy Years of Life and Labour: An Autobiography*, 1: 210.

[6]*Cigarmakers' Official Journal*, June 10, 1878, 1; Philip Taft, *A. F. of L. in the Time of Gompers*, 7-8.

[7]*Cigarmakers' Official Journal*, March 10, 1881, 1; June 10, 1881, 1, 3.

[8]Ibid., October 10, 1881, 5.

[9]Selig Perlman, "Upheaval and Reconstruction," in Commons et al., *History of Labour*, 2: 310; *Carpenter*, August 1881, 2.

[10]Chicago *Socialist*, July 5, 1879, 2.

[11]*National Labor Tribune*, June 21, 1879, 2. The best work on the ideology and roots of the Knights of Labor is Gerald N. Grob, *Workers and Utopia: A Study of Ideological Conflict in the American Labor Movement, 1865-1900*.

[12]*Journal of United Labor*, December 15, 1880, 73; see Grob, *Workers and Utopia*, 38-39.

[13]Powderly to O. C. Hegdon, April 22, 1880, Letterbooks of Terence V. Powderly, Catholic University Archives; *Journal of United Labor*, June 15, 1880, 21; December 15, 1880, 73. For a later statement by Powderly on "class" see Powderly to J. G. Schonfarber, July 31, 1890, Letterbooks of Terence V. Powderly.

[14]Powderly to Mooney, March 30, 1880; to Malachy Connolly, April 8, 1880; to D. H. Baumgardner, June 21, 1880; all in Letterbooks of Terence V. Powderly.

[15]Powderly to William White, March 12, 1880; to Hughes, March 15, 1880; to John G. Moore, April 13, 1880; to Egbert Hayard, July 6, 1880; all in Letterbooks of Terence V. Powderly.

[16]Knights of Labor, *Records of the Proceedings of the General Assembly*, Pittsburgh, September 7-11, 1880, 225, 246; Powderly to Bro. Feeker, February 22, 1880, Letterbooks of Terence V. Powderly.

[17]McGuire to Van Patten, January 9, 1881, Box 2, Socialist Labor Party Correspondence, State Historical Society of Wisconsin.

[18]McGuire to Van Patten, January 9, 1881, and April 15, 1881, Box 2, Socialist Labor Party Correspondence.

[19]*Cigarmakers' Official Journal*, October 10, 1881, 5; December 15, 1881, 4, 5.

[20]Ibid., December 15, 1881, 5.

[21]*Report of the (Education and Labor) Committee of the Senate Upon*

the Relations between Labor and Capital, 1: 373, 376. Compare this statement with that of Marx, quoted on p. 18.

[22]Ibid., 293-94.

[23]Ibid., 365-66.

[24]Ibid., 289, 297, 299, 300.

[25]Ibid., 367-68.

[26]*Labor Standard,* May 12, 1877, 1; *Rep. of the Sen. Comm. on Labor,* 1: 370.

[27]*Rep. of the Sen. Comm. on Labor,* 1: 375.

[28]Ibid.

[29]Ibid., 289, 366.

[30]Ibid., 374-75.

[31]Gompers, *Life,* 1: 97, 386.

Chapter 7

[1]Federation of Organized Trades and Labor Unions of the United States and Canada (FOTLU), *Report of the Annual Session* (1905-06 reprint), Pittsburgh, December 15-18, 1881, 3-5, 24.

[2]Ibid., 4; *Report of the (Education and Labor) Committee of the Senate Upon the Relations between Labor and Capital,* 1: 382.

[3]*Cigarmakers' Official Journal,* February 15, 1882, 4.

[4]FOTLU, *Annual Session,* Pittsburgh, December 15-18, 1881, 5, 21; Gompers, *Seventy Years of Life and Labour: An Autobiography,* 1: 224.

[5]Powderly to Layton, October 22, 1881; to Thomas William, January 3, 1882; both in Letterbooks of Terence V. Powderly. See also Powderly to McPadden and to A. M. Owens, October 22, 1881, ibid.

[6]Powderly to J. P. McDonnell, September 24, 1882; to John P. Bulman, October 1, 1882; both in Letterbooks of Terence V. Powderly; Gerald N. Grob, *Workers and Utopia: A Study of Ideological Conflicts in the American Labor Movement, 1865-1900,* 103.

[7]Powderly to Daniel P. Gallagher, December 4, 1879; see also Powderly to Wm. Halley, May 12, 1881; to Chas. E. Robinson, January 17, 1882; to P. J. Deegon, March 16, 1882; to Michael

A. Clark, May 17, 1882; all in Letterbooks of Terence V. Powderly; *Journal of United Labor*, November 15, 1880, 68.

[8]Powderly to Fred Turner, July 20, 1884; to Richard F. Trevellick, October 8, 1882; see also Powderly to Thomas Kind, October 30, 1882; to Hume H. Cole, July 22, 1884; all in Letterbooks of Terence V. Powderly. For more on Powderly's reform mayorship of Scranton, see Vincent Joseph Falzone, "Terence V. Powderly, Mayor and Labor Leader, 1849-1893" (Ph.D. diss., University of Maryland, 1970), Chapter 3.

[9]*Cigarmakers' Official Journal*, April, 15, 1882, 1.

[10]Ibid., February 10, 1890, 1; April 15, 1882, 1; October 15, 1882, 9.

[11]Ibid., February 15, 1882, 4; April 15, 1882, 1.

[12]Ibid., June 15, 1882, 4; August 15, 1882, 1. *John Swinton's Paper*, October 21, 1883, 1.

[13]Alex J. Miselson, "The Henry George Campaign in the New York City Mayoralty Election, 1886" (Master's thesis, Columbia University, 1950), 5-6; Selig Perlman, "Upheaval and Reconstruction," in Commons et al., *History of Labour*, 2: 442; *John Swinton's Paper*, October 14, 1883, 1.

[14]Gompers, *Life*, 1: 243; *Carpenter*, September 1881, 2; Philip S. Foner, *History of the Labor Movement in the United States*, 2: 33.

[15]*Progress*, September 20, 1882, 1.

[16]*John Swinton's Paper*, February 28, 1886, 1.

[17]*Progress*, Febuary 20, 1883, 1.

[18]Ibid., October 26, 1883, 1.

[19]Ibid. A more detailed historical analysis following this same trend of thought was offered by "J. F." and serialized in *Progress* under the title "The Natural Tendency of the Trades Union Movement," as follows: May 27, 1884, 2; June 24, 1884, 1; September 26, 1884, 2; October 24, 1884, 2-3; November 24, 1884, 3; December 20, 1884, 2-3; July 24, 1885, 3; August 21, 1885, 2; September 18, 1885, 2; and December 16, 1885, 2.

[20]Supplement to *Cigarmakers' Official Journal*, September 1883, 5.

[21]Ibid.

[22]Ibid.

[23]Gompers, *Life*, 1: 69, 88.

[24]Ibid., 1: 71, 190-91.

[25]FOTLU, *Annual Session*, Chicago, October 7-10, 1884, 8-9, 15.

[26]Norman Ware, *The Labour Movement in the United States, 1860-1895: A Study in Democracy* (New York, 1929), 103-12.

[27]FOTLU, *Annual Session*, Washington, D. C., December 8-11, 1885, 11, 17-18.

[28]Ibid., 16, 19.

[29]*John Swinton's Paper*, November 22, 1885, 3.

[30]Ibid., November 22, 1885, 3; December 27, 1885, 4.

[31]Ibid., January 10, 1886, 4; January 17, 1886, 4; February 14, 1886, 4; February 21, 1886, 4.

[32]Ibid., January 24, 1886, 4.

[33]Ibid., March 7, 1886, 4; July 25, 1886, 4; August 1, 1886, 4; August 15, 1886, 4.

[34]Ibid., February 28, 1886, 1; July 4, 1886, 4; August 8, 1886, 1.

[35]Selig Perlman, "Upheaval and Reconstruction," in Commons et al., *History of Labour*, 2: 446-453; George to James P. Archibald, August 26, 1886, Henry George Papers, New York Public Library. The most thorough treatment of George's career and ideas is Charles Albro Barker, *Henry George* (New York, 1955). George made a strong showing in the election; his 68,000 votes were second to Abram S. Hewitt's 90,000 and well ahead of Theodore Roosevelt's 60,000 in the three-man race.

[36]Gompers, *Life*, 1: 316.

[37]New York *Sun*, November 1, 1886, 1.

[38]For the work of the Progressives in unison with the CMIU, see ibid., October 11, 1886, 1.

[39]FOTLU, *Annual Session,* Columbus, Ohio, December 8-12, 1886, 8.

[40]*Craftsman*, August 14, 1886, 1; *John Swinton's Paper*, August 1, 1886, 4; August 15, 1886, 4.

[41]*Craftsman*, August 14, 1886, 1; *John Swinton's Paper*, September 19, 1886, 3; Gompers, *Life*, 1: 274-75.

[42]Powderly to Beaumont, December 16, 1886, Letterbooks of Terence V. Powderly: *John Swinton's Paper*, January 23, 1887, 4; Gompers, *Life*, 1: 277.

Chapter 8

[1]P. J. McGuire, "The Basic Drift of the Federation," *American Federationist* 3 (December 1896), 207-208; FOTLU, *Report of the Annual Session*. Cleveland, November 21-24, 1882, 18-19.

[2]*Carpenter*, February 1883, 3; FOTLU, *Annual Session*, New York, August 21-24, 1883, 9-10, 12.

[3]Arthur Mann, *Yankee Reformers in the Urban Age* (Cambridge, Mass., 1954), chapter 8; FOTLU, *Annual Session*, Chicago, October 7-10, 1884, 9, 11-12.

[4]FOTLU, *Annual Session*, New York, August 21-24, 1883, 15; Chicago, October 7-10, 1884, 7-8; Gompers, *Seventy Years of Life and Labour: An Autobiography* 1: 237.

[5]FOTLU, *Annual Session*, Cleveland, November 21-24, 1882, 18-19; Chicago, October 7-10, 1884, 11. See also Gabriel Edmonston, "A Practical Proposition," *Carpenter*, September 1884, 6. That McGuire's appreciation of the industrial aspects of the Federation did not signify a complete surrender of political interest is indicated by an editorial he wrote in the spring of 1886, discussing trade unions as "a large wing of the Labor Army: They are organized on the autonomic basis . . . they have a historic basis that insures their permanency . . . they will become the cornerstone of a Cooperative Commonwealth. . . . A trade union is distinctly an organization of wage-workers—it eschews politics until such time as the workers, through association and acquaintance with one another have acquired that degree of unanimity, to act in concert politically." *Carpenter*, April 1886, 4.

[6]FOTLU, *Annual Session*, Chicago, October 7-10, 1884, 16; Taft, *The A. F. of L. in the Time of Gompers*, 16; *John Swinton's Paper*, June 8, 1884, 4; August 3, 1884, 1.

[7]FOTLU, *Annual Session*, Chicago, October 7-10, 1884, 6, 14,

17. For the appeal of the Federation to the Knights, see Gabriel Edmonston to Fred Turner, June 8, 1885, and July 26, 1885, both in Letterbooks of Samuel Gompers.

[8]Powderly to T. B. Thurber, August 4, 1882; to Felix Adler, January 20, 1884; both in Letterbooks of Terence V. Powderly; Falzone, "Terence V. Powderly, *Mayor and Labor Leader, 1849-1893*," 109-110. Powderly later reflected on how the failure of cooperation had driven him toward an alternative program: "We found . . . that it was not practicable to inaugurate such a system while trusts and syndicates were permitted to absorb the earnings of the masses. . . . A more universal system of co-operation will first be necessary . . . until the avenues of distribution are within the control of the people. . . ." Powderly to William H. Coleman, August 31, 1892, in Letterbooks of Terence Powderly.

[9]George to Powderly, April 19, 1883, Knights of Labor Correspondence, Catholic University.

[10]Grob, *Workers and Utopia: A Study of Ideological Conflict in the American Labor Movement, 1865-1900*, p. 62; Powderly to friend Dever, September 22, 1883, to W. T. Raycroft, May 29, 1885; both in Letterbooks of Terence V. Powderly. For more on Powderly's interest in the land question, see Powderly to W. Goodwin Moody, January 31, 1883; to W. T. Raycroft, May 29, 1885; in ibid.

[11]FOTLU, *Annual Session*, Cleveland, November 21-24, 1882, 19-20. Gompers later commented on George to a correspondent: ". . . all the ills of our social and economic system cannot be cured by 'patent medicine.' " See Gompers to John O'Brien, February 7, 1889, as well as Gompers to H. M. Ives, April 3, 1893, both in Letterbooks of Samuel Gompers.

[12]Knights of Labor, *Proceedings*, Hamilton, Ontario, October, 5-15, 1885, 25; *Journal of United Labor*, February 10, 1886, 119.

[13]FOTLU, *Annual Session*, Chicago, October 7-10, 1884, 17; Foner, *History of the Labor Movement in the United States*, 2: 100-1.

[14]*Carpenter*, April 1885, 1; FOTLU, *Annual Session*, Columbus, Ohio, December 8-12, 1886, 8.

[15]Ibid.; Powderly to W. H. Foster, December 26, 1885, Letterbooks of Terence V. Powderly.

[16]*Report of the (Education and Labor) Committee of the Senate Upon Relations between Labor and Capital*, 1: 691.

[17]*Carpenter*, May 1886, 3.

[18]Powderly to Fred [Turner], May 1, 1886; to Ralph Beaumont, June 17, 1886; both in Letterbooks of Terence V, Powderly; *John Swinton's Paper*, August 30, 1885, 1; December 19, 1886, 3.

[19]*Carpenter*, June 1886, 3; October 1886, 1; Knights of Labor, *Proceedings*, Minneapolis, October 4-19, 1887, 1445.

[20]*Carpenter*, October 1886, 1.

[21]Powderly to Henry Dettman, August 11, 1886, Letterbooks of Terence V. Powderly. The charge of Gompers' intoxication was repeated in a Knights of Labor circular and was bitterly refuted by Gompers. See Gompers, *Life*, 1: 265-68.

[22]*Carpenter*, November 1886, 3; Knights of Labor, *Proceedings*, Minneapolis, October 4-19, 1887, 1528-31.

[23]AFL, *Proceedings of the American Federation of Labor* (1905-1906 reprint), Columbus, Ohio, December 8-12, 1886, 6, 17-18.

[24]Ibid., 16.

[25]*Craftsman*, October 30, 1886, 2; *John Swinton's Paper,* August 22, 1886, 4. It was estimated that New York had 90,000 trade union members in the mid-eighties; Chicago, 30,000; Cincinnati, 30,000; San Francisco, 20,000. See *John Swinton's Paper*, May 4, 1884, 4; August 8, 1886, 1; September 19, 1886, 3; October 31, 1886, 3; and *Craftsman*, October 2, 1886, 1.

[26]*Craftsman*, November 27, 1886, 1.

[27]For the decline of the George coalition, see Charles Albro Barker, *Henry George* (New York, 1955), 482-507. The interview was reprinted from the Haverhill *Laborer* in *John Swinton's Paper* July 31, 1887, 2.

Chapter 9

[1]Gompers to H. H. Davis, February 19, 1887; to W. H. Hoyt, December 3, 1887; both in Letterbooks of Samuel Gompers. On the purely working class nature of the movement, see Gompers to F. C. Decker, April 25, 1888; to Claude F. Drake, May 24,

1890; "Definition of the A. F. of L.," August 12, 1890; to H. P. Kimball, September 5, 1891; all in ibid. On the identity of interests among all workers, see Gompers to R. M. Burke, September 20, 1890; to Otto Bell, September 10, 1891, both in ibid. Concerning the historical basis of the trade union movement, see also Gompers to N. E. Mathewson, October 10, 1890; to E. H. Cheny, January 11, 1892; to J. H. McWilliams, May 25, 1896, all in ibid.

[2]Gompers to M. J. Dowling, January 11, 1888; to Professor Edward W. Bemus, April 25, 1888; to Louis Hartmann, June 30, 1888; all in ibid. For Gompers' use of the Phalanx metaphor, see Gompers to D. L. Alexander, February 14, 1890; to C. C. McGlogan, August 12, 1892; to David H. Roxburgh, October 4, 1892; all in ibid. Gompers' interest in attracting all workers, skilled and unskilled, was a favorite theme; see Gompers to Albert C. Stevens, November 1, 1889; to William Donovan and H. P. Hendricks, December 29, 1889; to M. R. Carrick, May 6, 1890; to Claude F. Drake, May 24, 1890; to Philip W. Danehy, December 9, 1891; to J. G. Nolan, February 7, 1894; to George H. Daggett, January 4, 1896; to J. F. Sheehan, January 30, 1896; all in ibid.

[3]Gompers to John L. Kirchman, August 20, 1887; to W. H. Hoyt, December 3, 1887; both in Letterbooks of Samuel Gompers.

[4]Gompers to the Officers and Members of the New York Stereotypers Association, February 23-27, 1888, in ibid.

[5]Ibid.

[6]Ibid. Gompers later enthusiastically seconded the similar thoughts of William Howard that, in Gompers' words, "there is no idea more absurd than that a man's wages should be regulated by the financial ability of his employer: that he must be held responsible in his wages, must be accountable in his life's necessities, for the condition of another's business, over which he has no control, in which he is allowed no interest, and about which he is never consulted." See Gompers to William Howard, January 30, 1896, Letterbooks of Samuel Gompers.

[7]Gompers to the Trade and Labor Unions of San Fransisco, June 13, 1888, Letterbooks of Samuel Gompers; "The Eight Hour

Day," *American Federationist* 4, (March 1897): 2; 4 (May 1897): 47.

[8]Gompers to George E. McNeill, February 15, 1888; to the Trade and Labor Unions of San Francisco, June 13, 1888, Letterbooks of Samuel Gompers; "The Eight Hour Day," *American Federationist* 4 (May 1897): 47.

[9]Gompers to George Hunter, February 14, 1889, Letterbooks of Samuel Gompers.

[10]AFL, *Proceedings of the American Federation of Labor*, Baltimore, December 13-17, 1887, 12; and St. Louis, December 11-15, 1888, 9. For further comment on the hidden function of amelioration, see Gompers to August Delebar, August 13, 1891, to J. H. McWilliams, May 25, 1896; both in Letterbooks of Samuel Gompers. Gompers was fond of comparing the educational aspects of the fight for amelioration to elementary education, counseling "start with the A. B. C. and the rudiments of their economic education" or, variously, that not to do so "is like an attempt at teaching an infant geometry and algebra, without the elementary rudiments of the alphabet and arithmetic." See Gompers to W. W. Armstrong, December 21, 1892; to Charles Kassel, July 14, 1893; in ibid.; *American Federationist* 1 (April 1894): 30-31.

[11]Gompers to Abe Spring, July 15, 1892, Letterbooks of Samuel Gompers, *American Federationist* 1 (September 1894): 147-49. In 1896 Gompers shared the thoughts of a correspondent on "the awful signs of the times." Gompers feared that should the trade union movement fail, the workers would be "forced into barbarism," compelled to resort to more ominous means. "That," he said, "makes me oftimes shudder." See Gompers to F. J. Webber, August 20, 1896, Letterbooks of Samuel Gompers.

[12]Gompers to Charles Heilman, March 2, 1887; to John L. Kirchman, August 20, 1887; to J. Johnston, October 13, 1887; to E. S. Eaton, January 13, 1888; to the Officers and Delegates of the International Trade Union Congress in London Assembled, October 27, 1888; all in Letterbooks of Samuel Gompers. See also Gompers to P. H. Donnelly, March 21, 1887, and April 23, 1888; to P. J. McGuire, February 24, 1887, February 26, 1887, and April 22, 1887; to Hackett, Carhart and Co., November 4,

1890; to James McGill, April 13, 1892; to M. J. Carroll, August 2, 1894; all in ibid.

[13]Gompers to John O'Brien, February 7, 1889; to John L. Kirchum, February 28, 1889; in ibid.

[14]Gompers to August Schmidt, February 23, 1889; to John L. Kirchum, February 28, 1889; to Edward T. Plank, May 20, 1889; to the Officers and Delegates of the General Assembly of Knights of Labor in Convention Assembled, November 9, 1889; to the Officers and Members of Typographical Union No. 3, May 5, 1890; to Messrs. Lauer and Mattell, May 21, 1890; all in ibid.

[15] Gompers to the Officers and Delegates of the Master Builders National League in Convention Assembled, January 25, 1890; to N. Yafter [?] of the *Sun*, March 11, 1890; both in Letterbooks of Samuel Gompers; Gompers, "The Eight-Hour Work Day," *American Federationist* 4 (March 1897): 2-3; (April 1897): 24; (May 1897): 47-48; (July 1897): 88; and editorials in the *American Federationist* 3 (March 1896): 12; (February 1897): 257; (August 1897): 116; Dorothy Douglas, "Ira Steward on Consumption and Unemployment," *Journal of Political Economy* 40 (August 1932): 543.

[16]Gompers to the Officers and Delegates of the Master Builders National League in Convention Assembled, January 25, 1890, Letterbooks of Samuel Gompers; AFL, *Proceedings*, Birmingham, Alabama, December 14-19, 1891, 49. Later, with the eight-hour movement well under way, Gompers assessed that "it has given courage and hope to the working people who for years were disheartened and acting on the defensive against the encroachments of the employing classes"; Gompers to August Keufer, May 9, 1890; also Gompers to the Officers and Members of Typographical Union No. 3, May 5, 1890; both in Letterbooks of Samuel Gompers.

[17]Gompers to Manager, Associated Press, February 20, 1889; to the Officers and Delegates of the General Assembly of the Knights of Labor in Convention Assembled, November 9, 1889; both in ibid.

[18]*John Swinton's Paper*, April 3, 1887, 1; Gompers to the Editor

of the *Craftsman*, April 19, 1887, Letterbooks of Samuel Gompers.

[19]Powderly to David D. Hill, January 8, 1887; to Edwin M. Blake, April 27, 1887; to the Order Everywhere, September 2, 1887; to Devlin, September 14, 1887; to D. Clifford, January 5, 1888; all in Letterbooks of Terence V. Powderly. See also Powderly to Committee, Conference, April 17, 1886; to Charlie, February 16, 1887; to Charles H. Litchman, October 31, 1887; to P. Wolland, August 18, 1891; in ibid.

[20]Powderly to W. L. Stewart, July 21, 1887, ibid.; *Journal of United Labor* 7 (November 19, 1887): 2527.

[21]*Journal of United Labor* 8 (March 31, 1888): 2603; (April 21, 1888): 2614.

[22]Powderly to James B. Weaver, October 3, 1888; to Ed [?], October 11, 1888; to F. Beyssier, December 29, 1888; all in Letterbooks of Terence V. Powderly; *Journal of United Labor* 9 (November 15, 1888): 2734.

[23]Gompers to William Weihe, February 25, 1887; to E. Moss, March 21, 1887; to P. J. McGuire, April 22, 1887; all in Letterbooks of Samuel Gompers.

[24]Gompers to P. H. Donnelly, April 23, 1888, ibid.; *Journal of United Labor* 7 (June 2, 1888): 2639.

[25]*Carpenter*, July 15, 1889, 5; AFL, *Proceedings*, Boston, December 10-14, 1889, 13; Gompers to N. E. Mathewson, October 10, 1890, Letterbooks of Samuel Gompers. The development of an impasse in the period between the two organizations' February harmony conference and the October meeting of their executive bodies can be traced in the following: P. J. McGuire to Powderly, March 20, 1889, and May 7, 1889; both in Knights of Labor Correspondence; Gompers to P. J. McGuire, March 11, 1889, April 12, 1889, and October 1, 1889; to H. J. Skeffington, May 24, 1889, and October 4, 1889; to the Executive Council of the American Federation of Labor, September 7, 1889; to Geo. E. McNeal [*sic*], September 16, 1889; to W. S. McClevey, October 4, 1889; all in Letterbooks of Samuel Gompers; Powderly to P. J. McGuire, March 22, 1889, May 9, 1889, May 19, 1889, and May 24, 1889; to J. S. Reynolds, May 31, 1889; to Samuel Gom-

pers, June 18, 1889; to Ralph, October 14, 1889; all in Letterbooks of Terence V. Powderly.

[26]Powderly to Albert C. Stevens, November 9, 1889, Letterbooks of Terence V. Powderly; Powderly, "The Plea for Eight Hours," *North American Review* 153 (April 1890): 468-69. Gompers continued to suggest a treaty based on the limitation of the Knights' activities to education through mixed assemblies, "the proper field for the efforts and usefulness" of the K. of L. See Gompers to Robert C. Utess, June 27, 1890; to G. S. Buchner, June 29, 1890; to John W. Hayes, December 28, 1891; to the Executive council, February 4, 1892; all in Letterbooks of Samuel Gompers. Powderly detested the persistent proposal, which he sarcastically summarized: "The advice of the Federation is to go on and educate, strengthen the K. of L. and we will help you if you only let us live on in the shadows of the dark ages where we won't receive any of the education you are giving out. The Federation should have added 'We are strong in our ignorance, in our invincible ignorance. . . .'" Powderly to Devlin, January 7, 1892, Letterbooks of Terence V. Powderly.

[27]See Powderly to P. G. Gilligan, January 22, 1887; to Charles H. Litchman, to Bro. Hagerty, and to Hayes, all on December 5, 1887; to Dave, December 7, 1887; to Funk and Wagnalls, December 27, 1887 and March 1, 1888; to J. A. McMurdy, September 24, 1888; to Watchorn, May 27, 1889; to Bolton Smith, May 20, 1889; all in Letterbooks of Terence V. Powderly; George to Powderly, January 31, 1889, Knights of Labor Correspondence; and *Thirty Years of Labor, 1859 to 1889*, Columbus, Ohio, 1889.

[28]Powderly to A. Wardall, June 15, 1889; to Charlie, December 3, 1889, both in Letterbooks of Terence V. Powderly. See also Powderly to Watchorn, May 27, 1889, ibid.

[29]Powderly to Tom O'Reilly, December 19, 1889, ibid.; Knights of Labor, *Proceedings*, Atlanta, November 12-20, 1889, 52; Gompers to N. E. Mathewson, October 10, 1890, Letterbooks of Samuel Gompers. For the course of Powderly's courtship of the farmers, see: Powderly to Henry George, February 17, 1889; to

Bolton Smith, May 20, 1889; to H. C. Dean, December 29, 1890; to Thomas Armstrong, January 30, 1891; to Hugh, January 30, 1891; to E. M. Chamberlin, February 23, 1891; to Henry George, February 23, 1891; to N. G. Spalding, September 15, 1891; to Ben Terrell, January 2, 1892; to John W. Hayes, February 17, 1892; to W. L. Stark, April 7, 1892; to Doctor, June 6, 1892; all in Letterbooks of Terence V. Powderly.

[30]AFL, *Proceedings*, Boston, December 10-14, 1889, 13-14. See also Gompers to Tom Mann, September 12, 1891, Letterbooks of Samuel Gompers. Gompers, "Organized Labor in the Campaign," *North American Review* 155 (July 1892): 91-96.

[31]Gompers to A. S. Leitch, November 28, 1892; to H. M. Ives, February 23, 1893; both in Letterbooks of Samuel Gompers. Gompers characterized the Knights of Labor as "dilletante middle class"; see Gompers to A. Furuseth, January 22, 1892, ibid. Powderly was overthrown in a Knights of Labor power struggle in mid-1893. The year preceding was marked by stormy battle between the Federation trade unions and the Knighthood. The coalition which seized power in the Knights from Powderly achieved no better relations subsequently, despite its initial pretense of peace. Gompers noted that the accession of Powderly's co-worker, John W. Hayes, was an ominous sign: "Hayes has always been the greater antagonist to the trade unions of the two, was always bitter, vindictive and relentless." A summit conference was proposed, delayed, and then held without significant results in April 1894. For the federation's relations with the Knights from 1892, see: Gompers to the Executive Council of the AFL, June 13, 1892, June 27, 1892, and January 31, 1893; to William Marden, January 23, 1893; to A. W. Wright, July 10, 1893; to P. J. McGuire, December 28, 1893, and March 23, 1894; to J. P. Sovereign and John W. Hayes, January 4, 1894; to George W. Perkins, April 21, 1894; all in ibid.

[32]Gompers to P. J. McGuire, August 7, 1893; to Mr. A. Topping, October 27, 1893; both in Letterbooks of Samuel Gompers.

[33]Gompers to O. P. Smith, February 10, 1892; to Alonzo Crouse, E. S. Brown and [?] August 31, 1892; to Alonzo Crouse, September 23, 1892; to J. C. Bean, December 12, 1892; all in

ibid.; AFL, *Proceedings*, Philadelphia, December 12-17, 1892, 17.

[34]Gompers to John McBride, February 6, 1893; to J. C. Bean, February 6, 1893; to W. E. Kerns, March 18, 1896; all in Letterbooks of Samuel Gompers.

Chapter 10

[1]Engels to Sorge, November 29, 1886; Engels to Florence Kelley Wischnewetzky, December 28, 1886; in Marx and Engels, *Letters to Americans, 1848-1895: A Selection*, 162-67. For the recuperation of the SLP after 1884, see Quint, *The Forging of American Socialism*, 25-36.

[2]*Workman's Advocate*, December 14, 1889, 1.

[3]Ibid.

[4]AFL, *Proceedings of the American Federation of Labor*, Columbus, Ohio, December 8-12, 1886, 8, 16.

[5]*Ibid.*, St. Louis, December 11-15, 1888, 13-14; *Workman's Advocate*, September 21, 1889, 1.

[6]Gompers to August Delebar, January 25, 1889; to the Executive Council of the AFL, May 21, 1889; to Ben Tillett, April 6, 1896; all in Letterbooks of Samuel Gompers; *Workman's Advocate*, October 12, 1889, 1; November 12, 1889, 1; November 23, 1889, 1; June 21, 1890, 1; AFL, *Proceedings*, Boston, December 10-14, 1889, 23-24.

[7]*Workman's Advocate*, June 21, 1890, 1; June 28, 1890, 1; July 12, 1890, 1.

[8]Ibid., September 20, 1890, 1; *People*, June 11, 1893, 2. Gompers sought to distinguish between Federation members who, outside their union, "wish to take action upon the economic question in its social and political bearing," and those who tried to convert local labor organizations into political machines. See Gompers to H. P. Hendrix, April 7, 1890, Letterbooks of Samuel Gompers.

[9]Gompers to P. J. McGuire, August 4, 1891, ibid.

[10]*People*, June 11, 1893, 2.

[11]Ibid., December 6, 1891, 2.

[12]Quint, *American Socialism*, 161-65.

[13]Gompers to Harry Glyn, June 23, 1892; to Lloyd, July 2, 1894; both in Letterbooks of Samuel Gompers.

[14]Gompers to the Delegates of the International Labor Congress, Brussels, Belgium, August 4, 1891; to Harry Glyn, June 23, 1892; to Jas. G. Bacon, August 11, 1893; to Wm. Saul, September 21, 1893; to L. E. Tossy, July 3, 1894; all in ibid.

[15]Gompers to A. S. Leitch, December 8, 1892, ibid.; *American Federationist* 3 (July 1896): 91-92.

[16]Gompers to Eva MacDonald Valesh, February 9, 1892; to John F. Tobin, November 11, 1896; to E. Kurzenknabe, December 5, 1896; all in Letterbooks of Samuel Gompers.

[17]Gompers, "The Influence of the Labor Movement on Human Progress," *Bakers' Journal*, August 1, 1891, 4.

[18]Ibid., July 25, 1891, 3.

[19]Ibid., August 1, 1891, 4.

[20]Gompers, "Trade Unions: Their Achievements, Methods and Aims," a paper read before the American Social Science Congress, September 20, 1891, printed in *Bakers' Journal*, April 23, 1892, 4.

[21]*Bakers' Journal*, April 9, 1892, 3; April 23, 1892, 4.

[22]Gompers to P. J. McGuire, August 4, 1891; to E. M. Cherry, August 10, 1893; to Samuel Goldwater, December 1, 1893; to Horace M. Eaton, July 3, 1896; all in Letterbooks of Samuel Gompers; *American Federationist* 3 (November 1896): 187. See also Gompers to Geo. N. Daggett, January 4, 1896, Letterbooks of Samuel Gompers.

[23]Gompers to Fred. Engels, January 9, 1891; to F. A. Sorge, November 27 and November 21, 1891; all in ibid. Gompers already felt Engels had drawn on erroneous information in the preface to the 1887 edition of his *Condition of the Working Class in England*. In a letter to Florence Kelley Wischnewetzky in 1888 Gompers complained that Engels did not even mention the American Federation of Labor in his discussion of the preparations being made for the inauguration of an eight-hour movement in May 1890. Gompers was also disturbed that Engels should have indicated that the Knights of Labor was the organization of the proletariat in America. He could only surmise that

Engels was confused by the bluster of that organization but still admitted, "I am really surprised at it from so keen an observer as Engels. There is no doubt that his observations need amending." See Engels, *Condition of the Working Class in England* (New York, 1958), 356-57; Gompers to Florence Kelley Wischnewetzky, October 17, 1888, Letterbooks of Samuel Gompers.

[24] Gompers to F. A. Sorge, November 27, 1891, Letterbooks of Samuel Gompers; Engels to Schleuter, January 29, 1891, Marx and Engels, *Letters*, 232-34; to Sorge, January 6, 1892, ibid., 238-41.

[25] Gompers to George A. Schilling, January 6, 1891; to L. A. Hutchenson, January 17, 1889; to Jacob Kilkene, May 25, 1891; all in Letterbooks of Samuel Gompers; *American Federationist* 1 (May 1894): 53.

[26] AFL, *Proceedings*, Scranton, Pa., December 5-14, 1901, 15. See Lloyd Ulman, *Rise of the National Trade Union: The Development and Significance of Its Structure, Governing Institutions, and Economic Policies*, 390-99.

[27] Gompers to S. R. Holmes, October 8, 1890; to John C. Riedel, December 7, 1891; both in Letterbooks of Samuel Gompers.

[28] Gompers to Geo. L. Norton, May 17, 1892; to J. F. Brown, March 2, 1896; both in ibid. See also Gompers to R. E. Pleasants, January 17, 1889; to Frank D. Hamlin, April 30, 1890; to Jere Dennis, April 24, 1891; to Fred J. Carr, December 8, 1891; to John M. Callahan, May 24, 1892; to David Watkins, July 17, 1893; to George L. Norton, December 7, 1893; to Chas. H. Archer, June 1, 1894; to S. Halpruner, July 24, 1894; to Robert Howard, March 2, 1896; all in ibid.; and Gompers to W. S. Griscom, April 16, 1897; to Martin Fox, April 20, 1897; both in Samuel Gompers Correspondence, AFL Papers, State Historical Society of Wisconsin.

[29] Gompers to Frank P. Sargent and Eugene V. Debs, August 30, 1890; to C. H. Trenholm, January 16, 1891; both in Letterbooks of Samuel Gompers. In a similar spirit Gompers urged that the Machinery Molders join with the Iron Molders Union in recognition that "the spirit of trade organizations of to-day is not toward division, but rather toward consolidation and drawing

more closely together." Gompers also strained to bring about national unity among the brewers on the grounds that the trend of all modern movements was toward unity and "it is the hope of intelligent workmen to bring the wage workers of the world into a closer alliance with each other, to recognize the internationality of the labor movement, and the identity of the interests of the wage-workers of the world." He encouraged the idea of amalgamating the various branches of the metal workers into one great organization. He also argued against chartering the Clothing Operatives National Union, because there were already two others in that trade and "there must be a concentration of effort and not a diffusion of it to bring about the best results." See Gompers to John A. Penton, June 26, 1891; to John O'Brien, July 29, 1891; to Geo. W. Appell, May 22, 1888, to Wm. J. Connolly, November 20, 1891; ibid.

[30]Gompers to W. Burns, November 4, 1890; to John O'Brien, September 15, 1894; to Tom Mann, September 20, 1894; Letterbooks of Samuel Gompers. For more on Gompers' advocacy of railroad union federation prior to the Pullman crisis, see Gompers to C. H. Trenhold, December 29, 1890, January 7, 1891, and January 16, 1891; to Chas. W. Martin, December 9, 1891, all in ibid.

[31]*People*, April 12, 1891, 5; April 17, 1892, 2.

[32]Chester McArthur Destler, *American Radicalism, 1865-1901, Essays and Documents* (New London, Connecticut, 1946), 169; AFL, *Proceedings*, Chicago, December 11-19, 1893, 37.

[33]Destler, *American Radicalism*, 170-74.

[34]H. D. Lloyd to Gompers, July 30, 1894, and August 14, 1894, Samuel Gompers Correspondence, AFL Papers. See also Gompers to H. D. Lloyd, August 9, 1894, Letterbooks of Samuel Gompers.

[35]Gompers to Samuel Ross, October 30, 1894; to C. L. Drummond, November 8, 1894; to Frank K. Foster, November 19, 1894; all in Letterbooks of Samuel Gompers; AFL, *Proceedings*, Denver, December 10-18, 1894, 14.

[36]Gompers to P. J. McGuire, August 4, 1891, Letterbooks of

Samuel Gompers; AFL, *Proceedings*, Denver, December 10-18, 1894, 14.

[37]Gompers to Wm. Montgomery, August 20, 1896; to E. Kurzenknabe, December 5, 1896; both in Letterbooks of Samuel Gompers.

[38]Excerpt from the Boston *Labor Leader*, December 22, 1894, in Samuel Gompers Correspondence, AFL Papers. Compare this statement with that of Marx, quoted on p. 30.

Chapter 11

[1]Marx and Engels, "Manifesto," in C. P. Dutt, ed., *Karl Marx: Selected Works*, 1; 228; Engels to Florence Kelley Wischnewetzky, December 28, 1886, in Marx and Engels, *Letters to Americans, 1848-1895: A Selection*, 164-67.

[2] According to Gompers' statement in the New York *Sun*, September 19, 1893, cited in Philip S. Foner, *History of the Labor Movement in the United States*, 2: 174.

[3]Gompers to S. R. Holmes, October 8, 1890; to Mr. Hacker, December 21, 1892; both in Letterbooks of Samuel Gompers; *American Federationist* 1 (September 1894): 147-49.

[4]Jonathan Grossman, *William Sylvis, Pioneer of American Labor: A Study of the Labor Movement during the Era of the Civil War*, 88, 274.

[5]John R. Commons believed Gompers was a serious theoretical thinker but credited him with a much more freelance and uninhibited testing of alternative concepts than is here suggested. See "Karl Marx and Samuel Gompers," *Political Science Quarterly* 61 (June 1926): 281-86.

Bibliography

Manuscript Collections

Library of Congress, Washington D.C.
　　Letterbooks of Samuel Gompers, 1881-1898.
　　Minutes of the Philadelphia Branch of the Social Democratic
　　　　Workingman's Party, January 1876 to March 1878.
Catholic University of America, Washington, D.C.
　　Letterbooks of Terence V. Powderly, 1879-1893 (cross-
　　　　referenced with Knights of Labor Correspondence).
State Historical Society of Wisconsin, Madison
　　International Workingmen's Association Correspondence,
　　　　1871-1876.
　　Correspondence of the Workingman's Party of the United
　　　　States, 1876-1878.
　　Correspondence of the Socialist Labor Party, 1879-1896.
　　Correspondence of the American Federation of Labor, 1888-
　　　　1898.
　　Henry Demarest Lloyd Papers, 1893-1896.
Illinois Historical Survey, Urbana

Thomas J. Morgan Papers, 1881-1896.
New York Public Library, New York City
    Henry George Papers, 1886-1895.
Samuel Gompers Library, AFL-CIO, Washington, D.C.
    Minutes of the Legislative Committee of the Federation of
        Organized Trades and Labor Unions of the United
        States and Canada, November 19, 1881 to December 17,
        1887.
    "Old Clippings Left by Mr. Gompers' Son," Scrapbook, 1891-
        1897.

Newspapers and Journals

American Federalist, 1894-1898.
Bakers' Journal, 1891-1893.
Boston *Labor Leader*, 1887-1896.
Carpenter, 1881-1894.
Chicago *Socialist*, 1878-1879.
Chicago *Workingman's Advocate*, 1864-1877.
Cigarmakers' Official Journal, 1876-1882.
Cincinnati *National Socialist*, June-September 1878.
Detroit *Socialist*, 1877-1878.
Journal of the Knights of Labor, 1890-1896.
Journal of United Labor, 1880-1889.
New Haven and New York *Workmen's Advocate*, 1886-1891.
New York and Paterson, New Jersey *Labor Standard*, 1876-1881.
New York *John Swinton's Paper*, 1883-1887.
New York *People*, 1891-1896.
New York *Populist*, 1894-1895.
New York *Progress*, 1882-1885.
New York *Socialist*, 1876.
New York *Union Advocate*, June-December 1887.
Pittsburgh *National Labor Tribune*, 1875-1896.
Washington *Craftsman*, 1884-1888.

Proceedings

Proceedings of the American Federation of Labor, 1886-1898.
Proceedings of the Federation of Organized Trades and Labor
    Unions of the United States and Canada, 1881-1886.
Proceedings of the Knights of Labor, 1878-1896.

Books, Dissertations, and Pamphlets

Aldrich, M. Almy. *The American Federation of Labor*. American
    Economic Association Studies, vol. 3, no. 4. New York: Mac-
    millan, 1898.
American Federation of Labor. *A Verbatim Report of the Discussion
    on the Political Programme, at the Denver Convention of the Ameri-
    can Federation of Labor, December 14, 15, 1894*. New York:
    AFL, 1895.
Andrews, John B. "Nationalization," in John R. Commons, et al.,
    History of Labour in the United States. Vol. 2, New York: Mac-
    millan 1918.
Aveling, Edward Bibbins. *The Working-Class Movement in America*.
    London: S. Sonnenschein, 1891.
Avineri, Shlomo. *The Social and Political Thought of Karl Marx*.
    Studies in the History and Theory of Politics. Cambridge:
    The University of Cambridge Press, 1968.
Barker, Charles Albro. *Henry George*. New York: Oxford Univer-
    sity Press, 1955.
Beard, Mary. *A Short History of the American Labor Movement*. New
    York: Macmillan, 1920.
Bernstein, Samuel. *The First International in America*. New York:
    Augustus M. Kelley, 1962.
Briggs, Asa, and Saville, John. *Essays in Labour History*. London:
    Macmillan, 1960.
Browne, Henry J. *The Catholic Church and the Knights of Labor*.
    Washington: Catholic University of America Press, 1949.

Buchanan, Joseph R. *The Story of a Labor Agitator*. New York: Outlook, 1903.

Buder, Stanley. *Pullman: An Experiment in Industrial Order and Community Planning, 1880-1930*. New York: Oxford University Press, 1967.

Burbank, David T. *Reign of the Rabble: The St. Louis General Strike of 1877*. New York: August M. Kelley, 1966.

Cahill, Marion C. *Shorter Hours: A Study of the Movement since the Civil War*. Studies in History, Economics, and Public Law, no. 380. New York: Columbia University Press, 1932.

Carroll, Mollie Ray. *Labor and Politics: The Attitude of the American Federation of Labor toward Legislation and Politics*. Boston and New York: Houghton Mifflin, 1923.

Christie, Robert A. *Empire in Wood: A History of the United Brotherhood of Carpenters and Joiners of America*. Studies in Industrial and Labor Relations, vol. 7. Ithaca: New York State School of Industrial and Labor Relations at Cornell University, 1956.

Cole, G. D. H. *A History of Socialist Thought*. Vols. 1 and 2. London: Macmillan, 1953-1954.

Collins, Henry, and Abramsky, Chimen. *Karl Marx and the British Labour Movement: Years of the First International*. London: Macmillan, 1965.

Commons, John R., ed. *A Documentary History of American Industrial Society*. vol. 9. Cleveland: A. H. Clark, 1910.

Costello, Lawrence. "The New York City Labor Movement, 1861-1873." Ph.D. dissertation, Columbia University, 1967.

David, Henry. *The History of the Haymarket Affair*. New York: Farrar & Rinehart, 1936.

Destler, Chester McArthur. *American Radicalism, 1865-1901*. New London: Connecticut College, 1946.

————. *Henry Demarest Lloyd, and the Empire of Reform*. Philadelphia: University of Pennsylvania, 1963.

Dorfman, Joseph. *The Economic Mind in American Civilization*. Vol. 3. New York: Viking, 1949.

Draper, Theodore. *The Roots of American Communism*. New York: Viking, 1957.

Dulles, Foster Rhea. *Labor in America: A History*. Growth of American Series. New York: Thomas Y. Crowell, 1949.

Durden, Robert F. *The Climax of Populism: The Election of 1896*. Lexington, Kentucky: University of Kentucky Press, 1965.

Dutt, C. P., ed. *Karl Marx: Selected Works*. New York: International, 1958.

Egbert, Donald Drew, and Persons, Stow, eds. *Socialism and American Life*. 2 vols. Studies in American Civilization. Princeton: University Press, 1952.

Ely, Richard T. *The Labor Movement in America*. New York: Crowell, 1886.

————. *Recent American Socialism*. New York: John Murphy, 1885.

Emery, Walter B. "Samuel Gompers, Spokesman for Labor." Ph.D. dissertation, University of Wisconsin, 1939.

Falzone, Vincent J. "Terence V. Powderly, Mayor and Labor Leader, 1849-1893." Ph.D. dissertation, University of Maryland, 1970.

Fine, Nathan. *Labor and Farmer Parties in the United States, 1828-1928*. New York: Rand School of Social Science, 1928.

Fine, Sidney. *Laissez Faire and the General-Welfare State: A Study of Conflict in American Thought, 1865-1901*. Ann Arbor, Michigan: University of Michigan Press, 1956.

Foner, Philip S. *History of the Labor Movement in the United States*, 4 vols. Vol. 2. New York: International, 1955.

Ginger, Ray. *The Bending Cross: A Biography of Eugene Victor Debs*. New Brunswick, New Jersey: Rutgers University Press, 1949.

Glocker, Theodore Wesley. *The Government of American Trade Unions*. Baltimore: The Johns Hopkins Press, 1913.

Goldmark, Josephine. *Impatient Crusader: Florence Kelley's Life Story*. Urbana: University of Illinois Press, 1953.

Gompers, Samuel. *The Eight-Hour Workday: Its Inauguration, Endorsement and Influences*. Washington, D. C.: AFL, 1897.

————. *Seventy Years of Life and Labour: An Autobiography*. 2 vols. New York: E. P. Dutton, 1925.

Grob, Gerald N. *Workers and Utopia: A Study of Ideological Conflict in the American Labor Movement, 1865-1900*. Evanston, Illinois: Northwestern University Press, 1961.

Grossman, Jonathan P. *William Sylvis, Pioneer of American Labor: A Study of the Labor Movement during the Era of the Civil War.* Studies in History, Economics and Public Law, no. 516. New York: Columbia University Press, 1945.

Gunton, George. *Wealth and Progress: A Critical Examination of the Labor Problem.* New York: Appleton, 1887.

Harris, Herbert. *American Labor.* New Haven: Yale University Press, 1938.

Harrison, Royden. *Before the Socialists: Studies in Labour and Politics, 1861-1881.* London: Routledge and Kegan Paul, 1965.

Hicks, John D. *The Populist Revolt: A History of the Farmers' Alliance and the People's Party.* Minneapolis: University of Minnesota Press, 1931.

Hillquit, Morris. *History of Socialism in the United States.* New York: Funk and Wagnalls, 1910.

Hollander, Jacob H. and Barnett, George E. *Studies in American Trade Unionism.* New York: Henry Holt, 1906.

Hurwitz, Howard L. *Theodore Roosevelt and Labor in New York State, 1880-1900.* New York: Columbia University Press, 1947.

James, Edward T. "American Labor and Political Action, 1865-1896: The Knights of Labor and Its Predecessors." Ph.D. dissertation, Harvard University, 1954.

Kirkland, Edward C. *Industry Comes of Age: Business, Labor and Public Policy, 1860-1897.* New York: Holt, Rinehart and Winston, 1961.

Knoles, George H. *The Presidential Campaign and Election of 1892.* Stanford, California: Stanford University Press, 1942.

Landauer, Carl. *European Socialism: A History of Ideas and Movements from the Industrial Revolution to Hitler's Seizure of Power.* 2 vols. Berkeley and Los Angeles: University of California Press, 1959.

Leiby, James. *Carroll Wright and Labor Reform: The Origin of Labor Statistics.* Cambridge: Harvard University Press, 1960.

Lichtheim, George. *Marxism: An Historical and Critical Study.* London: Routledge and Kegan Paul, 1961.

Lindsey, Almont. *The Pullman Strike: The Story of a Unique Experi-*

ment and of a Great Labor Upheaval. Chicago: University of Chicago Press, 1942.

Lorwin, Lewis L. *The American Federation of Labor: History, Policies, and Prospects.* Washington: Brookings Institution, 1933.

Madison, Charles A. *American Labor Leaders. Personalities and Forces in the Labor Movement.* New York: Harper, 1950.

Mandel, Bernard. *Samuel Gompers: A Biography.* Yellow Springs, Ohio: Antioch Press, 1963.

Mann, Arthur. *Yankee Reformers in the Urban Age.* Cambridge, Mass.: Harvard University Press, 1954.

Marshall, Ray. *The Negro and Organized Labor.* New York: John Wiley, 1965.

Marx, Karl, and Engels, Frederick. *Letters to Americans, 1848-1895: A Selection.* New York: International Publishers, 1953.

————. *Selected Correspondence.* Moscow: Foreign Languages, 1953.

McMurry, Donald L. *Coxey's Army: A Study of the Industrial Army Movement of 1894.* Boston: Little, Brown, 1929.

McNeill, George Edwin, ed. *The Labor Movement: The Problem of Today.* Boston: A. M. Bridgman, 1887.

————. *The Philosophy of the Labor Movement: A Paper Read before the International Labor Conference.* Chicago: AFL, 1893.

Montgomery, David. *Beyond Equality: Labor and the Radical Republicans, 1862-1872.* New York: Alfred A. Knopf, 1967.

Morgan, Howard Wayne. *Eugene V. Debs: Socialist for President.* Syracuse: Syracuse University Press, 1962.

Pelling, Henry. *American Labor.* The Chicago History of American Civilization. Chicago and London: University of Chicago Press, 1960.

Perlman, Mark. *Labor Union Theories in America: Background and Development.* Evanston, Illinois: Row Peterson, 1958.

Perlman, Selig. *A History of Trade Unionism in the United States.* New York: Macmillan, 1922.

————. *A Theory of the Labor Movement.* New York: Macmillan, 1928.

————. "Upheaval and Reorganization," in John R. Commons,

et al., *History of Labour in the United States*. Vol. 2. New
     York: Macmillan, 1918.
Pollack, Norman. *The Populist Response to Industrial America*.
     Cambridge, Mass.: Harvard University Press, 1962.
Powderly, Terence V. *The Path I Trod*. New York: Columbia
     University Press, 1940.
————. *Thirty Years of Labor*. Columbus, Ohio: Excelsior, 1889.
Quint, Howard H. *The Forging of American Socialism: Origins of the
     Modern Movement*. Columbia, South Carolina: University of
     South Carolina Press, 1953.
Rayback, Joseph G. *A History of American Labor*. New York: Mac-
     millan, 1959.
Reed, Louis S. *The Labor Philosophy of Samuel Gompers*. New York:
     Columbia University Press, 1930.
Saposs, David J. *Left-Wing Unionism: A Study of Radical Policies and
     Tactics*. New York: International Publishers, 1926.
Shannon, Fred Albert. *The Farmer's Last Frontier: Agriculture, 1860-
     1897*. New York and Toronto: Farrar and Rinehart, 1945.
Sorge, Friedrich. *Socialism and the Workers*. New York: Interna-
     tional Workingmen's Association, 1876.
Speek, Peter, *The Singletax and the Labor Movement*. Economics and
     Political Science Series, vol. 8, no. 3. Madison: University of
     Wisconsin Press, 1917.
Staley, Eugene. *History of the Illinois State Federation of Labor*.
     Chicago: University of Chicago Press, 1930.
Swinton, John. *Striking for Life: Labor's Side of the Labor Question*.
     Philadelphia: O. R. Keller, 1894.
Taft, Philip. *Organized Labor in American History*. New York, Ev-
     anston, and London: Harper and Row, 1964.
————. *The A. F. of L. in the Time of Gompers*. New York: Harper,
     1957.
Tannenbaum, Frank. *A Philosophy of Labor*. New York: Alfred A.
     Knopf, 1952.
Thompson, E. P. *The Making of the English Working Class*. New
     York: Pantheon, 1964.
Ulman, Lloyd. *The Rise of the National Trade Union: The Development
     and Significance of Its Structure, Governing Institutions, and*

Economic Policies. Cambridge, Mass.: Harvard University Press, 1955.

U. S. Congress. *Report of the (Education and Labor) Committee of the Senate Upon the Relations between Labor and Capital.* 4 vols. Washington D. C.: Government Printing Office, 1885.

Ware, Norman. *The Labor Movement in the United States, 1860-1895.* New York: Appleton, 1929.

Wesley, Charles Harris. *Negro Labor in the United States, 1850-1925: A Study in American Economic History.* New York: Vanguard, 1927.

Wolfe, Bertram D. *Marxism: One Hundred Years in the Life of a Doctrine.* New York: Dial, 1965.

Wolff, Leon. *Lockout: The Story of the Homestead Strike of 1892.* New York: Harper & Row, 1965.

Wolman, Leo. *The Growth of American Trade Unions, 1880-1923.* New York: National Bureau of Economic Research, 1924.

Yearley, Clifton K. *Britons in American Labor: A History of the Influence of the United Kingdom Immigrant, on American Labor, 1820-1914.* Studies in Historical and Political Science, series 75, no. 1, Baltimore: The Johns Hopkins Press, 1957.

Articles

Avineri, Shlomo. "Marx and the Intellectuals." *Journal of the History of Ideas* 28 (1967): 269-78.

Bernstein, Irving, ed. "Samuel Gompers and Free Silver, 1896." *Mississippi Valley Historical Review* 29 (1942): 394-400.

Bernstein, Samuel. "American Labor in the Long Depression, 1873-1878." *Science and Society* 20 (1956): 59-83.

Birdsall, William C. "The Problem of Structure in the Knights of Labor." *Industrial and Labor Relations Review* 6 (1953): 532-46.

Blicksilver, Jack. "George Gunton: Pioneer Spokesman for a Labor-Big Business Entente." *Business History Review* 31 (1957): 1-22.

Bloch, Herman D. "Craft Unions and the Negro in Historical Perspective." *Journal of Negro History* 43 (1958), 10-33.

———. "Labor and the Negro, 1866-1910." *Journal of Negro History*, (1965): 163-84.

Bremner, Robert H. "The Big Flat: History of a New York Tenement House." *American Historical Review* 44 (1958): 54-62.

Browne, Henry J. "Terence V. Powderly and Church-Labor Difficulties of the Early 1880's." *Catholic Historical Review* 32 (1946): 1-27.

Carman, Harry J. "Terence Vincent Powderly—An Appraisal." *Journal of Economic History* 1 (1941): 42-56.

Commons, John R. "Karl Marx and Samuel Gompers." *Political Science Quarterly* 61 (1926): 281-86.

Cox, LaWanda F. "The American Agricultural Wage Earner, 1865-1900: The Emergence of a Modern Labor Problem." *Agricultural History* 22 (1948): 95-114.

Destler, Chester McArthur. "Consummation of a Labor-Populist Alliance in Illinois, 1894." *Mississippi Valley Historical Review* 27 (1941): 589-602.

———. "Western Radicalism, 1865-1901: Concepts and Origins." *Mississippi Valley Historical Review* 31 (1944): 335-68.

Diamond, William. "Urban and Rural Voting in 1896." *American Historical Review* 46 (1941): 281-305.

Dubofsky, Melvyn. "The Origins of Western Working Class Radicalism, 1890-1905." *Labor History* 7 (1966): 131-54.

Durden, Robert F. "The 'Cow-bird' Grounded: The Populist Nomination of Bryan and Tom Watson in 1896." *Mississippi Valley Historical Review* 50 (1963): 397-423.

Fine, Sidney. "The Eight-Hour Day Movement in the United States, 1888-1891." *Mississippi Valley Historical Review* 40 (1953): 441-62.

Gitelman, H. M. "Adolph Strasser and the Origins of Pure and Simple Unionism." *Labor History* 6 (1965): 71-82.

Gompers, Samuel. "Organized Labor in the Campaign." *North American Review* 155 (1892): 91-96.

———. "The Lesson of the Recent Strikers." *North American Review* 159 (1894): 201-6.

Greenbaum, Fred. "The Social Ideas of Samuel Gompers." *Labor History* 7 (1966): 35-61.

Grob, Gerald N. "Organized Labor And the Negro Worker, 1865-1900." *Labor History* 1 (1960): 164-76.

————. "Reform Unionism: The National Labor Union." *Journal of Economic History* 14 (1954): 126-42.

————. "Terence V. Powderly and the Knights of Labor." *Mid-America* 39 (1957): 39-55.

————. "The Knights of Labor and the Trade Unions, 1878-1886." *Journal of Economic History* 18 (1958): 176-92.

————. "The Knights of Labor, Politics, and Populism." *Mid-America* 40 (January 1958): 3-21.

Gulick, Charles A., and Bers, Melvin K. "Insights and Illusions in Perlman's Theory of the Labor Movement." *Industrial and Labor Relations Review* 6 (1953): 511-31.

Gutman, Herbert G. "The Tompkins Square 'Riot' in New York City on January 13, 1874: A Reexamination of Its Causes and Its Aftermath." *Labor History* 6 (1965): 44-70.

Higham, John, "Origins of Immigration Restriction, 1882-1897: A Social Analysis." *Mississippi Valley Historical Review* 39 (1952): 77-88.

Hogg, J. Bernard. "Public Reaction To Pinkertonism and the Labor Question." *Pennsylvania History* 11 (1944): 171-99.

James, Alfred P. "The First Convention of the American Federation of Labor, Pittsburgh, Pennsylvania, November 15-18, 1881: A Study in Contemporary Local Newspapers as a Source." *Western Pennsylvania Historical Magazine* 6 (1923): 201-33, 7 (1924): 29-56, 106-20.

Kemmerer, Donald L. and Wickersham, Edward D. "Reasons for the Growth of the Knights of Labor in 1885-1886." *Industrial and Labor Relations Review* 3 (1950): 213-20.

Kessler, Sidney H. "The Negro in Labor Strikes." *Midwest Journal* 6 (1954): 16-35.

————. "The Organization of Negroes in the Knights of Labor." *Journal of Negro History* 37 (1952): 248-76.

Knoles, George Harmon. "Populism and Socialism, with Special Reference to the Election of 1892." *Pacific Historical Review* 12 (1943): 295-304.

Laslett, John. "Reflections on the Failure of Socialism in the

American Federation of Labor." *Mississippi Valley Historical Review* 50 (1964): 634-51.

Lindsey, Almont. "Paternalism and the Pullman Strike." *American Historical Review* 44 (1939): 272-89.

Mandel, Bernard. "Gompers and Business Unionism, 1873-90." *Business History Review* 28 (1954): 264-75.

———. "Notes on the Pullman Boycott." *Explorations in Entrepreneurial History* 6 (1954): 184-89.

———. "Samuel Gompers and the Negro Workers, 1886-1914." *Journal of Negro History* 40 (1955): 34-60.

Matison, Sumner Eliot. "The Labor Movement and the Negro during Reconstruction." *Journal of Negro History* 33 (1948): 426-68.

May, Henry F. "The End of American Radicalism." *American Quarterly* 2 (1950): 291-302.

McKee, Don K. "Daniel DeLeon: A Reappraisal" *Labor History* 1 (1960): 264-97.

McMurry, Donald L. "Labor Policies of the General Managers' Association of Chicago, 1886-1894." *Journal of Economic History* 13 (1953): 160-78.

Morgan, H. Wayne. "The Utopia of Eugene V. Debs." *American Quarterly* 11 (1959): 120-35.

Nolen, Russell M. "The Labor Movement in St. Louis from 1860 to 1890." *Missouri Historical Review* 34 (1940): 157-81.

Paul, Arnold M. "Legal Progressivism, the Courts, and the Crisis of the 1890's." *Business History Review* 33 (1959) 495-509.

Perlman, Selig. "John Rogers Commons, 1862-1945." *Wisconsin Magazine of History* 29 (1945): 25-31.

Reuter, Frank T. "John Swinton's Paper." *Labor History* 1 (1960): 298-307.

Rezneck, Samuel. "Patterns of Thought and Action in an American Depression, 1882-1886." *American Historical Review* 53 (1947): 1-29.

Taft, Philip. "A Rereading of Selig Perlman's 'A Theory of the Labor Movement.' " *Industrial and Labor Relations Review* 4 (1950): 70-77.

Varg, Paul A. "The Political Ideas of the American Railway
    Union." *The Historian* 10 (1948): 85-100.
Wish, Harvey. "The Pullman Strike: A Study in Industrial War-
    fare." *Journal of the Illinois State Historical Society* 32 (1939):
    288-312.
Yearley, Clifton K., Jr. "Samuel Gompers: Symbol of Labor."
    South Atlantic Quarterly 56 (1957): 329-40.

!

Index

267